D0571620

What Really Happened to the Class of

What Really Happened to the Class of

'93

Start-ups, Dropouts, and Other Navigations Through an Untidy Decade

CHRIS COLIN

Broadway Books • New York

Broadway Books titles may be purchased for business or promotional use or for special sales.
For information, please write to: Special Markets Department, Random House, Inc.,
1745 Broadway, New York, NY 10019.

PRINTED IN THE UNITED STATES OF AMERICA

BROADWAY BOOKS and its logo, a letter B bisected on the diagonal,
are trademarks of Random House, Inc.

Visit our website at www.broadwaybooks.com

First edition published 2004.

Book design by Chris Welch

Library of Congress Cataloging-in-Publication Data

Colin, Chris.
What really happened to the class of '93 / Chris Colin—1st ed.
p. cm.
1. Thomas Jefferson High School for Science and Technology (Alexandria, Va.).
Class of 1993. 2. High school graduates—Virginia—Alexandria. I. Title.
LD7801'A45C65 2004
373.755291—dc22   2003069550

ISBN 0-7679-1479-1

10 9 8 7 6 5 4 3 2 1

To great Amy

Contents

Contents

Introduction

The Army-Navy Country Club has already been booked—class officers, God bless them, are class officers for life. The e-mails have been sent, the volunteers courted. An understanding has been reached regarding alcohol; there will be lots. Sixty dollars covers admission, drinks, apprehension, blubbering confession, subsequent regret, and a light buffet dinner. It's been a decade since my high school classmates and I have all stood under the same roof, since we've filled each other with the same confusion and smallness and lust. Our ten-year reunion is nearly upon us, and at this moment millions of other Americans are planning for similar evenings of nostalgia and embarrassment, with roughly equal amounts of clamminess to their palms. Whatever that clamminess is, however scientists might classify it—I suspect the heart of this book lies somewhere nearby.

The nation's palms can go moist for a great number of reasons, many of them less absurd than an awkward roomful of former fifteen-year-olds demanding refills. There are planes to worry about, disease, nuclear bombs, wild dogs. But high school has its own special catalog of eeriness, its own constellation of high stakes, and it does not respond to reason. Nor does it vary all that much from person to person. One may spend those four years in countless circumstances—there are boarding schools, magnet schools, military schools, Catholic schools, wealthy schools and poor schools, happy schools and unhappy schools—but ultimately, impressively, something fundamental happens to every American high school student.

But what?

By the end of this book, my northern Virginia high school's class of 1993 will have flown in from all corners to answer that question. Hundreds of us—old friends and old enemies and old strangers—will have hugged each other or snubbed each other and otherwise processed the last decade. Between now and that day, I've decided to perform something of a warm-up.

In the year and a half leading up to our reunion, I tracked down as many of my former classmates as possible, though not nearly all 404 of us, and asked them to tell me about their lives since graduation. I Googled and dug through phone books and begged old classmates for other old classmates' numbers. I bothered these people at dinnertime and at breakfast time, lunch time, work time, and vacation time, insisting on impromptu high school reunion after impromptu high school reunion, cajoling mere acquaintances into sharing profound life moments as well as recollections of what high school itself had really been like.

The conversations about individual lives—Where do you work? Whom do you love?—became larger conversations over the course of my interviewing: What happened to us? Who are we? What country is this, exactly? Sometimes my classmates' answers opened windows onto a complex and momentous swath of American history; other times, just accounts of how a human being brushes teeth in 2003.

I suspect any high school class in history would yield just as much oddness and awfulness and hope as mine has—in that sense, these stories might as well be anyone's. But we also came of age together at a very particular time. In the decade since that last day of school, the country rose and fell, or fell and rose, or simply convulsed along a series of profoundly chaotic moments. From Rodney King to O.J. to Monica to the Boom to butterfly ballots to 9/11 to the war in Iraq, the last ten years accomplished a cumulative strangeness unlike anything ever seen in America.

I'm trying to carve out a decade here. Not just ten years, but a *decade*: the Twenties, the Sixties, and now, with slightly less of a ring to it, 1993–2003. I propose this *was* the Nineties. Just as the Sixties really went from '64 to '73, the Nineties were slow out of the blocks and then stretched enough beyond September 11, 2001, to see that famous optimism of ours fully evaporate. It wasn't just a *strange* decade—they're all strange, really. What's extraordinary about this one is where it deposited us. To interview Americans about their lives two and three years into the second millennium is to witness a sudden rush of people concluding that the nation, if not the world, has swung from prosperity and hope to someplace more worrisome.

Granted, someone or other has believed the end to be near since, well, the beginning. The Russians were going to destroy us; before that, the Japanese, and so on back to the witches of Salem. But Americans born at the jammed end of the twentieth century have seen something unique: a tech-fueled acceleration of incredible progress, followed by an acceleration of incredible crises—a proliferation of political, biological, environmental, and economic genies let out of bottles, with no discernible vision but chaos. This book is not about those things—we've read about them too much as it is. Rather, it's about the newly minted high school graduates who became full-fledged people in the midst of them. It's hard to imagine another generation knowing the same combination of potential and uncertainty ever again.

One can look in on an assemblage of classmates, gathered years after graduation, in a number of places. Jill Abramson wrote *Where Are They Now: The Story of the Women of Harvard Law, 1974*, journalist Karl Vick wrote a series about his high school class of 1951 for the *St. Petersburg Times* some years back, and of course Mary McCarthy's *The Group* got everyone thinking about the subject in the first place. Sherry B. Ortner's terrific *New Jersey Dreaming: Capital, Culture, and the Class of '58* brings an academic's eye to the years her classmates have seen since graduating—specifically, to the role social class has played in the group. On my desk is an old flea market find called *Harvard College Class of 1892: Fiftieth Anniversary Report*, full of wonderful, brief rendezvous with men like Rudolph Wieser Holmer, M.D. ("He cannot believe a new order of being, better than our past, can come from the world cataclysms that are upon us" and "His principal recreation is long-distance automobile driving.") But it's Michael Medved and David Wallechinsky's *What Really Happened to the Class of '65*, published in 1976, that *this* book takes its title and inspiration from. In it, Medved and Wallechinsky caught up with a group of fellow graduates from their wealthy Los Angeles high school and traced their paths through the upheaval of the late '60s. These stories, told mainly through oral histories, chronicled a remarkably different era, but one whose apprehension and uncertainty aren't wholly foreign, either. As with the 1965–1975 period, America between 1993 and 2003 changed at the highest and lowest levels. Confidence went to fearfulness and routine to disorder in a mood swing that couldn't be more American. What emerges from my classmates' lives is a glimpse of the decade itself.

AN OBVIOUS QUESTION arises: So what? That is, why would anyone in his or her right mind read about someone *else's* high school—isn't this like flipping through the neighbor's wedding photos, or riffling through her diary? After a year and a half of bothering my classmates, the answer I've come up with is: *Well, yes.* This is rubbernecking I'm talking about, the same thing we submit to upon passing a tangle of drama beside the freeway or spying a couple on their first date at the restaurant table beside us. We stare because we see ourselves in there somehow.

But whom, exactly, to stare at? Over the course of my interviews, friends would ask how I decided which classmates to zero in on. To be honest, I'm not entirely sure, but if I heard that a certain discipline case was now armed to the teeth, for example, or that a soft-spoken choir member was now singing show tunes in Japan, I penciled a little star next to his or her name on my list. This book is not science—it's a short roster of people whose stories seemed particularly interesting or particularly telling. Most of us had nothing to do with guns or show tunes. The period in question was a manic, messy decade and by rights there should be volumes on how veterinarians navigated it, not to mention stamp collectors and Avon ladies. This book here focuses on one particular little group, though maybe it's a little group reminiscent of other little groups from schools all over. Scattered then, among the individual profiles are chapters that zero in on milestones and trends that took us from graduation to here—certain recurring arguments, our time in the Boom, 9/11, and so forth, informed by conversations with a wider segment of the class. Finally the book ends with that singularly American and deeply peculiar convergence of all the above—our actual high school reunion.

There's no chapter on me in this book, though I tried not to remove myself too much from the stories—some of the people profiled here were more or less strangers to me, others were not. Besides, the high school reunion is in the eye of the beholder, and I figured my own biases ought to be transparent. A little more transparency, while I'm at it. These days I live in Oakland, California, with my girlfriend in 600 square feet that used to be the True Way Church of God in Christ, on a dusty street with stray dogs roaming around sniffing. Since high school I've had five lines of work, one car, two bikes, four years of college, five e-mail addresses, eight street addresses, two bad trips, and one cat. I had a lousy breakup with doors slamming— house doors, car doors. I lived in New York and California and Chile, and at twenty-seven am still disorganized. I think O.J. did it. I worry, but really I'm happy, though I worry. At the moment, I spend a lot of time thinking about high school.

I SHOULD SAY right off the bat that my high school class was peculiar. Ours was a special school, a public magnet whose mouthful of a name commanded respect and wedgies across town. Or at least that was the myth of the Thomas Jefferson High School for Science and Technology—I never heard of any classmates commanding anything, really. Nor did I ever catch anyone hollering our supposed school cheer: "TJHSS&T, that's who we are, that's who we be / We'll beat 'em high, we'll beat 'em low, our GPAs are 4.0!" In truth we were a mix, like all high school classes: bullies, eggheads, thespians, activists, outcasts, and none-of-the-aboves.

As with magnets such as Bronx Science or Stuyvesant in New York,

TJ was free but admission required an entrance exam. It was an intense place. Students there (*other* students there, at least) regularly set the nationwide record for the number of National Merit Finalists. In contests they won cash, scholarships, and even our own supercomputer. "With virtually unparalleled technological resources for a public high school and a string of high-profile academic achievements, Jefferson has secured an undisputed reputation as the premier high school in northern Virginia and one of the best in the nation," the *Washington Post* wrote in 1990. "By one measure at least, Jefferson is the best school in the country. In the nationally-administered preliminary scholastic aptitude test, Jefferson's pupils collectively did better in 1991 than any other school," the *London Guardian* wrote in 1991. Jefferson parents worried about the familiar stable of issues—drugs, alcohol, pregnancy, general apathy—but also hazards befitting our unique milieu: stress, lack of sleep, and excessive ambition. The New Economy, with its new enterprise and new hours, sprung in part from hothouses like ours.

We were atypical in many ways, but through a funny calculus, our various quirks balanced each other out at some kind of cultural midpoint. Jefferson nestles deep in the vast suburbs of Virginia, but it's also just fifteen minutes from Washington. Virginia is a conservative state, but the Democratic leanings of *northern* Virginia offset this somewhat. The school is exclusive, but it's also entirely free and public—and a fierce meritocracy, at that. We focused on science and technology (a few of us limping along in those departments), but a great many artsy types filled in the ranks, too. We weren't exactly normal, but we weren't wholly abnormal either. Anyhow, teenage code breaks down the same anywhere: The class officers and the football team and the cheerleaders moved as a single laughing unit. The counterculture "alternative" circle was hip within the alternative circle, disdained and ridiculed in every other. The theater people—honest to God, they were called drama fags—had urgent business in the auditorium. Drumming textbooks with fingers were the heavy-metal kids. The young specialists had their physics problem sets or their oboes or their sketches of dragons to keep them busy. First and foremost, we were teenagers in America.

WHAT DID THE last ten years do to us all, and vice versa? We know the last decade in and out, but less attention has been paid to *us*, the people who actually inhabited it. The girl who had a baby at sixteen, the lovable homecoming queen, the brilliant bigot, the son of a famous politician, my own first love—what happened to these people, and others, when they went out in the world? And perhaps one last question, upon seeing that the world has become a stranger place than we'd ever anticipated, and that our own circle wasn't immune to tragedy: Are we okay?

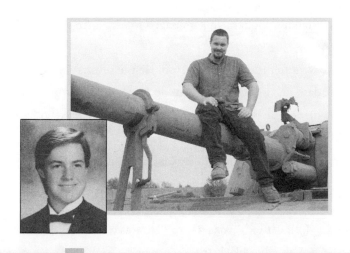

Brian McConnell

BRIAN MCCONNELL: *"I felt angry that the system would do this to me—I had been a good kid my whole life, had never been in trouble, had always been a good student, and the first time I make a mistake, I'm squashed like a grape."*

REBECCA (GRAY) LAMEY: "He was a character. He was always trying to get a rise out of people. He found out my locker combination at one point and I caught him rummaging through it. I came out of class and he had my private journal out and was reading it. So I punched him. Right on the left cheek. He just looked at me in shock. When I asked him later what he thought he was doing, he said, 'Well, I was just curious.'

"He was basically harmless—to humans. At one point he threw a live frog at me. I remember at one point him taking extreme pleasure talking about having managed to hit his first squirrel with his car.

"We went to the same college, too. He was always trying to seem very badass, and one of the ways to do that was being a gun nut. He always made sure people knew he loved guns. He tried so hard to build up the idea that he was a stupid redneck. Even though I never entirely believed it, I thought it was stupid how much energy he put into the act."

VANYA (SEAMAN) WRIGHT: "He was a lot of fun. I remember he had this big black truck he worked real hard to buy. He had mounted these huge spotlights on it and pointed them backward so he could blind people behind him. I knew people who got rides to school with him, and [they said] he used to swerve to hit squirrels.

"He's in love with the idea of being a good old boy—which obviously distances himself from the concept a bit. He had a white rat that he liked a whole lot, and he would give it beer. I think it met an early demise."

O f all the dates I make to visit old classmates, only one involves the promise of firing a Tomahawk missile at a slab of concrete. Brian McConnell proposes the activity as one might propose a stroll around the neighborhood. The day I get there, however—"there" is the Naval Surface Warfare Center in Dahlgren, Virginia—it's raining, and the missile plan is nixed. Outwardly I make like this is fine—all my high school reunions involve canceled detonations!—but inside I'm crestfallen. After a two-hour drive, not test-firing a cruise missile is a little like going to bed without supper (specifically, a supper of one W-80 conventional submunitions dispenser with combined-effect bomblets). From my disappointment, impertinence. Does the military call off war every time it drizzles? What, are we building cardboard missiles? But then this: Did I want to be alone with Brian and a warhead in the first place?

"People may have thought I was a bit of a nut back in school," Brian allows not long after I arrive at the base. I've cleared security and we're stepping over puddles to his bunkerlike office in the Light Weapons Branch building. "It would be easy for people to draw the conclusion that 'he works with guns all the time—he's just a big nut.'"

I'd wondered how long an informal reunion like this could last before the matter of a certain unpleasant reputation is alluded to— and there's the answer, just four and a half minutes. My classmates and I will prove it again and again this year: *You're never really done with high school.*

On the surface, ten years have smoothed "homicidal, gun-wielding madman" into the benign, wacky-sounding "big nut." On the surface. But things come out when you're holed up in a bunker, and over the course of the day it becomes clear that certain outrageous rumors, stemming from certain well-known incidents, aren't always left behind at high school graduation. Of course, Brian always knew the truth, the innocence behind those darkly spare sentences in the *Washington Post* ("The weapon was found in a car in a school parking lot, police said"), but innocence is a tough meme to spread.

For now we talk about the weather.

He is a big, tall engineer—one of several thousand scientists here at the NSWC. As we shake the rain off in his office, he explains that the rainstorm amplifies the noise of a missile test, causing crankiness in citizens living near the base. If I were neighbor to a Tomahawk or any of Brian's other toys, I would stop complaining and start watching. Do they know what happens with the, say, Extended Range Guided Munitions? Once fired, "Fins pop out, a rocket motor turns on and boosts the thing up to 70 to 80,000 feet. It acquires a GPS signal, calibrates its inertial navigation, and it can fly out 50 nautical miles and drop in within twenty meters, right in somebody's lap, boom." Do they know about the fuel-air explosives, which do their job via overpressure? "It only takes about two PSI of overpressure to start rupturing organs and veins and stuff." If you believe the seriousness of the faces here, the stuff of the NSWC is the booming, rupturing future of the free world.

Brian and I spend the next few hours talking, mainly in his teenager's paradise of an office—the light weapons engineering equivalent of a basement rec room. Found within are a twelve-pack of warm soda, a poster-sized photo of a Tomahawk test explosion in progress, a shelf of manly volumes (*Jane's, Fundamentals of Heat and Mass Transfer, Small Arms of the World, Valves and Fittings, Naval History of World War II*), and not a single window or fellow human to interrupt the privacy.

Brian is not a member of the armed forces, nor is he employed by a private weapons manufacturer. While the NSWC develops certain projects on its own, by and large it's a middleman. When the government awards a contract to a manufacturer, Brian helps make sure the manufacturer fulfills it promptly and thoroughly. That Extended Range Guided Munitions system is in Raytheon's hands, for instance, and the NSWC is keeping tabs on its development.

"We set up tests to make sure it's on schedule to do what they say it's going to do, before the government gives them the next chunk of money. We make sure the government and the citizens are getting their money's worth from the contractor."

Brian—a runner of tests, a designer of machine-gun mounts, an agent of civilian-Pentagon trust—has "a dream job," and it's fitting that it falls somewhere between military and civilian. Brian belongs to that special class of men who pride themselves on their independence and liminality, on the bootstrap do-it-yourselfness they sharpened over the rough years, without the harness of institutional allegiance. And Brian has certainly done it all himself. "Self-taught redneck," he says with a crack of the knuckles.

Rednecks have long since seized the slur and take pride in shouting it from the corrugated metal rooftops. More than once, Brian mentions the high school nickname John Doyle (Chapter 19) gave him: McRedneck. "I'm actually more dangerous than a redneck," Brian boasts now. "I'm a *well-educated* redneck."

And here the subject of Brian's saga becomes unavoidable. It's a well-worn, you-know-I'm-kidding smile that rushes across his face upon calling himself dangerous—the kind of smile you might hasten to display having uttered "bomb" in a crowded airport. There's just no getting around it: Brian's high school career is dominated by a single memory.

The newspaper articles cast him a long shadow after the incident. A case like Brian's was low-hanging fruit, obsessed as everyone was with youth violence and with the raft of new zero-tolerance policies at schools across the country. Columbine was still years away, but many school officials had already done their best to imagine such a scenario. And yet with all the fuss this story generated, few of us ever heard the full account from Brian himself, and were probably too scared to ask. Ten years later, I invite him to set the record straight, and he seems content to do so.

"It was a week before homecoming, senior year," he begins. "I had a big black Chevy Blazer, and I was going to tow the homecoming float. I was jazzed. I was going to have the top off the back, I was going to pile all the cheerleader chicks in the back of my truck, turn up the bass, it was going to be so cool. And my goddamn truck breaks down."

Bryan started catching rides to school that week with his best friend, Pete, while he tried to fix the truck. Knowing Pete to be a fellow gadget geek, Brian mentioned a recent engineering curiosity he'd come across. It was a "piece-of-shit pellet gun that I had gotten from a department store," the kind "you can literally shoot it right into your thigh, and it'll just leave a red mark. . . . Of course, being a piece of crap, it had broken. I, being mechanically inclined, had taken it apart and was trying to fix it."

While taking the gun apart, Brian—in the way only teenage engineers care to do—discovered a "stupid little trick" wherein he could remove a piece of plastic and "make the slide go *ch-chink*." He told Pete, and Pete wanted to see it.

"Well, he was picking me up for school that one morning, and somehow [the gun] came up, so I ran back inside, grabbed it, jumped back in the car, and he looked at it there in the driveway. And rather than going back inside and putting it away, I just stuck it in the mesh map-holder behind the front seat, didn't give it another thought, and we drove to school. I forgot about it.

"[A couple days later] we were sitting in first period and [school administrator] Mr. Hawkins came and got Pete. I just thought there was a permission slip he hadn't signed or something. Second period, I had calculus, and Mr. Hawkins came and got me. He asked, 'Do you know what this is about?' I was like, 'Is this about the soda can I threw out the car window this morning?'

"It wasn't until we were walking around the corner, up to the front office—I saw two cops standing there—it wasn't until then that it hit me that it could've even *possibly* been related to the stupid, broke-dick piece of BB gun that I had left in Pete's car. That was all my involvement. I never touched it on school property, I never had any intention of going into school with it. In my mind, they were going to give me detention or something.

"The cops sat me down, said, 'This is a very serious incident—why don't you tell us about the BB gun.' And I told them all I knew about the BB gun. They said, 'Well, since you're under eighteen, you're not going to be arrested.' They made me call my parents, they had them pick me up, and they said, 'As of now, you are suspended. It's an automatic ten-day suspension.'

"My parents were furious—at me, at first, but then I told them what happened. Mr. Jones [our principal], God bless him, was behind me, but he was required by law to report it to the police, and to recommend that I be expelled. The rules were set up so that, even though I had two appeal hearings before I got to the school board, the result was written before I even went in there. They automatically had to recommend that I go to the next level. Each time I'm telling my story, it's like it didn't matter. I was automatically ridden out of town on a rail. They took all discretion out of it—it's like a mandatory minimum sentence where you've got guys in prison on a life sentence for selling pot.

"I felt like I was being crucified. They kept Pete and me separate—Pete was ordered by his father not to talk to me, not to call me, not to interact with me. And Pete was my bud, we were joined at the hip. Now if I tried to say 'hi' in the hall, he'd turn around and walk away. It was crushing."

Brian's family appealed the suspension, and he was back in school after five days. They also hired a lawyer in anticipation of Brian's school board hearing, just before Christmas.

"That year over a hundred cases went before the school board for weapons policy violation, and Pete and I were the only two not expelled.

That, I guess, was the silver lining. [Still], they handed down a pretty stiff sentence. I had to do forty-something hours of community service, [and] I had to do speaking engagements at Carl Sandburg Middle School seven times. They had me speak to a combined total of almost 3,000 students, talking about the weapons policy. I felt humiliated.

"But what really got me was that I couldn't go to any after-school activities for the rest of the year. I couldn't go to basketball games, baseball games—of course, I missed homecoming. I wasn't allowed to go to my own prom. They revoked my parking permit without a refund. I wasn't even allowed to drive on school property without permission. And if I so much as looked cross-eyed at somebody, I would automatically be expelled, no questions asked. I was allowed to finish the year, but you could see how that could make somebody a little bitter. I withdrew. I felt like people hadn't stuck up for me."

At the conclusion of his story, Brian shakes his head a little and swivels in his chair toward his desk to regroup. For a moment we both gaze quietly at his computer screen. The desktop photo is of something beautiful—round, almost kaleidoscopic—but I can't tell what. "I built that," Brian murmurs. We're looking down the barrel of a ten-foot cannon.

"HIGH SCHOOL REUNION" poorly describes our meeting and the meetings I have with other former classmates over the course of the year. The phrase sounds like exciting confrontations—a kiss, a slap—all these years later, against a frolicky backdrop of Budweiser and Eighties rock. In fact, these encounters resemble nothing so communal. There is indeed confrontation, but often it's a private affair—a confrontation of the new self with the old. The engineer revisits the martyr, shakes his head slightly, and plows through the story.

But then he's done, free to move on somehow. Still seated in his dark, fluorescent-lit office, we proceed to the subject of Brian's impressive redneck qualifications. Whatever the label means to him, he does have his papers in order. In his backyard is a 100-yard shooting range and the enormous fire tower he recently bought—and dismantled. "On more than one occasion he's almost killed himself," his colleague, Vince, tells me later with some awed laughter. "He likes projects that are bad news." Soon Brian will build the tower up again. ("Why not?" is the official explanation.) The night before my visit to the base, he was up past midnight grinding venison from a deer he'd shot Thursday. He's an avid gun owner, and a creature owner, too: two boa constrictors, a couple turkeys, two cats, three dogs, and a dozen chickens, which he sometimes eats. How did he learn to butcher chickens? I ask. Started small, he answers—squirrels, rabbits, et cetera.

"Squirrel's a lot of work," he tells me. "My favorite way to eat it is to parboil it about ten minutes, pop it on the grill with some barbecue sauce, and eat it just like corn on the cob." In a testament to his powers of persuasion, Brian the chicken-butchering squirrel-eater convinced a former Hare Krishna vegetarian to marry him.

Brian, whose style could be called militia-casual—jeans, crew cut—wears a nearly squirrel-sized goatee on his face. Sometimes when he travels, he adds a concealed pistol to his ensemble. The pistol's legal. He wears the style of eyeglasses native to fifty-year-old shop teachers—big, square, serious—but under it all is a boy's face. He has big, kind brown eyes and the same ruddy cheeks he had at TJ.

Growing up, Brian was something of an outsider, even before county discipline policies made it official. As a Navy brat, he moved around every year or two and "was always the new kid."

"You might as well have a social disease," he says. "The only people who will be friends with the new kid are the dorky kid, or the smelly kid, or the poor kid—they're happy to get anybody to be their friends. So you end up being associated with them, and you end up [with] an esteem problem, because you think, 'I must be a shithead.'"

Once, in sixth grade, a group of kids held him down while one of them pelted him with red playground balls. In eighth grade, Brian kept a can of Right Guard aerosol deodorant next to a Bic lighter in his gym locker. "One day I had somebody get in my face, and [he] had to take a step back to avoid a ball of flame. I avoided certain conflicts by outthinking the next guy."

By high school, he says, he'd replaced his flamethrower with a crassness that kept classmates at roughly the same distance.

"I can remember sitting in government class watching the Waco standoff on TV. I was sixteen or seventeen and thought I knew everything. I remember watching the complex catch on fire and thinking to myself, 'Good!' I was happy to watch it burn. I was sitting there with a big old grin on my face. Me and Pete were high-fiving and stuff. It's something I'm still ashamed of. Karen [Taggart, Chapter 15] turned around and looked at me like I'd grown a third limb out of my forehead.

"I probably said things that offended a lot of people. Said and did things that were insensitive—I wasn't really thinking about how I was making people feel. I would've been one of the people to joke about 'the queers' or about 'the drama weirdos.' It's one of the things people dream about: If I had a chance to do high school over again, how would I do it differently?"

Even on the football field, where insensitivity rarely impedes chumminess, he recalls being shut out. He attributes his ostracization to a single play he botched in a preseason scrimmage.

"I think the [coach] had it in for me from that day. I never got into any of the games that season. The last game of the year, in November, we were playing Hayfield and it started to snow. We were down by, like, thirty-one points. There were five minutes to go in the fourth quarter, and I told the coach, 'You haven't played me all season. Can you just put me in so I can say that I've played?' But he just ignored me. I was the only junior on the whole football team who didn't play one second in varsity."

WE'RE NOT EXACTLY humans in high school—more like mice, trapped in the corner of a room. But at least we're trapped. After graduation we're free to bolt, and as with Brian's first years at Virginia Tech, it's not always pretty.

"I almost failed out of college. I grew up going to the gifted schools, the nerd schools, and I had a very domineering mother who was always cracking the whip, always controlling everything. I got to college and there were no parents there, nobody to stick their nose in my shit. So I found a million things to do besides schoolwork. I would skip class to go down to the river and fish, or go swimming, or go caving, or goof off, or play video games, or sleep in—I didn't care, it was like a vacation. My grades sucked. I had a 0.9 average one semester.

"I had actually gone to the Army recruiter's office in town, watched their little videos, and I thought, 'Maybe this is what I need to straighten myself out.' I fell into a funk there for a while. Everything seemed hopeless. It seemed that I had dug myself such a huge hole that there was no way I could ever get out. I just didn't feel good about myself at that point. I felt like a loser.

"There are distractions at college. I made myself a freaking suit of chain mail. I was one of those dudes fighting with the padded swords in front of the cafeteria. Anything I could do other than work, that's what I was doing. . . . There was that last eight weeks of one semester where my grades were already in the shithole when it was really the worst. Waking up every morning and puking my guts out just from the stress. Almost having an ulcer. If there's an edge of almost breaking down, I think I found it. I'm just glad I didn't trip off the end and roll over and die.

"It's good I changed gears when I did. I was right there at the edge. If I didn't ace everything and do a 140 percent, they were going to kick me out of school, game over. Well, I had never had to try as hard as I could before. Even at TJ, I knew what my parents expected of me and did just enough to get that. I never did anything for myself. Now I realized I *had* to do it for myself.

"When you strip away everything and get down to the core of who you are and hit rock bottom, then you can build yourself back up with the kind of person you really want to become. It's almost like being reborn. That tempering process was a big part of me maturing since high school and finding out what kind of person I wanted to be. Did I want to be a loser or somebody who someone might look up to one day? Once I started applying myself, and going to class, sitting up front, taking notes, actually doing homework, I started getting great grades. The lowest average I got any semester after that was a 3.25. I got straight A's my last semester there.

"I got into grad school—this was when the dot-coms were going crazy and everyone was going from undergrad straight into the job market, so I didn't have a hard time getting into graduate school. I ended up getting a dream job."

TEN YEARS SINCE his solitary confinement that last year of high school, Brian sits with me in the headquarters of his adult life and explains the new existence he's made for himself. A good bit of this existence involves the philosophy surrounding his work. I had planned to ask Brian—after the missile detonation, of course—whether he had ethical reservations about developing lethal weapons for a living. It turns out I don't have to ask. Without prompting, he assumes what his colleagues might call a defensive posture. It's probably a commentary on what's in the air in 2002 as much as on Brian's personal temperament.

"I'm not a policy maker—I design a tool. I've had people say, 'How can you design weapons that are going to kill people?' My answer is pretty simple: My dad was in the Navy for twenty-two years—he flew a plane and tracked enemy submarines around the world during the Cold War. When my dad would go away for six months at a time, I was really glad he had the best tools at his disposal to get his job done. It meant that he came home to us safe and sound.

"So I'm not building a weapon to blow someone up, I'm building a tool so that some serviceman or servicewoman can get their job done quickly and safely, keep our country safe, and come home safe to their families. My conscience doesn't have a problem with it, because I'm not pulling the trigger, I'm not deciding who the target set is. Do you want a soda?"

I do.

"For me, the government pays me a pretty fair salary to do a certain job. I am not paid to provide my opinion, unless it's asked of me. The way I see it, if there's a policy that should arise that I really don't agree with, I have avenues to voice my opinion in an appropriate and professional manner. If I want to go home and write 400 letters to my congressman, I'm free to do that. If I had a problem where I really couldn't sleep at night, I always have the option of finding another line of work."

Brian has grown noticeably animated, and it's no mystery why. We've sat down to talk at one of those times in history where so many lines of conversation threaten to converge on one or two single points: Afghanistan. Iraq. Terrorism. Brian and I agree, tacitly, not to go further, for the terrain there only gets rockier and the stakes higher. With my time at the base drawing to a close, we decide to take a tour.

"These are called rifle grenades," Brian says, presenting me with what could only be rifle grenades. "You just stick it on a rifle and shoot the bullet into it, and the bullet and the whole thing takes off. This is one of the possible systems that we're looking at [for a war in Iraq]. You'd try to get it through a window—you could get it through a window a football field away. I shot one of these in my backyard."

Next we enter a garage occupied by a Hummer prototype that had been ordered by the Marines. Brian climbs aboard and demonstrates a recent modification of his, a pneumatic lift for the .50-caliber machine gun in the back, which has made it considerably easier to raise and lower. "That was a real quick-and-dirty," he says. Next, a remote-controlled gun/video camera contraption that allows a person to fire at an enemy without inserting himself in the line of sight. Next, a digital photo of some chewed-up "witness panels" after a test firing. From these Brian will forensically deduce fragment velocities and ultimately a lethality rating for the projectile in question. "Whole lotta toys," he says, and then we conclude my visit with a look at some of the biggest toys ever made.

In Brian's truck we drive through the rain to the misty, silent gun range at the edge of the base, a border marked suddenly by the wide, gloomy Potomac River. Here an array of tree-long barrels point out solemnly at the gray water, a line of ancient Babe Ruths showing us where they'd be hitting it that day, were it not raining. Were it not raining, we would have seen an extravagant clearing of river traffic in preparation for the projectile that would come its way. This precaution alone costs $60,000 a day, Brian says. Another precaution would be parking his truck farther away. In the past, cars in the vicinity have seen their windshields sucked off like paper by the blast.

There's a sadness out on the gun line, and it's not just the mist and the gray. These huge, inert machines seem like dinosaurs. True, they aren't yet extinct—in the Gulf War of 1991, it was 16-inch guns on battleships such as the *Missouri* that hastened the Iraqi army's submission. (The enormous mortars would scream in from offshore, Brian explains, followed by leaflets rained on the devastation: *We'll be back tomorrow at 1—perhaps consider surrendering before then.*)

The sadness out here, of course, is the sadness risen at the end of the decade that followed that war and that followed our graduation from high school. September 11 clarified for the world that a new era had begun, one where America's gravest threats might no longer be found in the sights of our big weapons. Like most aspects of existing defense strategy, though, these guns will be maintained nevertheless—the death of conventional warfare hasn't been declared just yet—and on certain sunny days at the NSWC, the dinosaurs along the gun line just might let rip into the Potomac. Still, the paradigm shift isn't lost on Brian. "A bunker buster doesn't work when there's no bunker," he says with a resignation everyone learned after 9/11, and that Brian himself might have known years before that.

We head to the truck. We're probably a sight, two former classmates, all grown up now, sharing an umbrella and hopping over puddles after a visit to some absurdly large guns. On the way to my car, Brian tells me someone discovered that the barrels, melted down, make good razor blades—and so Gillette came and bought some. Everyone loves a good swords-into-plowshares story, and it isn't until I'm back on the highway that I realize I've heard not one, but two. How else to parse the saga of a young man with a pellet gun, beaten into sorrow and doubt and then, triumphantly, remade as his own squirrel-eating peace in adulthood? "Guns are serious," he tells me toward the end of the day, slightly out of the blue, and somehow this bit of news feels as hard-won as anything else one former teenager can say to another. Anyhow, he's got a permit now.

2 Charlotte Opal

CHARLOTTE OPAL: *"I wanted to belong in every group. I remember being really careful to not ever say anything bad about anyone. I didn't like the idea of anyone talking badly about me, and I never wanted to give anyone reason to."*

JOHN HELMANTOLER: "We were impossibly good friends. She's a genius, pretty, talented—where's her damn Achilles' heel? She loves to bring everybody into the fold, has no holier-than-thou sentiments in her at all."

DAVID LOBE: "We used to drive to school together. Charlotte always surpassed my expectations. She is one of the nicest people I've ever met. Very social, very extroverted—the kind of person who would reach out to someone who was being quiet. She was so down-to-earth, and yet so brilliant. She didn't show it off."

TU TRAN: "Charlotte was really pleasant to be around, but she was too polite as well. I often got the sense that she didn't say what she really felt. 'Confrontational' is not a word I would use to describe her. . . . I remember her being very private too. For instance, I knew her for a while before I learned that her father died.

"Charlotte was very humble in high school, too—which was nice because I think a lot of the kids weren't. . . . I always knew Charlotte was smart in that particular way, but I never got confirmation, because she didn't talk about it. I don't think she was into 'the game.'

"Charlotte was a co-captain on the lacrosse team with me, and though she wasn't one of the best players on the team, she was a very good captain. She was a morale builder and socializer, and the players needed that.

"Not much dirt on Charlotte—maybe that's because she never let any out?"

JUSTIN ROMBERG: "I remember her as being incredibly sharp and incredibly sarcastic. She was more open-minded than most people are at sixteen or seventeen."

JOE GIASSON: "I wrote one of my first songs about her, when I was sixteen—'Everybody Loves Charlotte.'"

■

At her mother's behest, Charlotte was always a nerd. In kindergarten, living in Austin, she took Spanish classes before school. Next she went to an immersion school where she studied French one day, English the next, then French, then English, et cetera. The other kids were learning to read, but Charlotte could already do that in English, so she did one day Spanish, one day French, one day Spanish, one day French. For fun, Charlotte and her mother sweated over logic problems. Charlotte began playing the violin in fourth grade and the viola in fifth and the oboe in sixth, and would sneak her instruments out of class so the other kids wouldn't see she was a nerd. Charlotte's mother had her eye on college from the beginning, and in fact she took Charlotte on her first college tour—in seventh grade.

Charlotte should have become a first-class loner, a sullen glue sniffer if not another terrorizer of squirrels; through sheer dedication to education, no parent has ever worked harder to guarantee her daughter a miserable adolescence. Instead Charlotte became one of the most popular people in our class, and one of the most successful.

Often popular means that a student is liked by a certain and influential set, but Charlotte brightened the faces of jock and punk alike. Sophomore year she was voted Homecoming Princess, and then Homecoming Queen senior year, but she was never an eyelash batter. She was politically active and she was an athlete. She stopped hiding her musical instruments and started winning honors with them. After college she received a Rhodes scholarship. She earned a Master's of Philosophy from Oxford and then an MBA. She salsas competently. She's funny (a recent e-mail to me began, "hi—how was mexico? enough about you—i was on the news last night!"). Her job is a noble one, and it takes her around the world, and though she's warm, she does not tolerate people who aren't dedicated or good. She has begun conversations by saying, seriously, "At the dinner with Mandela . . ."

Almost fifteen years since the first day of high school, I ask Charlotte how she turned out, well, even better than her mother had planned.

We're driving up the northern California coast when I ask this question, and it occurs to me that traveling with a former homecoming queen, one feels both protective and curatorial instincts. Charlotte is royalty, as per high school mythology, but she's also something of a relic—like other queens of the world, the homecoming variety feels increasingly ornamental these days, and possibly moribund. I suspect my class sensed this at some level when it chose to elect Charlotte. She was a sarcastic queen, though not a fully ironic one, and managed to bring a refreshing lightness to the throne without mocking it. "She wasn't the prettiest girl in our high school, but still she was the homecoming queen—that says something," classmate David Lobe tells me.

She was also an outsider. Some girls, one sensed, had been bred with the homecoming court in mind—and perhaps even in their blood. Charlotte had been groomed for study hall, and what's more, the grooming happened on the cheap. There wasn't much money in the Opal household, so her achievements were thrifty ones. She walked or used public transportation when other kids drove; she worked for scholarships, not for prestige but for cash. At lacrosse games, her mom was the mom who wasn't there—she always had to work.

The secret of my passenger's success? Contacts, she says. Throughout childhood, Charlotte's eyeglasses were thick and funny-looking. In middle school she got contacts and began dressing the part of the popular girl. This was the beginning. The transformation, she confesses readily, was conscious and deliberate. If there were any adults around to explain that happiness requires more than a change of wardrobe, Charlotte knew better than to listen. The person everyone saw on the first day of high school was assured and striking. She arrived with long blond hair and a smart gap between her front teeth that would make Lauren Hutton blush. "She'll never work for the

CIA," John Helmantoler says. "You'd always be able to pick her out of a crowd."

Still, a pretty foot in the door will go only so far. Charlotte proceeded immediately on to Phase Two of her plan.

"I was very strategic," she says, laughing at the recollection of it. "I never said anything bad about anyone, I said 'hi' to everyone in the hall, I called them by their names—nerds, jocks, misfits, everyone! Then I made a conscious effort to figure out who the popular people are and really insert myself in their group."

If at this point our queen sounds ripe for the guillotine, I should explain that Charlotte has a distinct way of talking. She's perpetually arch, forever speaking in *italics*. The effect can be confusing at times, particularly when there's sincerity beneath it. In high school, I had assumed her enormous Sweet Sixteen party was a campy, tongue-in-cheek affair, for instance, that she was too mature to take such a corny ritual seriously. A dozen years later Charlotte disabuses me of this idea.

"I invited everyone I'd ever met. I had sixteen sheet cakes that were black and white checkerboard. I spent my life savings on it—probably $300. It was really stressful. I had a headache because I was doing everything at once, and trying to introduce my friends from summer camp to my orchestra friends to my school friends. It wasn't fun at all. Why did I do it? Why did I feel the need to throw myself a huge party? To say that I invited 300 people to my Sweet Sixteen party?"

A big guest list in high school is a remarkable thing: a defiance of conventional rules of popularity, for it forsakes exclusivity. It's a Jeffersonian gesture, to be sure, and the sign of a committed free-floater. There was no shortage of floaters in our class, people who preferred making their own rules to following convention, but I can't think of anyone else who did so from so close to the center. Charlotte wasn't smoking cigarettes in the parking lot, she was wearing a tiara on the football field at halftime.

"I could never be categorized. I didn't know which group I belonged in. I wanted to belong in every group," Charlotte says. "There was the popular group, with all the jocks and pretty girls. Then there were the cool people who eschewed all those things. I wanted to be in everything."

So she was. She was an officer in Students for the Ethical Treatment of Animals, she co-captained the women's lacrosse team, she was the oboe section leader in band, she was the viola section leader in the D.C. Youth Orchestra, and she was one of two TJ students selected for the Fairfax City Public Schools Anti-Drug Council. Recently I came across an old videotape documenting our senior-year talent show; in one number, I had played guitar while Charlotte and her sister Barbara sang—gawd—a song by the Indigo Girls. Ten years later, I was excited to find the awkward adolescent performance so I could tease the grown-up Charlotte with it on one of our visits. Upon watching the tape, however, I discovered that Charlotte never was an awkward adolescent, or really even an adolescent at all, for that matter. Beside me on the stage was precisely the same woman I see walking around today.

There's one in every crowd: a person who disobeys the laws of his or her high school student genre, who freely crosses the boundaries of his or her clearly ordained set. In the highly codified sphere of teenage protocol, a funny, idiosyncratic, independent-minded vegetarian feminist should have traveled exclusively in the artsy circles; our homecoming queen hung out with jocks instead. For a politically and socially circumscribed class, this was a confusing move. Wasn't she consorting with the enemy? Weren't these the people who, say, made fun of animal rights?

"I was never a missionary," Charlotte explains. "In some ways I thought I could lead by example—if I'm normal, yet have these different views, people might accept the views. . . . If you purposefully reject everything about someone, why would they listen to you?

"Also, I hate awkwardness, so I hate talking about things that aren't going to have a happy ending. So I just don't go there. I would never talk about 'Why are you an investment banker? Don't you think you're hurting poor people when you bet on their currencies?' I'm afraid of the answer. I hate conflict."

Charlotte and I are driving up the coast on this day because I want to show her the gorgeous hippy enclave of Bolinas. I've taken it upon myself to lead her around the state since she relocated from the East Coast, and I'm curious what a straightlaced but progressive person like her will think of a bunch of New Agers. Also, I wanted to trap her in my car long enough to squeeze some candor out of her. Charlotte offers a fellow classmate little in the way of grit or scandal. She is, and always has been, a charming person adored by those who encounter her. One longs for at least a little ugliness.

"I didn't want anyone ever to have anything on me that was negative," Charlotte explains with a shrug. "I don't know why. I guess I saw how much people talk about each other, and I didn't ever want to be that person who was talked about. I wanted to be perfect so that no one would ever say anything bad about me."

BEHIND EVERY ELECTED homecoming princess is an awkward moment alone with pencil and ballot.

Determination of the homecoming court is a thoroughly democratic event, and sophomore year Charlotte had to cast her vote knowing she herself was a contender. Would it be more graceful to vote for someone else? It would. But come on. She scribbled "Charlotte Opal" and handed the paper to her math teacher, the hip and beloved Mr. Thomas, who was collecting the ballots. He opened hers and beheld her vanity. Charlotte was mortified, but she'd also had her reasons. Freshman year her father had been diagnosed with cancer. She wanted to be princess so he could walk with her at the big homecoming game.

"He died my sophomore year," she tells me in one of our very few conversations about him. "He was still living in Texas, so we didn't see him very much, but he would fly back. It was terrible. We flew back. He died. It was awful. And then I went back to school and my [guidance] counselor had told all my teachers. And I remember being really pissed that my chemistry teacher, who I hated, had something over me. I remember thinking, 'I don't want his pity.' I was really angry. I would think, especially in chemistry, 'This isn't important. What's important is that my father died. And I hate this class even more now. And I hate that I'm thinking about him, and [my teacher] knows I'm thinking about him, and I'm sad.' It was terrible.

"Then I remember kind of wanting people to know and feel sorry for me. And then thinking that was selfish. It was weird. Wanting people to know *how strong and brave I was*—that this *terrible thing had happened to me* and I was *still carrying on*, and *wasn't I cool*. But apparently those are normal sentiments. I remember I was in the bathroom one time, crying, and Laura Griffin came in. And I had these mixed feelings. I was embarrassed that she'd seen me crying, but then I was like, 'Now she knows what a hard time I'm having.'"

Aside from walking in on her in the bathroom, there was one other way a person could have learned what kind of time Charlotte was having: Cry Club. Officially, the extracurricular grieving group went by something more sensitive, but as long as Charlotte and her sister attended, they regarded it with Opal archness. "Everyone in the group had a story of someone saying, 'I understand,'" Charlotte remembers. "And we'd all say, 'No, you don't understand!'"

At twenty-seven, Charlotte will sometimes look straight ahead when she's talking about certain things—sort of a glassy look—and this is what she does on the subject of her father. But she doesn't cry. The sadness that remains is a diffuse kind. "It's weird because I didn't know him. I was fifteen. I wish I could get to know him now that I'm an adult, and I could get more out of it." And then there's the double pain of being with those who did know him as adults. "It's very sad visiting his parents, because they're still devastated. And then I feel like they're really wrapped up in me and my sister, because we are *him* to them. They want us to succeed so much."

SENIOR YEAR, CHARLOTTE applied to more than a dozen colleges. She submitted music applications, for both oboe and viola. In the end she picked Wake Forest, in North Carolina, because it gave her a full scholarship and she knew she could be "a big fish there."

Big fish didn't mean following the crowd. After two days of rushing, she decided to avoid the Greek system. ("So segregated!" she recalls. "And you walk into those rooms and it's like the parakeet cage at Kmart!") She spent her time doing lacrosse, orchestra, and karate. She sang in a local gospel choir, too—her favorite activity. She was one of two student members on a faculty race-relations committee. "They asked the white girl in the gospel choir, and then they asked a black girl," she says with something between a laugh and a sigh.

Charlotte liked college—she tends to like everything she does or else she stops doing it, she says plainly—but she does call Wake Forest a sheltered existence. Having come from Jefferson, where the level of activism never dipped below red, the political idleness at college frustrated her. Upon graduating from Wake, she went straight to an economic development consulting firm in Washington for a summer. In October 1997, she moved to England to begin graduate school for development studies, spending one of her summers in Zambia working with a microcredit agency—she'd already lived in Swaziland, teaching there the summer after high school. Now, after receiving her M.Phil, she took a job in African urban development at the World Bank. Then she went back to Oxford for her MBA. In early 2001, she worked again in Washington, at a nongovernmental organization (NGO). Later that year, she moved to New York for a job at Peaceworks.

In 2002, the year I began tracking down classmates, Charlotte broke up with a longtime boyfriend and left New York for Oakland, California. She came to Oakland to become New Products Manager at Transfair USA. Transfair is the international organization behind the "Certified Fair Trade" sticker ideally found on your bag of coffee, a ten-year-old group dedicated to promoting a sustainable model of international trade. As Charlotte tells it, Transfair works to level the playing field for disadvantaged farmers in Latin America, Africa, and Asia by implementing "the 'triple bottom line'—a fair deal for farmers and workers, environmental sustainability, and profitability for all parties in the chain of production." Most of Charlotte's work happens in the office, though she travels some, too; on one occasion, she took a buyer down to Oaxaca, Mexico, to meet the farmers behind the beans that his store was buying.

Recently, she accompanied me to the place where I did a lot of the writing of this book, and I saw her brand of activism at work. The Café Macondo is a dark, shabby room with peeling posters of Colombian revolutionaries and Simon Bolivar wisdom, and a brooding clientele mostly of old "U.S. out of _____" types. (A person would be hard pressed to find an office better suited for concentration, on account of the hypnotic, never-ending Louis Armstrong CD.) This is an old San Francisco place for Conscientious People, and though the political atmosphere is pretentious and undercooked, I thought Charlotte might appreciate the spirit. I should have known spirit doesn't count for much in her book.

"Hi. Do you know if your coffee is fair trade?" she asked the woman at the counter.

"What's that? Like, local coffee?"

"Well, it means that it was certified, saying the farmer was paid fairly for it."

"I think it's local, not imported."

Charlotte smiled and wrote a brisk note to the manager and left it with the woman. At our table she took a bite of her spinach empanada. "*Local* coffee?" With her non-empanada hand she phoned her office.

"Hi, it's Charlotte. I'm at Café Macondo, in the Mission, and they're serving Bodega Coffee Company. Is Bodega on the list?" The list lists every company that sells fair-trade products—about ten chocolate companies, five tea, one banana, and 175 coffee—out of 1,600 nationwide, Charlotte says.

Bodega was not on the list. She hung up. Her impatience at well-meaning liberalism came out. "What, exactly, is revolutionary about this place? Can't you do your work somewhere else?"

Perhaps because she herself is largely self-made, Charlotte is particularly attuned to how other things are made. If success comes about through cut corners, she wants to know about it. Even her Rhodes scholarship is an ambivalent achievement for her—that money came originally from de Beers and its slave labor, she points out.

"Of course, show me any foundation or scholarship that has clean money at the bottom of it—they don't exist. My undergraduate scholarship was R.J. Reynolds, my college at Oxford apparently was founded by arms money. And my business school was founded by an arms dealer. So if I don't fight the good fight, I'm going straight to hell."

This past year Charlotte returned to South Africa for the fifth time in her life. She was there to attend the celebration of the hundredth anniversary of the founding of the Rhodes Trust as well as the launch of the Mandela Rhodes Foundation, which was started with money from the Rhodes Trust and assembled to invest only in projects in southern Africa. It was a good cause teeming with Rhodies who *weren't* fighting the good fight.

"I was just kind of snobby the whole time," she admits, describing a "schmoozy cocktail party" where the likes of James Woolsey and other luminaries circulated. "There were a lot of consultants and lawyers and i-bankers there, and people kept coming up to me saying, 'I *so* admire what you do! I'm not getting that kind of fulfillment out of my job.' And I did not know what to say to them. I kept saying how happy I was, but what I really felt was: *Then do it. You have to give up a lot of stuff—you're going to have to sell your nice car and maybe you won't have a nice flat—but you spend a third of your life at your job. Get some fulfillment out of it.* . . . Because I'm someone who's good at changing my situation if I'm not happy with it, I have little sympathy for people who wish they were doing more, but don't actually do it."

IT IS POSSIBLE, with just a little stretching, to think of America itself as the clique, or sorority, or cocktail party at which Charlotte becomes a star, and to which she ultimately won't commit. She and I arrive in Bolinas, park the car, and stroll through the funky streets and onto the beach. Surfers and drum circles share the sand with us, and on Charlotte's face I think I can make out some vague distaste. How, in America in 2003, can this look like anything but indulgence and solipsism? It's only a matter of time, I suspect, before I call to find she's packed her bags for South Africa. Rhodie mixers aside, her recent trip was a reminder of what might well be her favorite place in the world.

Charlotte could sell time-shares in Cape Town on any number of points. The country's constitution is a monument to institutional thoughtfulness. ("The most progressive and most liberal constitution in the world. It enshrines not only political and civil rights but also economic and social rights, like housing, jobs, health care, and education.") And the way business gets conducted sounds awfully enlightened in her telling. (She recalls going to a nightclub with an openly gay, openly HIV+ constitutional court judge talking about G-strings—"This would never happen in America. It's a small country, so you can be real, you don't have to be political.") Appropriately enough, what moves Charlotte most about South Africa is the self-determination that allowed these developments to happen in the first place. The italics in her voice vanish when she describes it.

"They just decided everything had to be changed, and they never gave up, and they never lost hope. I mean, they were singing in the streets for *years*. They came together and even agreed to make changes they knew they weren't ready for. The average South African wasn't comfortable with homosexuality, for example, but as a nation they understood that *everyone had to be free*.

"Being in South Africa now is like being in America in 1780," she tells me later, not a little depressingly. "People haven't given up over there. It's such a fresh, new democracy—everyone's forward-thinking and civic-minded. And it's a small enough country that you can actually see changes happen. There are a lot of problems that need to be fixed, and I feel like they can actually *be* fixed."

"And in America?" I ask. The homecoming queen shrugs sadly. A shrug looks out of place on Charlotte—she always seemed to know what she, and the rest of the world, was capable of. But uncertainty, she tells me toward the end of our interviews, is finally catching up with her.

"This is the first time in my life where I don't know where this chapter will end," she says. "Until now, I always knew what I'd be doing in a year. High school, college, jobs, grad school—everything was temporary. But suddenly this is *my life*, it's starting now. I'm very happy with it, but it's scary. I don't know what happens next."

Lorraine Bembry, Adam Rice

LORRAINE (BEMBRY) RICE: *"What did I care about? Music. Feeling good. Or feeling anything. I wanted everything to be raw, to experience everything. That part of me has changed a little since then."*

JEANNIE WONG: "Lorraine in high school: a liberal-minded activist who rallied around women's and civil rights, self-assured and collected, will debate/discuss theories with well-thought-out points, sadistically funny, enjoyed reading and writing fiction with an autobiographical twist; has a vast knowledge bank of pop culture, songs on the radio and movies from past to present day, has an amazing talent for acting, does not like carrots.

"Adam in high school: liberal-minded, nontraditional family, underachiever with great potentials, enjoyed reading philosophical texts, discussing abstract ideas, always searching for new ways of being. Favorite book was *On the Road,* had many Kerouac books he dog-eared and underlined. Didn't care about getting good grades or traditional schooling at all, much to the disappointment of his teachers—and this in a place where grades, scores, and placement was of utmost importance to many; had a comic book collection of about 3,000; did not like mixing Coke with chips and salsa."

MIKE JANSSEN: "[Adam was] often quiet, even enigmatic, but clearly alert and thoughtful about what's going on around him. . . . Maybe it was his reticence that seemed to give what he did say added weight and focus. His exuberance, when it surfaced, always seemed so genuine and up-to-the-brim, or his delight in something funny. I remember once when he walked out of the bathroom, came right up to me, and said, 'Mike Janssen, isn't peeing GREAT?' And I knew what he meant.

"Another time we shared a very odd moment when, almost by accident, we faced each other in the course of doing something else—I think we were leaving a house, walking through the doorway—and we looked into each other's eyes and suddenly seemed to see very deeply into each other's, well, souls, for lack of a better word and at the risk of sounding mushy. It lasted just a split second, but we both knew what had happened and it was almost as if we were embarrassed by it. . . . That's perhaps never happened to me save for a few times, and Adam is definitely one of the few people I know with whom it could happen—that's the kind of person he is. Sometimes difficult to 'read,' but ultimately open.

"I really didn't know Lorraine well, but we were in a few classes together. . . . I recently learned something terrible from her—once in AP Journalism, I edited something she had written and was apparently (not uncharacteristically) blunt in my criticism, and my bluntness was enough to make her feel insecure about her writing not just for months, but for YEARS. She told me this for the first time last year, and I felt awful. I still do!"

JOHN HELMANTOLER: "Adam and I went to elementary school together—he was always the quiet, underachieving genius. He was so damn smart. In fifth and sixth grade, he was the one staying up till three in the morning. I don't know doing what. Probably reading Tolstoy. He was always in all the accelerated classes, but got terrible grades. School was not his thing—he was a life learner.

"Lorraine was quiet, shy, sweet. Impossibly sweet—I felt impure talking to her. Very accepting. Soft-spoken."

JOE GIASSON: "I have a song about Lorraine. I think she's an amazing person. She's authentically nice. I always wanted to see her mad—she always had an enormous smile that you couldn't get past."

Me, I kept quiet our freshman year, not shooting-spree quiet, just quiet enough to ponder where the Smiths stood in relation to Lou Reed, and whether my pants looked dumb. I disliked TJ at first, because it was hard and my good friends attended the nonmagnet neighborhood school, and because I was, like everyone else, lonesome. I scratched pictures on my desk and watched the leaves blow across the parking lot out the window—deep stuff. Eventually my chin came up, and I got sucked into the good diversion that is bad high school drama. My sense, from all these interviews, is that this happened to many of us—we strained and strained against school until, one day, we were simply part of it. A decade later, the ordeal can even strike us as worth revisiting, if only for its unique sadness and funniness. But seldom do we return beyond contained and liquored affairs like the ten- or twenty-year reunion. Seldom do we spend a year talking to former classmates, and more seldom still do we track down our first loves and expect reconciliation.

Lorraine Bembry and I came to each other with the excitement of two Arctic explorers who discover each other crossing the tundra. If high school can be a frigid and lonely landscape, a science and technology magnet high school will have certain types actually muttering at the musk oxen. Lorraine and I met in our sophomore-year Spanish class—home of the blessed group project, public education's answer to oysters and Spanish Fly—and I still recall that immediate recognition that we'd been put on the planet to locate each other and begin construction of our separate and preferable universe. We didn't get A's that semester in Spanish. *No nos preocupabamos.*

Lorraine liked things that were not popular in our forward-thinking school—things I happened to know were unbeatable, like certain Simon and Garfunkel songs, and cutting class, and intrepid stares delivered to the almighty jocks. Many thought she was shy, because she was quiet. I didn't. I thought she had an elaborate energy-expenditure plan, and that the average person simply didn't make the cut. (I was above average; this was inexplicable to me, but great news.) Lovably, Lorraine distrusted authority even more than I did—she didn't even *talk* to it if avoidance was an option. She was a sharp, sweet, good old soul, and could inconspicuously knock your head off with some quiet sarcasm. Lorraine was very pretty, with one tooth that peeked through her smile when her mouth was closed—a genuine snaggletooth. The tooth suggested many great things to me: reluctance, strangeness, and, ultimately, irrepressible goodness.

Each of us had "dated" other people before, but mainly in that preadolescent summer way, via string bracelets and polite phone conversations. Not until each other did we have someone with whom we could *not* exchange bracelets. We forswore all things juvenile, not to mention treacly, square, stupid, smart, quaint, and modern. We invented our own creaky world, a miscellany of pretentious bohemia and mild rebelliousness. At times we were a Leonard Cohen song, other times a minor crime syndicate, still others an old Mike Nichols film that never was made. We took walks at the zoo. Moreover, we adored each other.

What was love at fifteen and sixteen in 1990 in America? I don't know, but it usually happened in a car. Cars equal independence and cars equal coming-of-age, and both of those require privacy, and cars also equal that. One night Lorraine and I parked and left the radio on. My father had to come jump-start the car, back there behind the Safeway after midnight. "What were you doing back there?" he asked, and that now strikes me as an interesting question. We did it again weeks later, killed the same battery. He didn't ask that time.

Another night we drove into the parking lot of a darkened middle school. Around back we went, beyond the Dumpsters and milk crates, over to the dark corner of the parking lot, beside some empty tennis courts. We faced a line of wooly pines and cut the engine. A testament to love was our failure to notice the squad car enter the parking lot a while later. It skimmed its searchlight across the tennis courts and pine trees and into our window. Next it sped forward across the asphalt. It appeared he would hit us; we were not so lucky. Instead he stopped at the last minute, ten feet from the old Toyota at that urgent policeman's angle, and proceeded to step out of his vehicle. The next forty-five minutes involved interrogation, shame, disgrace, solemn paperwork, threats of jail time, and, at one point, even a second police car. Why the backup? I wonder now. Did he think we were going to overpower him and resume necking?

In retrospect, it's unclear what Lorraine and I actually talked about. We didn't talk about classes, or teachers, or friends much, and probably not politics, or art, or religion, either—those things were understood. If a good book was being read, that was noted—I remember Salinger being passed between us meaningfully—but I don't think we lingered on literature much, particularly. One would assume, then, that it was ourselves that we talked about—our hopes, our thwartings, our ambivalence about later Woody Allen. But really I think most of our communication happened through code. "Hi," we said to each other a lot. "Hi," we wrote on scraps of paper on lockers. It went without saying that we'd understand each other's deeper meanings. Hi. Hi. Hi.

Someone asked me recently if we ever talked about race, since Lorraine is black and I'm white. I remember only one conversation in which it came up. What will our kids look like? we wondered aloud one afternoon in the back of a bus. My—our?—exposure to such things must have been awfully limited, for I remember us sharing a kind of thrill: Here two teenagers had inadvertently discovered the cure for racial strife—love. It's not that we made light of race, but rather we made heavy of our more fundamental connection. Had someone described the aching race conversation we would have in her kitchen a dozen years later, we would have laughed and driven off to another parking lot.

A COUPLE GOES deep underground for a period, then in spring emerges and rejoins the world. By the second half of our sophomore

36

year, we were still great, and it was warm, and we had Van Morrison songs in our heads, and we rolled back the rock to let others in. A guy named Adam Rice began to hang out with us sometimes. Adam was a wry, taciturn, generally miserable, morose, funny, and fun person. Like us, Adam enjoyed making jokes, listening to superior music, cursing The System, and generally talking nonsense.

As odd birds go, he came with excellent credentials; there's just no competing with a lesbian mom who practices astrology. Adam was born in California—the Amazon, as far as we were concerned—and when he was five, his father got a job in Virginia, so the family moved east. His mother (still married at the time) came a few weeks later than the others, and when she arrived, she had a boyfriend with her. The boyfriend moved in, too. Adam recalls just one middle-of-the-night fight, out in the yard.

Most of the time when I saw him, he was with Jeannie, his girl-friend. In fact, if I ever saw either of them alone, it was safe to assume the other was either angry or deathly ill. They were the kind of couple that seemed to have been together forever. In Adam I found a fellow lost but occasionally contented soul, though sometimes we stumbled upon minor differences in our global strategies. I remember driving him home one day and sitting in the driveway with the engine on and talking about capitalism. We were fifteen. "This is meaningless," he said at the climax, referring to the $10 bill in his hand. "I should burn it." He raised a lighter.

"Then I'll take it," I said.

"You're missing my point," he said.

"*You're* missing *my* point," I said.

"*You're* missing *my* point," he said.

"*You're* missing *my* point," I said.

Thus our discussion of capitalism concluded. Ideally, there'd have been a third person in the back seat who informed us that was no point to *either* of us, and who proceeded to light *us* on fire, but it was a small car.

LORRAINE AND I dated from November until June. I went away that summer, and we wrote letters, but when I came back something was different. One of us had ventured too far from underground, and we couldn't get back to normal. We were sad soul mates. We pitched and tossed for weeks, and finally I pulled away. I think I said, "We need to see other people," or something similarly awful. The night we broke up, each of us spent a great deal of time talking to our friend Adam on the phone. "I couldn't believe it. It was devastating," he says now about that evening, generously.

Lorraine and I tried to stay friends. Nowadays, she says it was me who tried hardest—to her displeasure. By the end of high school, it was pleasantries between us. The next fall she went off to Hampshire College, where her new (and older!) boyfriend awaited her. Once, in the middle of college, home on vacation, I called her and we met at an all-night doughnut place. Lorraine looked at me funny for the duration of a glazed cruller, and then we lost touch entirely.

Adam and I had better luck staying friendly, but there was drifting between us, too. By the end of high school, he'd fallen in with C.R.A.P.— a club to which I belonged, officially, but rarely in practice. The Coalition for the Righteous Application of Plants had been Mike Janssen's brainchild, a response, I suppose, to mounting hysteria over animal rights in our politically minded class. Our circle of friends had always made fun of things with straight faces, but C.R.A.P. marked irony's institutional arrival at Jefferson. (That some C.R.A.P. members happened to be vegetarians didn't diminish the point, as there was no point.)

Adam and his girlfriend Jeannie went to Hampshire together. There, Adam proceeded to push the concept of "college student" as far as he could.

"Rather than do what most students do, which is go to class and do homework," he says, "I set up a Web server in my room and taught myself everything I could about it." It was the kind of project any liberal arts academy would have applauded—he's one of the few people who can say he was building Web sites back in 1994—but Adam never told any professors what he was doing. Not all that long after arriving, he dropped out.

I asked Adam recently if he ever thought about going back to school, though of course he's realized that dot-com economy dream of rendering higher education unnecessary. He told me he *did* go back to school—some time after leaving, he returned to Hampshire to try again—but again he couldn't focus. Nevertheless, he occasionally contemplates taking another stab. "Looking back, there's still part of me that just wants to knock it out. Get a big aluminum bat and destroy Hampshire once and for all. In a good way. Figuratively. Yeah."

IN NOVEMBER 2002—almost exactly a dozen years since that group project in Spanish class—I finagle a dinner invitation from Lorraine and Adam. Lorraine and Adam are now husband and wife. Ian Sol is there, too—Ian Sol is their son. The wedding happened in 1999. Adam performed a silent vow in which he washed Lorraine's feet. Lorraine performed the talking kind, and ad-libbed it, no less. Ian is twenty-three months old. His eyes are huge and brown, and they stare and stare. I don't blame him. Before it's through, the evening will be unaccountably strange.

The Rices—Lorraine changed her name; it had ceased to hold meaning for her—were a long time in the making. "We were messing around in a messy kind of way in college, and the end of high school, but it wasn't really until later [that the relationship began]," Adam says. They moved to Brooklyn together when Lorraine graduated from Hampshire, and got married soon after. When Lorraine got pregnant, they moved back to northern Virginia, into a small, carpeted apartment in a quiet subdivision not far from their high school homes.

Lorraine greets me at the door when I arrive, and we move into one of the more awkward hugs ever performed. Next I meet Ian, who is curious and bold and far less inept at saying hello. Adam is still at work, so the three of us sit on the carpet and waste no time beginning some marker drawings. Ian is interested in fireman- and truck-related art. When he finishes coloring on paper, he colors on the carpet. Lorraine treats him with respect in situations like this. When she tells him she'd prefer he colored on the paper, she explains why.

Lorraine, I think. It's not a sophisticated thought, but it's heavy. What else is there after so many years? What else is there when suddenly you're on the carpet with your own past—and a big aspect of it, at that? I launch into a barrage of nervous questions about her and Adam's lives. He's doing freelance Web work, she tells me, and she's taking care of Ian and working on writing when she has time. They think about buying a home. They miss New York. Ian passed his first coin yesterday. Then she just looks at me. It's the same look she used to give adults who were pestering her.

"I'm different," she says to me finally. She says it again, almost anxiously. She's in the presence of a ghost, after all—the kind that hasn't been briefed on certain transformations. Like all visits from the past, mine threatens to undo the careful progress that's been made. Ex-boyfriends are trouble.

So why bother? There are plenty of other classmates to intrude upon—nothing required that I speak with Lorraine. I called all these years later having gotten it in my head that we could sit down and figure out something deep. It was an amateur archaeologist's fantasy, some variation of which lies behind every one of these interviews. With Lorraine and me, we had known love at its earliest—just an excited young thing in the hallway—then gradually moved on. Couldn't we examine it dispassionately now, so many years later, from the safety of our respective happinesses? Wouldn't we learn something important to us, poking at it there under the microscope? What had we been like? How had we changed? All those phone calls into the night—what had we said? Or maybe just this: Hadn't it been nice? More recent and tumultuous unravelings, with their adult-scale cruelties—these are not to be treated as curios. But a sweet high school love affair?

"You told me we should see other people," she says twenty minutes into my visit.

"I know."

"I was bitter for a long time."

"I'm sorry."

LATER, AT THE end of the evening, when I've left the Rices and found a computer, I will read the Web log Lorraine keeps, and to which she alludes somewhat anxiously before dinner:

"He is from a time I would like to forget, more because of who I used to be, than anything about him," she's written in one entry, after my first phone call to the Rice household. Elsewhere, amid terrific descriptions of Ian and beautiful observations about life, there are writings on race that catch me off guard and shed light on some of the tension that rises and falls—and then crescendos—over the course of our dinner:

"For someone who has little patience these days for the racist bumblings of well-meaning whites, I sure do have a lot of white folks in my family. And I'm not talking about the man whose name I wore for years because he took it upon himself to help himself to my great-grandmother. Not the so-and-so who contributed to the fairness of my skin or the smoothness of my sister's hair. I'm talking about the folks I see on a regular basis; the ones who frequent our dinner table; the ones who make up our holiday gatherings. . . . When I say that my in-laws are racist, I mean in that liberal-minded, intellectualized, best of intentions sort of way that begs to differ, begs to be excluded from any generalizations or inappropriate labels that only serve to further hostility between the races. Racists in denial. It gets tiresome—the fascination with my hair; the singling me out for my expert opinion when the topic of race is raised; the insistence on relating to me on the level of my blackness, or rather their perceptions of it."

EVEN BEFORE READING Lorraine's writings, though, coloring there on the rug with Ian, I'm aware something has changed. It's a relief when Adam gets home. He does so tired, with the look of someone who often does so tired. He wears an iPod connected to headphones, and presents a gentle kiss to Ian. Ian knows "iPod," and repeats it while climbing up the legs in front of him. He's on his father's shoulders in two seconds flat, and from there discoursing confidently on trains. "I'm as happy as I've ever been," Adam told me earlier on the phone. "It's hard not to sound clichéd, but I don't think I had a sense of the depth of love I was capable of feeling. It's absolute."

It's also a secret, at least from Adam's great-grandmother—who he's convinced won't read this book.

"[She's] not allowed to know that I'm married, because Lorraine's black. She doesn't know she has a great-great-grandson. The way it was put to me, my grandparents were literally afraid that she'd have a stroke, and that would be it. She's in her nineties. So we don't even visit my grandparents, because she lives across the street from them.

"I do sometimes have the 'fuck 'em if they can't deal' feeling, but it would be hurtful and damaging to Lorraine [to confront them]. She would be like a bomb I'm dropping, and that's not really my place."

To marry Lorraine, Adam had to undergo a kind of sensitivity training on the subject of race. He was already very sensitive, but as Lorraine points out in subsequent conversations, that's precisely where a lot of liberal white people get complacent.

"I loved him," she tells me later, "but I couldn't have married him if he didn't make race a major focus of his life."

"I had to do a lot of reading before we got married," Adam says. "I had a lot to learn."

Lorraine felt that she, too, had a lot to learn, and did so after high school. Her concentration at college (Hampshire's equivalent of a major) was Women's Studies and African-American Studies, and these classes altered deeply how she'd long understood race. In that "intellectualized" way she writes about, to the extent that a black person and a white person can begin to, I think we once thought about race in the same way: We were lovers of Dr. King. We believed we were brothers and sisters. The civil rights message of justice and brotherhood was ultimately the right path, we thought, even when it seemed mild or the vocabulary outmoded. At college Lorraine looked deeper at these beliefs, questioned their implicit assumptions and omissions—in short, she learned the same depressing lesson everyone learns upon revisiting race: It's more complicated than they taught us in high school.

In high school Lorraine eschewed our Black Student Union, and for this received reproach from friends in the group. But she'd held her ground, saying (to me, at least) she wouldn't spend valuable time relating on a skin-deep level. At Hampshire she started attending the school's black student group and criticized other black students who didn't. What she'd concluded is that black student groups offer community and "a place where you can *not* be the only black person in the room."

Lorraine also adopted a new definition of racism: prejudice plus power. It's a popular but controversial interpretation that draws fire from both blacks and whites, as it implies that black people—fundamentally lacking power in this country—cannot be racists. (The debate, like so many contemporary debates on race, is a mess of misunderstanding. Nobody's arguing that black people can't be bigoted. It's just that their bigotry differs systemically from white racism.)

Back in reunion-land, the evening teeters between niceness and minidrama. Adam is casual and dry and self-deprecating—same as I remember him. Is he still the boy holding the $10 bill and the lighter? He's holding a twenty-three-month-old instead, and his hands seem pretty full. Ian sings. We all chop potatoes. At one point, Lorraine brings out a portrait I'd drawn of her. But at another, she confronts me about the surprise party I threw her, post-breakup, when she turned seventeen. She didn't like surprises.

"I thought everyone liked surprises!" I protest, and suddenly, as only exes can manage, we've wandered into a deeper wood. If lovers communicate in code—"Hi," we once said momentously—so, too, do *former* lovers. Lorraine's response to my protest is a look that assures me I'm annoyingly naive, a solipsist who assumes his good intentions are good enough in this world. I am well-meaning but callow; she is oppressed or at least irritated, an unwitting subject of my careless benevolence. In turn, I give a look that says I can't believe we're talking about a surprise party. (Adam, likably, tries to keep things simple. What he remembers from that party was hearing *Nevermind,* Nirvana's allegedly generation-defining album, for the first time. "That was big," he says with ample gravity.)

Ian, who had been on a toy-gathering mission, returns with a song instead, and we abandon our discussion. Politics and symbolism and other species of absurdity have a gnat's life span in homes with young singers. It's 8 o'clock, and this one happens to be rambunctious. Lorraine puts a cartoon into the VCR.

"We swore we'd never get a TV. Anyway . . . we're very careful about what he watches," Lorraine says. I make a face that I hope will establish that Ian can watch all the TV he wants, and that I'm sorry for a great number of things and that I still believe everyone in the world can get along one day.

Lorraine and Adam take Ian's education seriously and will be administering it themselves. The home-schooling plan wasn't ever really discussed, Lorraine says—"It was just understood he wouldn't go to school, unless he tells us he wants to."

"Schools are fucked up in so many ways," Adam adds. "There's so much institutional racism, to begin with."

"Everyone says, 'What about socialization? How will he be socialized?' And I'm thinking, 'High school? *What* socialization?'" Lorraine says. Here her eyes fall on me for just a second.

AMY ARRIVES WITH dessert. Amy is my girlfriend—from my real life, not high school—and in the planning of the evening, it was agreed that more would be merrier, or at least more interesting. With

Amy around, the tension between Lorraine and me lifts. More wine is opened. We sit down for vegetable burritos and proceed, in the manner of two couples just introduced, on to the reliable subject of babies. Before Ian, we learn, Lorraine had two miscarriages. Then, when she was twenty-five weeks pregnant with Ian, doctors told her something was wrong with her cervix, and that the baby could pop out any minute. She was bedridden for eleven weeks, five of those in the hospital. She passed her days watching TV, reading, and knitting.

"But being pregnant is the most incredible feeling I've ever had," she says, nevertheless. "I can't wait to feel it again."

Adam nods; Ian is holding his hand. We talk about fatherhood and the various insanities our own fathers might or might not have passed along. Lorraine's was "a slacker," and when they were living in Harlem, he was "doing something with numbers—gambling of some sort."

"It's funny," she says, turning to Adam sweetly. "You're such a slacker too, but I never worried about it, and you do just fine supporting our family."

"It's true, I'm a slacker."

"Well," she says after some thought, "it's more like you can't be torn away from whatever you're doing."

"Sleeping?"

"I was thinking computers."

Amy and I laugh, everyone laughs. We've all loosened up, and Lorraine and Adam are being sports about presenting their lives to a guy with a notepad. And so it happens I'm caught off guard by—by what? A memory? An accusation? A step toward healing? "Come on," I cajole Lorraine playfully, thinking something had finally repaired between us. "What do you remember about *our* relationship?"

Something had *not* repaired. On the contrary, I'd simply stumbled upon an odd moment of levity before the bomb doors were flung open.

"Well," Lorraine replies without hesitation, "one day, out of the blue, I remember you told me that you didn't think of me as black."

The room is silent for several moments.

"That doesn't sound like anything I'd say," I answer finally.

"You said it."

"I *really* don't think I would've said that."

"You said it," she replies.

And here, finally, is the high school reunion laid bare. It's the excavation of moments—truly, moments—we were too young to parse at the time. Lorraine's excavation has revealed me to be a kind of racist. The racism I'm being assigned is the race-blind variety—once ubiquitous among liberal whites (and some blacks), possibly a hair less so today. What began to dawn on people was that turning a blind eye to race is not only impossible—like trying to level the playing field on the side of a mountain—but wholly dismissive of meaningful racial differences. "Race has no place in American life or law," Kennedy declared in 1963, and decades later that putatively progressive thesis remains deeply divisive.

Lorraine and I had never talked about race, but for that one question on the bus: *What will our kids look like?* Now, picking at my burrito, I spiral into doubt. Could I have said something, anything, that denied her her blackness? Even knowing, as we did then, that color blindness was a flawed paradigm? This rings false. Besides, what shy sixteen-year-old would feel comfortable saying something so stupid? Anyhow I *did* think Lorraine was black, and I thought I was white. I just thought it didn't matter.

The evening has officially fallen to its knees. Zombie-like, we trudge into the living room to wind things down. Ian—oblivious, thankfully—is carried off to bed.

"I had a huge crush on you," Adam tells me when we're on the couch. I believe he's trying to make me feel better. Then Lorraine joins in, too, strangely enough.

"You were kind, and wanted everyone to be nice to each other. You really believed in that," she offers. "Even when those bullies were being assholes, you were kind to them somehow."

This last bit might be more patronizing than nice—a tribute to my simplistic faith in that childhood fantasy, equality—but I've heard worse. I mumble an awkward thank you and soon we're all at the door. "I'm sorry," Lorraine says quietly. "I didn't mean to come across so . . . You know, after we broke up, I really was bitter for a long time." Adam and Amy—technically civilian casualties by now—shift on their feet, and finally we're in Adam's car being driven to the Metro station. "Was that weird for you?" I ask as I'm getting out.

"No, no," he says. "You?"

"Definitely." We hug and agree to keep in touch.

THE SHOCK, NOW, is in discovering old alliances to have shifted, but at the time high school was always abuzz with accusation. As a class we challenged one another's ideologies constantly. The fights weren't lofty. They were probably *hormones*, actually. But at some level we were bickering about life itself. Admittedly, life seldom presented itself to us as anything deeper than a series of inflammatory questions demanding our yea or nay. Is affirmative action the right path? Should the environment take precedence over human interests? Are gays and lesbians—and through certain events, this became our flagship concern—treated fairly in our school, or our society for that matter? Our Weltanschauung was hardly a Weltanschauung, but the impulse came from someplace truly ontological. What is life, how is it to be lived, and—that inevitable teenage corollary—who's standing in the way?

A twenty-seven-year-old channeling a sixteen-year-old—that's the high school reunion in a nutshell—I can't now stomach the idea that I've been one of those standing in the way. The next time I speak with Lorraine is a month later, the day Senator Trent Lott appears on Black Entertainment Television to make amends for his recent public nostalgia for Senator Strom Thurmond's 1948 segregationalist campaign for president.

"To be a racist, you have to feel superior," Lott explains moronically to interviewer Ed Gordon. "I don't feel superior to you at all."

Lorraine answers the phone, and we skip the chitchat. Am I racist? Lorraine hems and haws, then says yes. I may not be bigoted, she reminds me, but all people have prejudices, and white people have power. I tell her she's not judging me by the content of my character. She asks why she has to talk about race when race is just a part of who she is. I say you can't call someone racist in America and then talk about the weather. She says she gets tired of sensitive white people thinking they understand. I ask why she married one and dated others. It's complicated, she says. An hour of this passes, and finally we agree that everything is complicated. Agreeing feels good. We even agree that we probably agree on quite a lot, when it comes down to it. Which it doesn't, very often.

Race is as swampy as it was in high school. There everyone had talked about it polemically, abstractly, and adolescently—those class conversations were a herding of cats: here, a boy calling blacks lazy; there, someone waving a bell hooks essay; here, a debate about genocide in Rwanda; there, a girl unconcerned with the whole thing and focused on her calculus homework. To say anything on the subject of race relations was to watch it ricochet throughout the vastly different corners of the classroom, and ultimately into meaninglessness.

Ten years later, things still ricochet. I'd wanted to talk about love, not race, but maybe love would have been just as charged. And who knows—maybe we *were* talking about love, sideways at least. In a subsequent e-mail, Adam remarks that he was surprised Lorraine and I were "both so unresolved around that relationship." "Unresolved" strikes me as a perfectly acceptable word in a book about high school.

4 "I Want to Be Everything"

M y classmates and I grew up in an age of good-hearted but insipid affirmations. *You can be whatever you want to be. Nothing is impossible. Life is what you make of it.* These bits of fuzzy Disney wisdom, improvements no doubt on what the previous generation had been told as kids (*Cut that hair*), were precise about one thing: The sky was the limit. Ours was a generation designed to have more than our parents did, and given the bounty of possibilities, our sole charge was to follow our bliss. Ten strange years later, my classmates give an account of how the following of bliss actually played out.

If it's an accounting of promise—ultimately squashed or otherwise—the last decade must surely begin with Clinton and that crisp January day in 1993 when he was inaugurated. The scene is still clear. We're jumping around on this day, watching our breath, wondering briefly about security along the inaugural parade route, mainly absorbed by our own proximity to history. We cheer and cheer, us high schoolers and others too, all types, even a boy in a beanie. A beanie: It's that kind of day, redolent of those optimistic years after World War II, confetti over everything. Not everyone likes this fellow from Arkansas—some here despise him—but there's excitement of one stripe or another on all sides, for change and youth are about to enter our era. "Tolerance" is the idea that swirls about, trailing this election and vibrating in our own little circles, too. It's a complex notion for teens, with its double meaning of enlightened acceptance and patrician concession, but we're thrilled to be discussing life itself at the end of the twentieth century. The beanie propeller spins patriotically, rekindlingly. *Hillary Next!* says a T-shirt. Elsewhere a dog wears sunglasses, like the big guy himself. Anything is possible, these signs indicate. Overwrought comparisons to Kennedy are forgiven, for we've lacked occasion to make them all our young lives. All our young lives we've wanted to feel like our own generation.

Bound up in the story of my class, and my generation, is our much-noted and occasionally overhyped sense of hope, which for us had so perfectly coincided with adolescence, when everyone's hopeful anyway. The peak of that hope has been misremembered by history— in truth there were only a few years between the dawning of our awareness of the Boom and its rapid collapse. If anything, our generation will one day be known not for its sense of hope, but for the historically small window that hope was squeezed into; by the age of twenty-six or twenty-seven, most of us had seen terrorism and unprecedented economic collapse obliterate any feeling of assurance. Nevertheless, for that brief moment in time, we did seem to believe we could do anything. What my classmates describe was a unique sensation, bolstered by technological advancements, by money, by a feeling in the air, and by those encouragements we'd heard since childhood. It wasn't optimism, for optimism can exist only in contrast to a kernel of pessimism. Ours was simply the warless, depressionless reality we'd always known, and we behaved as though impediment didn't exist.

"I never thought about *not* going to college," classmate David Lobe tells me, articulating our nearly unthinking assumption of upward mobility. "I don't know why I was so sure—my mom didn't do a four-year college, neither did my dad. Theirs was a different time. You went to college to get a job. They were the generation where you still heard 'college boy' and it meant something negative. I just wanted to go to a good school as an end in itself."

"As I was growing up, I was told I could do and be anything—and they weren't just telling this to *me*," Laura Wilbur, who now works for AAA in San Francisco, tells me one night over drinks. "It was a sheltered existence, like nothing bad was ever going to happen to you."

It wasn't just indulgent parents and teachers daring my class to dream. All around us were indicators of a vast easy street up ahead. The recession of the early '90s was lifting, the Internet became more of a reality every day, and American culture's love of youth grew steadily. Clinton was in his fun years, pre-Monica. People got jobs—great jobs, creative jobs. Globalization sounded nice.

My class set out to realize its abstract potential just as the boom years were beginning. Those not swept up in the optimism were exuberantly disregarded, and Americans on the losing side of the culture wars, NAFTA, or welfare reform got roundly buried in the good vibes. We had mourned the Rodney King verdict, weathered the Gulf War, and rebounded from the recession—now it was time to look forward.

"This is a special moment in history," our class heard over and over, and it was special for all the hardship it lacked. Certainly tension and danger swirled around us—we saw varieties of bigotry in our halls, and profound hatred just beyond. "Kill all niggers and Jews," someone painted on the elementary school beside our building one night. Later, five days after Clinton's inauguration, Mir Aimal Kasi went to CIA headquarters in Langley, fifteen miles from our school, and walked from car to car shooting passengers stuck in traffic— revenge for U.S. treatment of Muslims, he said later. But most of us failed, by and large, to regard these as signs. We were eighteen. They called it a hopeful era, so it *was* a hopeful era.

Cut to five years out of high school. The arc of our optimism can be picked up again in, say, an e-mail sent from California. The feeling of possibility is stronger than ever. The e-mail says *come out.* It is upbeat, mature, far from home—at twenty-three the writer has found her voice. San Francisco has these moments, the e-mail continues, the fog burned off and the outdoor bar packed around the tables, there's something in the air. It says out with the old. It says these dot-com jobs are the new thing, minimal bullshit. It says the times they are a-changin'. This may be the peak, it says, life may go downhill after this. But probably not all that far.

Skip ahead two more years. In this final glimpse of the trajectory of our hope, a dozen brief scenes intermingle. The cuts aren't sharp, like a movie montage, but blurred at the edges like dreams. There's the initial phone call and the turning on of the TV, and the sickening angles of the airplanes slicing through. There's the busy signal on the calls to Manhattan, to D.C. There's crying, still, months later. There are the plane dreams and the waiting. Then there's the learning of new terms, the Seymour Hersh articles, the wondering about box cutters, dirty bombs, strangers who'll die to kill us. Finally, there is war, then another war, and arguing all over again. The arguing doesn't feel energizing, as it did so many years ago in high school. There is bafflement at the relative smallness of politicians or dot-com jobs, the smallness of the self that once engaged with such trifles.

WHAT HAPPENED TO that vague but steady conviction that we could become anything we wanted? Terrorism can't be blamed entirely for its disappearance. If anything, 9/11 just signaled a change whose seeds had been planted in us far earlier.

John Doyle (Chapter 19) puts it like this: "I think there's a lot of unhappiness out there right now in our generation. And I think a lot of that has to do with people who don't know what they want in life. . . . Our parents, and our parents' parents, worked to survive, to establish themselves and set their kids up for success. Whether they hated work or not, they were going to always go there because they had a goal. Now that we've been set up for success—and many people *are* successful in their jobs—[we're] just not happy."

Classmate Alo Basu was voted most likely to appear on the cover of *Time* magazine when we were seniors. Around the time of our graduation, the *Washington Post* ran her photo and mentioned a few of the accomplishments that might have helped lead to the *Time* prediction: "Her near-perfect score of 1570, out of 1600, on the Scholastic Aptitude Test, her having been admitted to the Massachusetts Institute of Technology and her medical research project, 'The Action of 2-aryl-3-indoleacetamides (FGIN-1) on the Amnesiac Effects of Dizocilpine Maleate.'" She speaks English, Bengali, Hindi, and French, and sings Indian classical music; a presidential commission named her one of 141 Presidential Scholars nationwide, the *Post* reported. "I want to be everything," she says in the article. "That's the problem."

Ten years after leaving high school, Alo has yet to grace *Time*. And though her achievements haven't gotten less impressive over the years—she graduated from MIT with degrees in biology and brain and cognitive science, then went to Harvard for her Ph.D. in neuromedical science—she has revised the dream of being everything. "I'm less career-oriented and more life-oriented than I expected to be after [high school] graduation," she says. A year ago she married a fellow academic, and the two have decided against the life of long-distance romance so common to university-bound couples. Instead, she says, they're going to take turns following each other, even if it means a temporary career setback.

The classmates who are doing something, anything—but not the *ultimate* something or anything—are legion. Amanda Rieder, a good friend and a pianist in high school, and always the first to hear about a good new band, never lacked for direction at Jefferson. Since college she's led a happy but decidedly roundabout professional life. She tended bar in California. She spent several years as an assistant private investigator, working to get death sentences reduced to life. She quit and went back to bartending. She's an excellent and amiable bartender—I've seen her patrons adore her—but this past year she quit again, this time for New York. There she'll begin a graduate program in forensic psychology. With her master's under her belt, she'll go back to working on capital cases.

"I was told, growing up, that I could do whatever I wanted," says Lesley (Kato) Cook (Chapter 7). "And I fully believed I could. And therefore I had no idea what to do. I still feel that way. There are a lot of different directions I can go in, and I'm still totally caught in all the options: Art. Learning how to tattoo. Learning how to work on antiques. Going back to school and getting my English degree. Or going back to school for art. Or going to school for something entirely different, like forensic criminology. Or going to San Francisco and going to mortuary school. It's maddening."

What happened to our conviction that we could be whatever we wanted, that life was there for the taking? Did we take it? Are we in a temporary rut, or was it our earlier confidence that was anomalous? A young man once forsaken over a broken pellet-shooter now designs lethal weapons for the Naval Surface Warfare Center. A homecoming queen realizes she doesn't know what will happen next in her life. An old friend marries an ex-girlfriend, and an ex-girlfriend finds racism all around her. *Life is what you make of it*, they kept telling us as children—no doubt, but apparently life also makes things of itself, and we're not always consulted or prepared.

5 Brenda McEldowney

BRENDA MCELDOWNEY: *"I'm still searching for my voice, but I didn't feel like I had one at all back then. I was quiet. I was under my parents' thumb, my boyfriend's thumb, whoever's thumb. I didn't feel like I could have opinions back then. 'What movie do you want to see?' 'Oh, I don't care.' As for what other people thought, in my yearbook they'd write, 'You're so sweet!' I did a lot of observing, as opposed to participating, which I do very much now."*

SAM ZEITLIN: "I met her freshman year in choir. She was shy, sort of unsure of herself in the beginning. A straight-A student with perfect handwriting who couldn't spell! She was studying dance all the time. But she wasn't an exhibitionist—I don't think she did it to get attention. She loved music and dancing. We were all amazed that she could convince her parents that it was okay to possibly become a starving artist."

RICH VUDUC: "She was quiet, but there was something elegant about her. She was attractive, and she spoke French, and was very talented."

MARCUS GROENIG: "She and I were boyfriend and girlfriend in high school and a year into college. She was very smart, very talented . . . very naive, very sheltered, very kind. Emotional. Very well-read, cultured. At the core, she was a very simple, kind, caring person—the kind of person you could take home to Mom."

■

Alo Basu was on to something—a decade after high school, that which most impacts my classmates' love lives might be busyness, of all things. The years after our graduation didn't invent busyness, but they saw to its upgrade: productivity levels skyrocketing, leisure time dwindling, and so on. Faster technology never quite freed us to pass our hours on riverbanks, as once predicted; instead our lives got faster, too, as if to keep up with all the time-saving. Not just for the cubicle set, busyness as a way of life washed over the farthest noncorporate corners of my class during the late nineties. This should have been no surprise for a group of young people weaned on the double gospel of individualism and ambition—isn't that the recipe for busyness?—but for a certain half of us, time expenditure became yet another political issue. My high school class came of age amid the oddly persistent debate over the mythical Busy Woman, aka the Career Woman. We saw the blood pressure of conservative scolds and feminists alike skyrocket no matter how often the tired matter was revisited. At the heart of the matter was the busy woman's love life: a stepping-stone to her family life, as some saw it, and so the foundation of our very nation.

One side of the quarrel saw domesticity threatened by busyness, the American suburb itself threatened. The other saw anxious old men wringing their hands over having to heat their own pot pies. Ten years after we left high school, I spoke with one of the busiest women I know, who happens to be trying to make it in the busiest city I know, and who is busied by emerging arts careers, in which individualism and ambition come in spades. She has also spent the bulk of her twenties in a serious, long-term relationship.

Brenda McEldowney's day begins in an elevator so narrow that a man carrying a sandwich would have to eat it before entering, in a cramped, midtown Manhattan office that opens to several pods of computers, each staffed by professional transcribers, or rather *impostor* professional transcribers. Nearly everybody in this office, if not everybody, is actually an actor. This is the day job they haven't quit. At any monitor at any given time, one may find the unspooling transcript of a Nicole Kidman interview, or a *Dateline* exclusive on JonBenét Ramsey's parents, or testimony from a grisly murder case in Florida; also at any given time, any one of the transcribers may quietly push back his or her chair, throw on a jacket, and hurry away to dance, sing, or act.

Brenda, who in high school sang and danced and acted but offstage kept a low profile, is now a tornado of activity in New York City; on a Tuesday afternoon she calls slow, she lets me tag along through the wreckage. Out of the office, into the corner grocery she walks briskly for her lunch, a banana. Then back to the office, up the tiny elevator, into a tiny lunchroom, sitting only for the length of the banana. Then down to the street, onto the A train, more brisk walking to the small Upper West Side studio on the park to rehearse for a benefit. Some quick theater chitchat with the music director happens—costumes, certain singers' heights, et cetera—then it's over to the green piano in the corner of the apartment.

He plays, she sings. On the wall above them is a Renoir-ish reproduction of angelic, alabaster figures at a piano, and this is more or less the impression Brenda herself gives. Admittedly, she lacks the flowery Victorian dress—in fact, she's wearing Japanese jeans she got when she performed in a Broadway revue in Tokyo recently—but with her porcelain skin and simple, white-tennis-shoe style, she has a way of making even a rushed lunch-hour moment look pastoral. "Jack and Jill prefer the hill / and they're a thrill / beneath the silvery moon," she trills. Irving Berlin carries the next forty-five minutes, lyrics tending toward spooning or springtime, sometimes both ("Springtime is the best time to spoon"). A person singing such things is an innocent. If she had a theatrical prop, it would be an oversized lollipop.

Back on the street, we rush down to midtown again. Another banana lunch and two auditions will take place tomorrow. She auditions five or six times in a normal week, plus callbacks, plus rehearsals. She'll find out about one callback tomorrow, and if she gets the part, she'll back out of the benefit for which she just rehearsed. Benefits don't pay. Why do them in the first place? Brenda recently switched agents and wanted to give the new one a chance to see her work. "A couple headliner types" from Broadway were also doing the benefit, and sometimes they attract attention, and you never know. On Fifth Avenue, trailing a half-step behind, I ask Brenda what the big-picture goal is. "Best-case scenario is no more typing, [and] I support myself completely with my theater," she says. "I would like to do a mix of everything."

There's that word again—*everything*. It seems to me Brenda *does* do a mix of everything. She spent several months at Japan's Disney-Sea, singing and dancing. She's spent half a year on board a Norwegian Cruise Lines ship, performing in three shows as a principal dancer. ("We had weekly weigh-ins. Cruise ships are just nuts.") She spent another few months in upstate New York, in a production of *Phantom*. She had a part in a small independent film. Last December she had a supporting role in a ten-episode Russian miniseries, shot largely in New York. Her part had originally been given to a Russian actress, but this was shortly after 9/11, and when it came time to begin shooting the American scenes, the actress wasn't allowed into the country. Brenda took over, à la Darren in *Bewitched*. ("My character was the girl-next-door Russian who comes to America and is sold into stripping, and decides she likes it. We had a scene in a strip club. I was clothed head to toe. I didn't want to be in any kind of G-string.")

Brenda keeps a key to her office so she can transcribe at 3 A.M., she says. This pace is not atypical in this or other cities, but Brenda is not, at heart, a city girl. She doesn't come across as corn-fed, but there's no trace of world-weariness in her, either. "Gosh only knows," she says at one point. Her bangs and her pink scarf luff in all the rush. Back to the A, back to work. We part for the day, and I propose scheduling another get-together. Brenda keeps her calendar in her head. "Let's talk tomorrow," she says.

FOR ALL THEIR lying on couches, high school students are among the busiest people going. They wake early, toil in a variety of unrelated and boring fields, negotiate family concerns, struggle to keep over a thousand peers' faces in some kind of social grid, and in the remaining hours squeeze in a lifetime of worrying. Brenda fell squarely in the normal range of most high school indices. She didn't get pregnant at sixteen, didn't play with pellet guns, and didn't engage in many of our fierce political debates. She didn't wear elaborate piercings, and she didn't wear a cheerleader uniform, either. Were her character to be written into a screenplay, a bewildered script doctor might well scratch his head at her seeming ordinariness and finally give her lupus. Brenda was a soft-spoken, friendly, and unostentatious girl who quietly dedicated herself to theater.

Brenda first learned to share her devotions our senior year, when she asked a boy named Marcus to homecoming. This was Brenda's central high school romance, one she calls "a twisted, sordid nightmare." The date had its foundations in symmetry more than passion—Brenda's friend was going with Marcus's friend—but somehow Brenda made an impression. For a long time after the dance, she says, Marcus insisted rather inimitably on a prolonged arrangement.

"I remember him coming in with these scratches all over his wrist and being like, 'Look! This is why I'm so depressed, because you don't want to be with me!'" Brenda says. "And so finally I was like, 'Fine! I'll go out with you!' And we started dating, and we stayed together for that entire year."

And then they continued to stay together, though Marcus's devotion had mutated into criticism. Brenda's decision to major in musical theater at the University of Michigan, she says, just didn't strike him as a good idea. "Here I am in acting class, with Marcus in the back of my head going, 'You're too smart! What are you doing? You should be doing something that's actually worth your time!'"

While Marcus wanted Brenda to devote less time to a frivolous arts career, Brenda wished Marcus would devote a little more to the subjects that truly interested him. "His passion was history. He loved history. I always kept thinking, 'You should go into history. Be a history professor, be this eccentric older man—I could totally see him in a classroom. But here's what he said to me: 'Your job is to make money, that's why you work. So from nine to five I'm going to be miserable.

But I'm miserable from nine to five so I can have a life outside that.' There was something really warped about that, to me. I want my life to be full 24/7."

I call Marcus expecting to find Brenda has exaggerated his commitment to professional misery. By now I know that the particulars of a high school romance can be remembered rather differently by those who were involved—in fact, I'm a little anxious to look in on how another TJ relationship has fared over time. But what I encounter in Marcus is a voice I scarcely recognize as that of a classmate; he sounds instead like a Gen-Xer's parody of the previous generation.

"I have a fairly strong philosophy on work," Marcus tells me from his office in Austin, Texas. He's something called a process architecture engineer for Samsung—responsible, he explains, for "overseeing DRAM products." "I know a lot of people who are doing what they always wanted to do. But some of us do jobs because they allow us to live a lifestyle that we want. There are jobs that are *not* engineering-related that I would *like* to do, but . . ." He trails off here, picks up with a proud enumeration of all that his career supports. "I have a six-year-old house with four bedrooms, I have a nice big garage. I'm about to get a new car, and I already had one before the current one. I'm able to purchase what I like. It sounds shallow, but physical possessions are a way to measure happiness. At the end of the day, I can go home and play with my toys."

Marcus and I go on to talk about life in general since high school. He isn't crazy about Arabs these days, he tells me before going on to explain that writers like myself don't have *real* jobs. Which reminds him of those nonengineering majors at college who "had fun on Friday nights while I was doing problem sets"—he suggests that some kind of "bad karma" will eventually pay them back for their whimsy. Finally, I ask what he thinks of Brenda and her current professional arrangement—a subject, after all, that figured prominently in the dissolution of their relationship years back. Marcus is characteristically frank:

"I think she could've succeeded at anything she put her mind to. She was very focused on doing what made her happy, to the exclusion of doing certain things well. She could've succeeded as a scientist or a computer programmer. I have a lot of respect for her perseverance, but I certainly wish she'd chosen otherwise. I have a difficult time understanding how somebody can turn their back on realism. [People like Brenda] pour their life and their essence into this fantasy."

BRIAN IS THE name of Brenda's nonfantasy boyfriend. She's been with him for five years—most of her adult life, really, at least since the end of college. "I've felt like I've always wanted to have somebody else in my life," she says. "That's just always been one of my priorities. I feel better, I need that, it's important to me."

We're having breakfast when she tells me this, at a restaurant near St. Mark's. Brian, in a skullcap and wearing a contagious grin, sits beside her. The three of us discuss the politics of love and career. She is not unaware of the pressures that attend otherwise happy arrangements like hers.

Now, as our waiter freshens our coffees, she describes a rolling conspiracy of lifestyle directives, and then a chorus of defiance from people—from women, really—that leaves her equally skeptical. Most recent is a barrage started by the magazine industry, she says.

"It almost seemed like the publishers called each other and were like, 'Okay, we're all gonna put out as many covers as we possibly can about the fact that you can't get pregnant after forty.' And all the women were like, 'Aaaahh!!' There was this big outcry, like 'Don't tell us what to do!' But I think people have blinders to a certain extent. 'I can be Superwoman. Madonna can have a baby at forty-one, so can I.' I'll be really curious to see what happens to us . . . in twenty years when we think we can have and do it all."

This is just breakfast, and I don't think Brenda means to be saying anything overly provocative. But to speak of women having and doing it all is code for women reaching too far beyond what was historically out of reach, and whatever follows tends to be heard by pricked-up ears. What follows in this case is Brenda saying this: "There's a finite amount of time and energy and biology."

Brenda devotes much of her energy and biology to Brian, in particular, because his nose lights up, and he passes saltshakers through wood tabletops, and he has shaved his head even though it will limit his marketability. Brian is a clown. Also a magician, a mime, a juggler, a singer, an acrobat, a dancer, an actor, and an "interactive street theater" performer. He is tall and gentlemanly. At times he suggests a young Bill Murray. He holds doors, head down butlerlike, and comes into the city from Queens just to meet Brenda on her lunch hour.

The challenge of negotiating individual pursuits and couplehood will be relatively minor for the next couple weeks, which will find both actors living in New York. The hardest part is coordinating auditions and rehearsals so that certain meals can be shared, and this has proven feasible. It's not usually so simple. Over the last five years, Brenda says, they've spent a total of two and a half in the same area code.

A glance at the résumé on the back of Brenda's headshot—an approachable, wholesome image—gives a sense of why her love life often happens telephonically. Brian is no less busy. And while the ultimate goal for both actors is to establish stable enough careers that work outside New York can be declined, that's a long way off. Two weeks from today, Brian boards a cruise ship gig of his own. For about three months he'll do clown work, juggling, and assorted variety arts—"Blue Man Group meets 'Stomp,'" Brenda says. Does the ship have e-mail? How often does it port? These are the kinds of questions she and Brian ask these days.

SEVERAL MONTHS AFTER following Brenda around in New York, I phone to see what's changed. She informs me that Brian returned safely from his time on the cruise ship—and then left again, for a summer job at Hershey Park. The past few months have had their share of trying moments.

"We calculated. This year we might actually have seen each other *less* than half the time," she tells me. "We sort of went into crisis mode around the time he was on the ship."

Since then, things have improved. She and Brian got better about scheduling phone conversations when one of them is away, and not talking when either is exhausted. At the same time, Brenda says outside pressure on the relationship has picked up.

"My family went back to '*When are you getting married?*' We had a big blowout over it. *They* see Brian and me as not willing to make a commitment to each other; *we* feel like we just don't know each other enough yet. My mother told me, 'Our priority was relationships and yours have been careers.'"

Just to keep things straight at this point, I tally in my head. Brenda's got a family urging her to ease off the career a smidge, an ex-boyfriend reproaching her—in absentia, at least—for not taking her career seriously enough, and a magazine industry reminding her biweekly that her biological clock is ticking louder than ever. Fortunately, Brenda is either too talented or too busy to suffer any real injury in this pileup. In fact, she's more or less casual.

"My mother's right to an extent," she adds, "but I think [Brian and I] are just dealing with it in a different way than their generation did. Anyway, we're rolling up our shirtsleeves these days."

6 Tim Yerington

TIM YERINGTON: *"I was a mostly awkward guy who was kind of angry in a lot of ways. I was bitter that I was gay, that I didn't fit in, that I wasn't athletic like my brothers, that I wasn't one of the popular kids. It was more or less the standard high school things. I had friends, but I didn't have any clue who I was. I was really immature. I was the youngest of my siblings and wasn't expected to be mature."*

BRIAN MCCONNELL: "I had been friends with Tim Yerington throughout high school. When he started saying that he had bisexual tendencies, I was leaning toward that knee-jerk conservative club, very closed-minded, 'those mother-effing blah blah blah.' But when you have to step back and think about it, it was like, 'I know Tim. He's a good person. I don't want to hate this person. He's a nice guy.'"

WAYNE STEWARD: "His reputation was a little unfair: Before he came out, people talked about him as being sleazy or slimy—getting around, I guess. I don't think that was fair. I'm not sure I did my part to counteract that when it would come back to me. He was a nice guy."

JOHN HELMANTOLER: "Tim Yerington was the biggest horn-dog ever freshman year. He was all over every girl I knew, and was notorious for that. I'd be talking to a girl, and he'd come up behind her and start giving her a backrub. And then *he's* coming out? What? Don't tell me he's coming out to get more chicks! It was a slightly unbelievable change—he went from major to minor in a single bar."

SAM ZEITLIN: "He was a little geeky, not super geeky. Our lockers were next to each other all four years. He was kind of flirtatious. Senior year we started talking a lot about our parents not understanding us—he was coming out at the time, although he was describing himself as bi then.

"We dated briefly that year. I got mono from him. I had it for several months—it was awful. It wrecked all my auditions for music school. I always kind of wondered if he's why I didn't become a musician. I was really upset at the time, especially because he lied—he'd told me he just had chronic fatigue syndrome. He admitted it to me later that he'd pretty much known. I broke up with him because of it."

LESLEY COOK: "We'd known each other since we were nine or ten, and used to walk to elementary school together. . . . The difference from before he came out and after was huge. A world of difference. He was pretty miserable, he was worried about coming out to his friends. He was so full of life and happy afterwards."

■

When I say I'm finding old high school classmates, people ask, *What are they doing?* Implied here is that we are, indeed, *doing* something—reinventing our high school identities, rethinking our positions, playing strippers in Russian miniseries—and not that things are being done to us. What about chance? What about plans falling aside, scrambling to regroup after the *un*planned takes place? Lest it be overlooked exactly how much plans can change—and in just a year's time—here is what Lesley Cook had heard about Tim before they lost touch:

"Tim is married now, has been for a long time, to a much older guy named Dan. Don't know if they're legally married. Tim is getting his Ph.D. in Texas, I think, so he can be in a program about gay and lesbian psychology. Tim's goal is to have a housekeeper, who speaks Spanish and English, to raise his children for him! He wants kids, he just doesn't want to raise them—and he wants them to speak Spanish!"

FRANKLY, I CALLED Tim to see what he remembered about Lesley. I expected to be off the phone in fifteen minutes. I won't say politics and bigotry and other high school detritus had wholly disintegrated by the end of our conversation an hour and a half later. Tim, who speaks of life with the restraint of a reformed romantic, would find that an all-too-elaborate misapprehension. Nor will I say I was depressed, or even sniffling, by the end of that first talk, because Tim says this: *Life is really rather happy.* So I'll just start with high school.

In high school Tim was a skinny kid with glasses and a stud in each ear. Tim did not seem terribly anxious about fitting in, though he was not unpopular. He had superstar older brothers—they went to Jefferson ahead of him, were great swimmers, and went on to become doctors—and had some individuality to carve out. Lesley recalls in him flare-ups of "little-brother syndrome." Tim sometimes wore a smirk, but the sass he dispensed now and then was good-natured. Finally, as with an uncommonly high percentage of us, high school seemed to split into two eras for Tim. To be precise, they were straight and then gay.

Right up till senior year, the straight Tim (or maybe the Tim who *thought* he was straight) was known for his efficacy at being straight. "He was getting laid by all sorts of chicks" is how Helmantoler puts it. But as Tim remembers it, his heart wasn't always entirely in it:

"My friends and I would go to a movie and they'd be all into the boobs, and I'd be like, *hmm*," he recalls. "It's not that I wasn't homophobic—I was. You can't not be. You're raised in this country believing being gay is gross."

Senior year was when our classmate Wayne Steward came out—to lots of fuss but little surprise. But no one saw it coming with Tim. Lesley remembers getting the news:

"One day he told me he was house-sitting for some people, and he was like, 'I need you to come over to study with me.' I thought this was strange, but I figure 'Okay, I'll bite.' Really what he wanted to do was come out to someone."

It didn't go so badly. For all the buzz at TJ about harassment of gays and lesbians, Tim never felt any directly. He likens the school's mass coming-out, cautiously, to the Civil Rights movement—he's not the only one to do so—but it was Civil Rights toned down many notches. There were no firehoses at Jefferson. For all the arguing and dirty looks and concerned parents, our school's introduction to gay pride seems to have left few truly *scarred*—though it left many with the righteous feeling of participating in history itself.

"It's something we should be proud of, I think. It was tolerance," Tim says. "I think we were raised and taught to act like leaders. Not that we were great moral people, and not sleeping around, and not acting like teenagers, but it was still an expectation."

As for Tim's parents, they were just relieved when he told them: "They knew—parents *know*—and were worried I [had been] repressing."

"Who knows—I was sixteen," he says about the whole experience. "I came out when everyone else did, Wayne and those guys. It was cool to do it that way, it was a socially comforting way to do it, but it wasn't necessarily a good way to figure out who I was. You do that by yourself, later."

IN HIGH SCHOOL we're warned of well-heeled kids cutting loose at college, losing control like monkeys. It's a cliché, and it's exactly what happened to Tim when he went off to Mary Washington.

"My parents are very dominant at my house—not controlling, just dominant. There weren't any drinking parties, and I never did drugs—not a lot of self-exploration possibilities. I went to college and was on my own, and I completely fucked up. I tried drugs, had a 2.1 GPA, didn't go to classes. One day I showed up high to an Italian class. I wasn't even in the class. It was the funnest year I've ever had, and a great way to figure what I *didn't* want to be."

Having squeezed about eighteen semesters of debauchery into that first year, Tim was ready to settle down by sophomore year. He did so as ferociously as he'd partied the previous year.

"His name was Dan. I met him that summer after freshman year, while lifeguarding," Tim says, his voice trailing off. "He was older, wiser. We found domestic bliss."

Tim spent another year at Mary Washington, then transferred to George Mason to be closer to Dan, who lived in Maryland. In 1996, the two went to Rehoboth, Virginia, and got married—meaningfully, if not legally. Tim was twenty-one, Dan thirty-four. "I became the perfect poster child for the gay movement: married, monogamous, volunteering for charities," Tim says. It was what he thought his parents wanted.

"We lived merrily, I finished my bachelor's in psych, then got into the University of Houston for grad school, so I took us to Texas of all places. I was getting a Ph.D. in clinical psychology for a year but gradually began to doubt what I was doing."

And then domestic bliss frayed. In Virginia, Tim had always been home while Dan was at work; he was *around*. Now he worked 100-hour weeks, leaving Dan friendless and lonely about the house. In his busyness and his reluctance to consider defeat—"My parents are still married, and divorce was just not an acceptable option for me"—Tim says he ignored certain signals. That became impossible the night he came home to a strange man in his bed with Dan.

"I just stood there," Tim says.

"Did you say anything?" I ask.

"I said 'Hi.' 'Hi' is what I said."

Eventually Tim wandered back into the spare bedroom to write a paper. The two didn't talk for the rest of the week, then finally screamed.

"[Dan] said he needed to get counseling, but that didn't really work. It went on for another six months or so, and in April of 2000, it was done. I was tired. I didn't want to deal with it anymore. Two weeks later, he moved to Florida with another guy."

Tim had been thinking of dropping out of school, but as his marriage dissolved, friends advised him to postpone additional life changes. He stuck it out at the university for a little longer and behaved the way one does when one's husband moves to Florida with another man. "I'd dated a little in high school, but not much. So I went a little crazy after the divorce, took some risks."

IT RAINED AND therefore poured after the divorce. A general flood swallowed him, and little in the way of noticing distinct afflictions took place. When his health suffered, he simply didn't pay attention. Finally, he got it in his head he had cancer.

"I had pneumonia a couple times, and was losing weight. They were testing for lymphoma, and allergies, and other stuff. In December I flew home for Christmas, and while I was home, I got a 106 temperature. I was really sick and delirious. My brothers, who are doctors, had me on an IV in the house.

"When I got back to Texas, the doctor said, 'Let's get a follow-up test.' The whole thing was a mess for a while. The blood work took a long time, and they lost the results to the test. Meanwhile, my sinuses were terrible and I couldn't sleep. It was a Monday, and I was in the [doctor's] office—I wanted drugs so I could sleep. The guy said, 'Okay, let me just check your chart.'

"His name was Sunday, I'll never forget that. It was his first year. He came back out and just lost it, started crying. I didn't know what to think—cancer?—and I couldn't get an answer out of him. Finally he said, 'You have HIV.'

"At first—it wasn't rational—I was relieved that it wasn't cancer. Then it sank in. He kept bawling, so I went into psychologist mode and shut down. I started figuring out immediately what I needed to do, what tests to get done, that sort of thing. It's frightening how calm you can be at these times.

"I got in my car—it was pouring down rain and hail—and I was driving home and crying, because I'd lost it at this point. I finally got home and called friends from the program—everyone was in the student lounge, so the whole department found out that day."

Calling his parents was another story. "I didn't want to tell them. It's so shameful to get HIV—I know better, I had no excuse," he says. Worse, HIV had already touched the family. "My uncle had it, and he killed himself—he blew his head off because he didn't want to be a burden. That was [my mom's] one take on HIV."

Tim called his older brother instead. "We had a crying session over the phone, and then he got off and promptly told my father. I'd told him not to, but it was good. I would've lost it, and he probably did too, but as a doctor he could also tell them it's treatable, and that it's not a death sentence.

"My parents and I talked after their initial breakdown. They said, 'It's fine, we'll deal, we'll take care of it'—they weren't hysterical. It was just what you'd want your parents to do. They were wonderful."

There were still more phone calls to make.

"When you find out you're positive, you have to do the callbacks. Very fun. I called everyone, and [the man who gave it to me] was the only one who turned out to be positive. He hadn't known. He was this guy I knew was bad—seedy character, I knew he was doing drugs, if not selling them. His personality was enthralling, he was fun to be with, and was amazing in bed. But he was nobody you'd ever bring home."

Tim says the condom probably broke—his behavior was risky, but not *that* risky. "I was sexually active, but not fucking everything that moved. I was smart. I used condoms."

I TELL WAYNE Steward that Tim has HIV, expecting—I don't know—emotion. Wayne, who paved the way for coming out at our school, is now a postdoctoral fellow at the Center for AIDS Prevention Studies at the University of California–San Francisco. His exact response is "Uh-huh."

Of course, *uh-huh* is politics, not indifference. Responding to the report of a peer's infection is tricky business in both the gay and AIDS research communities. The receipt of staggering news must be weighed against the mantra *HIV is not a death sentence.* The mantra isn't just insistence on hope, Wayne says, it's remonstrance against pity and, by extension, blame.

Tim has his own strategies for processing the news. "At first you dwell, and get angry, and find blame. Then you realize: You can be bitter and have HIV, or you can move on and have HIV," he says. "Being angry and bitter and [HIV] positive is kind of a joke, you know? This is not a maturity thing, though it sounds like it. I'm not wise—I just don't have a choice."

As proof of his lack of wisdom, Tim offers up his current bachelorhood. Love has been a sporadic and sometimes clumsy proposition since he found out about being positive. "HIV makes dating difficult. You meet someone in a bar and try to slow things down enough to bring it up. I've tried so many different ways, none of them works great. I've tried the casual slip-in, having a friend bring it up. I've tried to date just positive men. There's no socially appropriate way to tell someone you're positive, and no socially appropriate way to respond.

"I've had the whole gamut of reactions: from not caring, to them telling me they're positive too (and relieved), to them flipping out. Full-on wig-out. I guess there's a most popular reaction: There's a PC component in the gay community, where you're not supposed to care. You're supposed to say, 'That's fine, doesn't matter.' But two weeks later, they always end up saying, 'You know what, I'm really wigged out about the HIV thing.'

"The truth is, I'm kind of in an awkward age range when it comes to dating. Not many guys going on thirty have it—most people [my age] knew better. The younger guys are more likely to be positive because they take more risks—everybody's been on the cocktail, so nobody's dying right now. It's going to be different in ten years."

By coincidence, the day of my conversation with Tim is the same that conservative activist Jerry Thacker withdraws his name from consideration for a presidential advisory panel on AIDS, amid reports that he'd referred to AIDS as the "gay plague" and the gay lifestyle as a "deathstyle" in the past. This news is on my mind—as are four long years of similar analysis from right-wing high school classmates—when I find myself taken aback by something Tim says. The most promising of his recent relationships was with none other than Dale Carpenter, ex-president of the Log Cabin Republicans.

"I didn't want to move to Minneapolis, and he didn't want to quit his job. Other than that, I might've married him," Tim says.

I confess to Tim that the concept of gay Republicans still eludes me all these years later.

"You have to make a distinction between Christian conservative and politically conservative," he explains. "Republicans are actually better on the issues than Democrats, oftentimes. Democrats treat gays like they treat blacks—they don't do squat for them, since they assume it's a guaranteed vote."

"I don't remember George W. Bush knocking down the door of the gay community to get our vote," Wayne says incredulously when I relay Tim's theory. "To be a gay Republican is a little deluded," he says. But Tim is adamant. When I ask where America is with regard to homosexuality these days, he replies with a Republican's economic perspective:

"The last gay-pride parade I went to, there was a *plumber* there. There was a time it was just frou-frou floats and guys in Speedos. Now there was a plumber there, with a rainbow flag on his truck. He just wanted to plumb for gay people! Gay people are finally just another group of people that a person can get money from."

TIM LEFT TEXAS: "Fuck it, I have HIV, I don't want to be in grad school." In accordance with his new life strategy (roughly, *be happy*), he got to work on a more pleasant existence and jettisoned any extra weight.

"I went onto Monster.com and found out, to my surprise, I'm very marketable," Tim says. "I got a job in San Diego and moved out just after 9/11. I'm a statistical programmer. It pays really well, and it's not the hardest job in the world. I come home, no homework, and I have a life again."

It's now been two years since his diagnosis, and the particulars of that life remain optimistic:

"My viral load is zero or really low now that I'm on the cocktail. I've had no problems so far. I've never felt as well as I do now. The healthier you stay, the longer you live. You eat better, you exercise, and you don't make excuses. There are days I'm nauseous, but apart from that, there isn't a day-to-day impact from the HIV.

"HIV's shitty, but it's not the worst thing that can happen to you.

It's not painful when it's in check, it's not disfiguring. And being gay and positive, you're part of a community. I think it'd be much harder to be straight and have HIV. When you're gay, everyone's used to having 20 percent of the population be positive. And even though it's going to obviously kill me, I could get smacked by a bus a lot sooner.

"I'm happy with who I am now. My parents are happy with who I am. I have really great parents and didn't realize that until I was twenty-six. They set a really high standard for us but didn't care when we missed! And one of the benefits of HIV is it forces you to prioritize things. You've got this looming nastiness that you can compare everything else to. Credit-card companies? They can kiss my ass. Student loans? I'm not too worried. You focus more on what's important. Spending time with family and friends, that kind of thing. Chances are they're going to bury me, so I want to make it right."

When I next check in with Tim, his father has just retired after over thirty years at the Department of Energy and will be moving out to Ohio with Tim's mother to be near their other sons—who live across the street from each other. Tim has been invited to join the fun, but he's declined. ("I don't do winter," he explains.) He has moving plans of his own in the coming weeks—to Los Angeles, for a better-paying job. The position, and the perks, are roughly the same: "I use my brain, but the work doesn't follow me home and interfere with the rest of my life."

"What's the rest of your life?" I ask.

"Oh, nothing special," he replies with a patient sigh. It's the kind of sigh one gives to someone asking heavy questions long after lightness has become the rule. "I go to the beach, I go to the gym, I play computer games—you know, *life*."

7 Lesley Kato

LESLEY (KATO) COOK: *"People find me hard to approach. Which is funny, because I'm not mean or rude without provocation."*

ANNE BARNHILL: "We've known each other since third or fourth grade. She was always outspoken and pretty rebellious— tough and sassy. Very individualistic, and a little bossy. . . . Her parents let her do things that my parents didn't let me do. She had free rein, she could sort of do whatever she wanted around the house.

"I think it was beyond the pale for me [when she got pregnant]. It seemed not very real. She was very resolute, from the beginning, about what she was going to do. We didn't talk about her options— she was clear immediately about keeping the baby. I think she thought that having an abortion would be wrong. Why she chose not to give him up for adoption, I don't know. It does seem plausible that her decision was motivated by wanting to be strong, and to be able to handle anything. She's very willful."

BRIAN MCCONNELL: "I sat next to Lesley Kato in chemistry class. We weren't the closest of friends, but we were friendly, and she had expressed bisexual tendencies. If you're honest with yourself and you say, 'My first gut instinct is to think they're sick in the head, or it's gross'—you need to think more logically about it."

WES BLACK: "She got pregnant—that was the big thing—but she was also supposedly bisexual. I couldn't tell whether those people really were gay, or just wanted to be part of something that was sort of popular at the time. She was pretty outspoken politically."

L esley Cook doesn't talk about what I think she's going to talk about. Not at first, anyway. We're in a café in Washington, D.C.'s Dupont Circle, not far from where she lives, and she's slouching before a big cup of tea. After some catching up, I've asked her about her time at TJ, and what she describes, of all things, is the politics.

"I thought TJ was conservative—until I started doing stuff. Then I found out there were a lot of liberal people there who'd been keeping quiet, and there was a lot of liberal faculty that was keeping quiet."

In Lesley's parlance, "liberal" seems to mean gay, and "doing stuff" means rabble-rousing. If she sounds a bit encrypted, it might just be a holdover from when her various political actions made encryption necessary. Lesley was an activist—the sort who wound up explaining herself to administrators from time to time. But she wasn't always a grizzled veteran of the debate trenches. Her former classmates would come to think of her overwhelmingly as that goth-tinged firebrand, that liberator of closeted gays, *that girl having orgies in the ceiling*, but Lesley was none of these for the first half of high school.

In the beginning, it was theater tech work, not politics, that she cared for. Theater tech people wear black jeans and carry tools on their belts even where the need for tools isn't apparent to civilians. Lesley's focus changed in a day, at a speech sponsored by a club called the Medical Explorers, to which she belonged briefly.

"One day we had an AIDS speaker come talk to us. The students [at the meeting] behaved so badly during the speech—muttering at him and mocking him [about homosexuality]—that I went up to him at the end and all I could get out was 'I just want to tell you—' The next day was when I went to talk to [our principal] Mr. Jones about setting up a student group for gay and lesbian issues."

It's hard to say what was more formative for Lesley—her emotional introduction to homophobia or the postscript, in which she learned her student group was forbidden. What followed was a fight, and then ten more years of fights. It's what she does best, or at least most.

Lesley stands out among the school's militants as the only one said to have assembled an army more or less in her likeness. As Lesley tells it, she was a Pied Piper to the school's fellow gays, lesbians, and bisexuals (she considers herself the latter). While some of us exchanged fire with homophobic meatheads in class, her work happened largely in the closet. To students' homes she would go—she made house calls!—to offer support as they mulled coming out. She estimates nearly a dozen did so with her help, though she hastens to add that she never *converted* anyone.

She must have had a special skill. She recalls lying in bed with a then-boyfriend—his parents were out of the house—who turned to her at 4 A.M. to say, "I just remembered something. When I was in junior high school, I used to go over to this guy's house and we used to jerk each other off while we played video games. Do you think that makes me bi?"

"People I didn't know came out to me," Lesley says, "[even] before they came out to their friends. . . . It was after I started doing stuff in school that the activities director and that science teacher wore cat suits and gay pirate outfits on Halloween."

As for her own sexuality, she says she's identified as bisexual since childhood—again, she's casual about it: "People are people, a kiss is a kiss."

Lesley mentions more than once to me that her childhood home was a politically silent one—"My parents never spoke of anything"— and even her sexuality failed to get their attention. "They were ignoring it, like they did everything else. . . . When the woman wrote the article about us in the *Washington Post*, she called the house and wanted to talk to my mom. I was like, 'Mom, this woman wants to talk to you about what it's like having a bi teenager.' [She said,] 'Why should she want to talk to *me* about—oh, okay.' And she never said anything about it afterwards—though she said great things in the article.'

"When I did the gay underground paper," she says, "some people had volunteered to pass it out, and one of those people—bless their heart—had taken them into a boys' bathroom and put them on the door. It was a little less discreet than, say, handing one to your friend in class. Well, [the administration] called me down and they were like, 'Stop.' And I was like, 'Didn't do it!' And they were like, 'Yeah, but we know you know how it happened, so stop.'"

It's hard to imagine an underground newspaper—a flier, really—

causing a fuss these days; the idea of it seems more like an under-ground newspaperman's fantasy, really. But college, the Internet, and other mind-expanding developments were still years away at the time. Quaint as it now appears, "Queer Life" led to yet another skirmish in TJ's culture wars.

"After I did the gay paper, somebody else did a parody that was all gay-bashing," Lesley says. She suspected her "archrival," Chris Sununu (Chapter 9), and proceeded directly to the administration with this opinion. In an effort to get them to search his locker, she says, she claimed she'd seen contraband inside; it was a tactic she used more than once. Unlike the school's daintier activists—we took our cues from the likes of Amnesty International and Mandela—Lesley could stoop to conquer.

If the increasing wrangling over homosexuality sometimes led to almost playful Spy vs. Spy shenanigans, it also drew on deep reserves of anger and hatred.

"Something happened my senior year [when] a friend and I were setting up a queer street patrol in Dupont Circle [Washington]. We would have training sessions every week, where we'd go learn differ-ent self-defense moves, have speakers from the police, whatever. One day I come home and my brother says, 'I think Lawrence called'—he's the guy I was working with—'he says practice has moved to this address, at this time.'

"It was on Army-Navy Drive, and had I been able to find the address, I probably would've gotten the shit kicked out of me. I'm sure that's what would've happened, because that whole area back there is secluded and dark. [When] I called Lawrence, he was like, 'No, I never called your house.'"

I can't print the name, of course, but Lesley is convinced she knows who made the call. "But do you really think he would've hurt you?" I ask. "Laramie," she answers without missing a beat, referring to the 1998 murder of gay college student Matthew Shephard in Laramie, Wyoming.

AT THIS POINT in the conversation a dark-haired child approaches Lesley and asks for money to buy a snack. This child is Jacob, the baby Lesley had at the beginning of our junior year of high school, and the subject that hasn't really come up for the last half hour, though he's been drawing in the corner of the café the whole time. The baby who was famous at our school—he was the only baby born to any of us—is now a full-fledged boy: eleven years old, nearly Mom's height, sweet and thoughtful-looking. Lesley puts a dollar in his hand with a look that says *I love you and thank you for being patient, but no junk food.*

Lesley is by no means secretive about Jacob—she beams when he comes up, beams over stories of his intelligence—but her recollections of high school do not revolve around him. Maybe it's because everyone *else's* recollections do that *for* her. Nothing focuses people's attention like an eleventh-grader with a baby. Indeed, before anthrax, before dirty bombs, before *Clash of Civilizations* became water cooler small talk, there were pregnant teenagers; our hands had to wring about something. Nowadays, amid all the muss of a newly disordered world, it's possible to forget to ask: What becomes of the high school junior who has a child?

The answer to this question, at least for one day, is that she tabulates gossip.

"I've heard some rumors about me," perhaps the most whispered-about girl in high school now whispers to me with a gleam in her eye. She rattles them off like they're old friends: "Abandoned Jacob, moved to New York, got AIDS, and dropped out of [college] to 'fight for the cause.'

"None of them true," she adds, just to be clear.

Unlike Brian McConnell, who stumbled into it haplessly, Lesley *courted* whispering throughout high school, and did so from the opposite end of our limited cultural spectrum. She wasn't a redneck tinkerer, she was a lefty agitator, often rather agitated herself. She raised as many eyebrows as could be raised, and ten years later she's got a new clutch of exaggerated gossip to her name.

Lesley, who is half Japanese and half midwestern, is almost wholly pierced these days. She wears two eyebrow rings, one nose ring, one tongue ring, one lip ring, one navel ring, five earlobe rings (three on the right, two on the left), one daith ring (through the cartilage just above the hole in her ear), two rooks (through the cartilage ridge below the ridge on top of her ear), and one barbell through the cartilage "bowl" of her left ear. She has downsized, she says—she used to wear something called a tragus and something called a labret.

"People who don't want to talk to me because of my piercings, well, *I* wouldn't want to talk to *them*. It's a sieve, see?" she explains.

The metal nubs are new, as are her nerves. She is exhausted and rattled. Nervous, twitchy things happen with her hands, leaving the impression she's smoking a cigarette even when she's not. "Sorry, the drugs made holes in my brain," she says when her train of thought derails. Today is potentially nerve-racking not just because she's come to rehash the past but because she's out of bed at all, which hasn't happened much in a while. More on that later.

There was a time she was never *in* bed. During high school, if you wanted to locate Lesley, you would look in her secret ceiling hangout, then around the theater, then in an orgy, then wherever a coming-out teen needed counsel, then on the hour-and-a-half drive to daycare, then at her after-school job, then at her homework spot, and finally in class, just in case. But bed? "I slept an hour a day."

Lesley was a sophomore when she got pregnant.

"When I found out, I was leaving town for a debate meet at Harvard. I told my mom in a note. Basically [it] said, 'Look, I've made my decision, whether you support it or not. The reason I wrote this to you is not to not talk to you about it, but I just don't want to get that initial reaction from you. If you overreact or scream or cry, I can't take that right now. So there you go.'"

For the rest of the school year, she went to class and watched her classmates wonder. "I know there were lots of rumors going around about me being pregnant, but only some people knew for sure. When I finally did have Jacob, there were still people calling and asking why I wasn't in class that day."

She gave birth the first week of school her junior year. Her maternity leave was astonishingly brief, and not even absolute—the county, ever protective, sent teachers to her house. ("We sat at my kitchen table. It was retarded.") A month after delivering her son, she returned to high school. "I was lucky, because my parents had the wherewithal and desire to be supportive," she says.

Lesley considers one of her happier high school memories a speech that she delivered to her English/history course soon after returning to school. "The premise of my speech was, just because things had to change didn't mean they had to be bad. In the media and in commercials and in magazines, teenage pregnancy meant gloom and doom. But it didn't ruin my life, and I didn't want people to feel sorry for me."

To this day, Lesley resents the bad rap given to teen moms. Depending on their tax bracket, it would seem, they're regarded as either victims or, as with Lesley, political gestures—when the teen mom is middle-class and ambitious, she is no less than a deliberate affront to family values.

"I'll never forget this teen pregnancy poster they had on the wall when we were in intermediate school," Lesley tells me in one of our phone conversations, recalling the "propaganda" against young people getting pregnant. "It said, 'It's like being grounded for eighteen years!'"

After Jacob arrived she spent a lot more time in her car, shuttling him around, and she did get a C in physics that first semester of motherhood, but Lesley doesn't describe anything resembling a grounding. She doesn't even describe a major transformation, though her nonchalance asks to be poked at now and then. Even her parents soon took the whole thing in stride, she reports. Was there ever a Big Talk? I ask. "Nope." The closest thing was an argument about where to send Jacob for preschool. Lesley wanted him in a Montessori school but refused to support the churches where many of them rented space. In the end, she found a sufficiently secular program.

Indeed, the way Lesley talks about being a high school mom, she might as well have had chicken pox for a couple weeks. Suspiciously casual or not, the majority of her high school recollections sound like those of a person who had fun and mischief but not offspring.

"I have fond memories—mostly of things I wasn't supposed to be doing. The first semester of senior year, I missed twenty-one days. Had it been twenty-two, I would've failed. I just wasn't there. I was hanging out in the ceiling."

By ceiling, she means the extensive fort she and some friends built in the roof over the drama department. To give an example of why, exactly, the ceiling was compelling on the order of twenty-one days, Lesley explains that it was divided into two sections: "One had a beanbag and a Nintendo and lights and posters on the wall. The other had carpeting, a sleeping bag, and whipped cream, cherries, and chocolate sauce," she says with a knowing smile.

"I don't think anyone in that school was having as much fun as I had. I was having sex all through high school, but the closer we came to graduating, the more often it was more than one-on-one. Everything everybody in the school thought we were doing together, we practically were."

TOWARD THE END of senior year, the implications of having a son got less abstract. NYU had been the plan, and the school admitted her on early decision, even courted her with a strawberries-and-champagne brunch. Lesley canceled her other applications when she found out NYU offered family housing.

"Then I called them again and found out they didn't. Then I called them again and found out they did. Then that they didn't. Finally, the official word from the dean's office was that kids aren't allowed to live in student apartments. And I couldn't afford to go to New York, pay $30,000 a year, plus raise a two-year-old if I had to pay rent. So I stayed here and went to [George] Mason.

"After high school I was completely alone, so I went back to where I'd hung out when I was younger: They used to have *The Rocky Horror Picture Show* at Fair Oaks [Mall], and we all used to hang out at Denny's in the middle of the night afterwards. So I just started hanging out there again. Made all new friends there, and it just so happens that a lot of the people at the time were pretending to be cool punk rockers, and therefore were homeless squatters. So they all came and lived in my house. It was fun for a while, but if you ever think to yourself 'I should count how many people are living here,' don't—the answer's probably like twenty-two."

It was the dorm experience Lesley never had. She loved it for a while—was even briefly engaged to one of the squatters—but eventually concluded he wasn't surrogate-father material. As for raising Jacob in a punk-rock headquarters, she insists he only benefited. In true parental plume, Lesley remembers a teacher of Jacob's marveling then at his social skills. "I kept him insulated from any bad stuff we were doing. It's not like he stayed up until dawn with us, or went clubbing or something. I think he stayed very much a little kid."

The night after breaking it off with her fiancé, Lesley went to see a band with a friend "who I'd sworn I would never date." The concert was several hours away, and the two spent the whole drive talking. The rest, of course, is history. She and John married three years later, in 1999.

"He's as abnormal as I am. It's a good fit. He's an engineer, perfectly intelligent, capable human being, but a lot of the drugs he did when he was younger left holes in his brain. He did a lot of huffing that really fucked up his memory. But other than that, everything else is so good. I have such a great time with him. And me being a Sagittarius—he's a Virgo, and it's probably the only thing that could counter my off-the-wallness. He's the only person I ever met who's happy. I call it John's La-La Land."

THERE IS, PLAINLY, no La-La Land for Lesley.

This is a theme repeated by nearly every classmate I found—the real world can be stunningly real. Lesley has battled depression since adolescence, she says, and if she's winning, it's a slow, measured victory. She tells a frightening story from that first year after our graduation. She had just begun antidepressants (she's since concluded that these medications don't work, though she's still on "a lot of Prozac"), and her depression came to a head in a startling episode.

"What they told us in school was, when you go on antidepressants, you have to be careful, because when they kick in, one of the first symptoms they relieve is apathy. So if you're suicidal and apathetic, now you're no longer apathetic and you can get off the couch and kill yourself," Leslie says in a tone that doesn't quite succeed at casualness. "And sure enough I woke up one day and I was like, 'Oh, yeah, I'm going to kill myself.' It wasn't a decision, it wasn't a *thinking about it* thing, it's just that I woke up feeling that way.

"I felt that way all during work. I went down to my car to go get Jacob, and the feeling went away. And I was fine. So I told [my therapist] this story, and she was like, 'I don't want you to be alone at night.'"

Lesley proposed spending the night at her boyfriend's house, but her therapist wasn't satisfied with this idea and suggested she might call Lesley's mother—a violation, Lesley says, of a long-standing agreement they'd had. What happened next is chaos.

"I flipped out on her. I called her a lying whore, I called her everything I could possibly call her. I left the office, she called my mom, I got in my car, [the therapist] stood behind it, I tried to back over her—she moved. I left, realized I only had a credit card, which is totally traceable, went back just as my mom got there. I ran over to her car, told my mom, 'All I'm asking is that you talk to me before you talk to her.'"

Lesley's mom assured her that the police hadn't been called, but moments later they showed up—they'd been told Lesley had a gun. Lesley says she negotiated with the officers for an hour through a crack in her car window, then eventually surrendered.

She spent one night at the psychiatric ward of a local hospital. Her recollection of the experience: She "got real hostile" and "gave the nurses a really hard time." She was released the next day, on the condition that she speak to her therapist again. She did, telling the woman that she hated her and that she was a terrible shrink. That last session ended early.

What's happened in the intervening years is an evolution of Lesley's depression. She says that adulthood has taught her not to trust all her feelings and impulses.

"In high school, it was really fatalistic—I always felt that when I was depressed, I was looking at the world as it was, and the rest of the time I was lying to myself. It's a really bad way to look at things," she says. "[Later] I learned to do the opposite of what my body was telling me—if my body was telling me to stay in bed, I wanted to get up."

THE NEW STRATEGY almost worked. Lesley hated northern Virginia's conservatism, its attitude toward piercings, its traffic, and decided that this time—unlike with NYU—she wouldn't miss her chance to leave. And then the door more or less hit her on the way out.

"We were going to move to San Francisco, and I was going to be pregnant [again] by that October," she says. "I was painting a room in my house, and suddenly my back didn't feel very good, so I stopped, took some anti-inflammatories to keep the swelling down, and went to bed. And it just got worse, and worse, and worse."

She's not talking about hours here. Lesley's last two years have revolved largely around the pain that began that day with the paintbrush. Much of that time has been spent in bed, and even then the agony often persisted.

"It's been so bad that I couldn't walk—physically, I couldn't move my leg because the nerves were so abused from firing all the time. There was no comfortable position to sit or lie in. People who haven't had back pain, they don't know.

"It fucked up my life so badly. As much as I love to be active—to rock-climb, to work on stage crews and stuff—I can't do it. I still don't do *anything* if I can help it. I just lie in bed, watch TV, do the Internet thing."

Finding help, particularly pain relief, became Lesley's career. As she tells it, brain surgery would have made for easier work.

"I had a piece of disk this big pressed up against my spinal cord. Because I'm young, and pierced, and female, it took me two months to get anybody to take it out. I couldn't get an MRI from anyone, because everyone just thought I was drug seeking.

"By the time they took the piece out of my back, it was really raw, and totally painful. I called [the doctor] after three days and was like, 'Not working, lot of pain, out of drugs.' His answer to that was 'Hang in there.' I was really on a track to kill myself."

Lesley describes a long and amazingly fruitless saga of looking for pain relief, for doctors willing to help, and for simple distraction. Eventually, through a Web site for chronic pain sufferers, she found a doctor willing to prescribe the controversial drug OxyContin—"a very, very, very potent painkiller." The pain vanished and stayed gone until the day her doctor lost his license. As luck would have it, Lesley's mother is a pharmacologist, and thus began another cat-and-mouse chapter in the pain-relief book. Lesley says they had an odd little ritual at periods when the pain was at its worst. "I would call, she would say she didn't have any. I would wait till she went to work and go [to the house] and steal them. Then she would refurbish that, and tell me she didn't have any, and I would go over and steal them."

Some months after our afternoon at the Dupont Circle café, Lesley tells me she's weaning herself from pain medication. Judging from her voice, this process might be more exhausting than finding the drugs in the first place. But it also seems to be an improvement.

"Things are reasonably good now," she writes to me one day. "At least I feel like me and I'm not living in my bed anymore."

LESLEY HAS AN endearing air of perpetual effort about her. The effort isn't about back pain or bigotry or Virginia provincialism, but rather ambivalence over how to pass the time. They say lack of direction is our generation's specialty—I picture millions of cheap compasses—and Lesley sees this as a response to our rearing.

"There are just so many options. This was definitely my problem growing up: I could play whatever sport I wanted. I could do art. I could play any instrument that I wanted. I could do many, many things, and I cared not about any of them. It was like I was spread too thin to care about any one thing. . . . We grew up with people [saying], 'You guys are going to run the world someday!' And so many of us are not even *trying* to do anything like that.

"When I was growing up, there was no emphasis whatsoever on being happy. As soon as I realized that, I was like, *I'm going to try to work on this.* It took me two years before I felt completely comfortable just sitting down to have a glass of tea. It was so beaten into me that I was being lazy. That's my main goal, as long as my husband can support us—just to be happy."

Lately, Lesley's been planning to be happy elsewhere—she's tired of northern Virginia and tired of being angry at it. So far happenstance has foiled her exits, and depression has made it hard to surmount happenstance. But the fighter who took on homophobia, a wary school administration, and common wisdom about when to have babies hasn't surrendered. For Lesley, having another baby has come to stand for forging ahead, for starting over—a rebirth, I suppose. And once again, she talks of having an army in her likeness.

"Someday I'll be better. [After I] get off the drugs, I plan on working out, so I can find out if I can even *have* a baby. If I can't right away, I'm going to keep working out and we'll adopt. Then try again down the road. . . . Even when I'm old, I plan on fostering kids forever. If I can afford it. I would have *ten* kids—if I could make sure they were all boys." She pauses just a moment, and here that gleam comes back to her eye. "I'm terrified of girls."

8 "The Aura Was Just Charged"

L ooking back, it seems like those clumsy adolescent attempts at defining ourselves—a cigarette before class, a practiced laugh, an argument about homophobia—had something to do with that sense of hope hovering above us. We were told we could become anything we wanted, but deciding who we were at present was hard enough. Basic social ordering helped for a while—cheerleaders over here, geeks over there, and so on—but when that ceased to be enough, a deeper reorganization was required. My class found a new mode of being. We argued, habitually, about politics.

A combustible new social order arose in our class, and it seemed to be firming up everywhere: liberals over here, conservatives over there. We argued and argued and argued—it tends to be the first thing my classmates remember now. We argued about issues and culture, believing we were arguing about life. Was Clarence Thomas lying? Was capital punishment moral? What to make of gangsta rap? And

NAFTA? The Soviet Union fell our junior year, and when the great, absurd culture wars puffed up to fill the consequent vacuum, we anointed ourselves an unofficial front: high school's tired jocks-vs.-geeks contest rejiggered as left vs. right.

To have attended high school from 1989 to 1993 is to have seen the world begin shifting, albeit through the haze of adolescence. Supposedly, we were relieved at America's preeminence in the new post-Soviet world order, but in truth we'd never truly shared our parents' Cold War discomforts in the first place. Nuclear weapons had been pointing at us all our lives, after all; unease having always been normal, its mitigation was only so impressive. Besides, replacement concerns had already been established. What to do about gang violence, and spotted owls, and teen moms? The battle enjoyed many fronts. People with long hair went out of their way to hate people with short hair, and vice versa. Once I wore a "Free Pee-Wee" T-shirt, and a boy named Geoff made fight faces when the teacher wasn't looking. In one yearbook photo, two students pose with mouths full of meat before a Students for Ethical Treatment of Animals display.

And then Wayne Steward told us he liked boys.

It was the summer before our senior year, and Wayne became the first in our class (some said in the history of our *school*) to declare himself gay. We had seen nothing like this in our short, suburban lives—not in a peer, at least. An anthropologist on duty in our halls would have found a population in shock—and a population gearing up to argue more than ever.

Before this moment our ideological friction was urgent but abstract. The meat-eating matter, the Pee-Wee matter—these were too minor to truly galvanize the school. As for deeper issues, with the single exception of the racist graffiti at the elementary school next door, we'd simply been born too late to hear "nigger" or "kike" in our halls like our parents had. This was good for obvious reasons, bad because we lacked a clear enemy—a recipe for trouble where teenagers (and presidents) are concerned. Like so many fellow children-of-Boomers, we longed for a Governor Wallace to unequivocally despise or support.

Then came Wayne and his great sashay, hips swinging nearly out to both rows of lockers. And then Tim. Then Lesley. And Lesley's dozen. In a discernible instant, homosexuality arrived at our school like Beatlemania or pot. Of course, like pot it had quietly been there all along, but suddenly the halls and bleachers and classrooms shook with it. Unlike, say, race, sexuality still seemed black-and-white to us—no factions beyond "tolerant" and "intolerant," to our minds. When Wayne and others forced the issue, we drew up the bitter lines happily. We had what all seventeen-year-olds hope for: something to get wound up about.

"Certainly homosexuals are people just like all others who should be loved and not verbally abused," wrote Ruth Young, class of 1994, in a letter to our school paper in November 1992. "However, by no means should we condone or accept homosexuality."

"The Bible explicitly states homosexuality is a sin," Wendy Branco, a freshman at the time, said in our senior-year yearbook.

"I went to golf camp for a week. I had a roommate who was an admitted homosexual," said John Helmantoler, from my own class, in an article from that same yearbook. "It was really awkward. I'd heard about homosexuality before, but this really struck close to home. . . . I was very cautious about which cup I used, and to use a toilet seat cover."

From the opposition, came burning entreaties for what was called "open-mindedness." We dashed off editorials and chanted in front of the school board. We spoke augustly of civil rights, and liberal society, and our counterparts' tiny little brains.

It should be clear at this point that the climate for coming out at TJ then was awfully different from what it might be today, just a few years later, with mainstream TV shows like *Will and Grace* and *Queer Eye for the Straight Guy*—think Siberia, but with football players. The idea of teen homosexuality wasn't just edgy, it was *dissent*, and dissent simply wasn't *in* yet in our provincial wasteland. Leather jackets and loud music were fine, but anything truly countercultural failed the cool test. The anti-establishment gloss that now feels ubiquitous and easy—rebellious-seeming soft-drink ads and the like—had yet to take hold at the beginning of the '90s, at least among Virginia teens. We were primitive.

Our pivotal contention found its epicenter in a tiny clause in the *Fairfax County Student Handbook* prohibiting harassment of fellow students on the basis of race, religion, handicap, and gender, but not sexual orientation. At the beginning of our senior year Sean Bryant (Chapter 20), our student representative on the school board, asked members to add such a clause to the text. He might as well have requested pure cocaine, given the uproar in the school, and then throughout Virginia. "Condones homosexuality!" some cried. "No it doesn't, and so what if it did?" others replied. "Sexual Preference" was indeed appended to the handbook, but after months of racket, the board softened its language into something both sides could agree was stupid: "matters pertaining to sexuality." Clunkier words have never burned on so many brains.

Matters pertaining to sexuality—years before the New Economy, we had the feeling of a bubble all our own. Yet as finite and narrow a cause as it might have been, it emerged quite logically from the moral lessons we'd learned as kids. Indeed, "tolerance" and "acceptance" might have become buzzwords in the '90s, but my generation had dealt in those concepts since *Sesame Street.* By the time we were teens, in big and little ways, they were everywhere. Here were Gorbachev and Bush shaking hands, Arafat and Rabin—Mandela actually *holds* the hand of his former guard after twenty-seven years in prison. Even Simon and Garfunkel got together again in Central Park. From the tumult of the '60s came the coming together of the '90s, right down to pop culture. We didn't come of age watching Cool Hand Luke snip off parking meter heads, but rather Tom Cruise learning to love Rain Man. Reconciliation, not revolution, became the predominant dramatic gesture for people my age.

The terms of our arguments over tolerance, like everything in our adolescent lives, were overstated. But at the same time, we'd unknowingly stumbled on an issue that would only swell over the next ten years: How ought the business of living be done? If the stakes were exaggerated, so too was our sense of duty and importance.

"We wanted to take the world's problems on our shoulders," Rebecca Lamey says. "We thought we could fix everything."

TEN YEARS AFTER clearing out, my classmates look back at our high school politics and shudder. So many do this that I can recognize the shudder immediately—a blinking mix of awe and embarrassment, like the morning after a bachelor party. A kind of guarded incredulity has sprouted: What were we so bent out of shape about?

"I don't know why it happened the way it did," Seth Bleiweis says, a little dumbfounded. "The whole aura was just *charged.*"

And now, one gathers, it's not. Which stands to reason, because that aura was never entirely about ideas and politics in the first place. Those were surrogates, to some extent; the squabbling and the ideology arose when we needed a way to talk, a thing to talk about. Certainly our convictions were genuine, but often they also stood for more: the things a high school student *really* feels when surrounded by a building of peers (a combination of fear and loathing, one also gathers).

A decade later, the fear and loathing have largely vanished along with the building full of peers. We are, with some exceptions, a more agreeable and comfortable group. When my conversations with classmates list toward politics, we tend to find the subject not barren—surely the world offers more to argue about now than ever before—but simply *manageable*, and possibly less compelling as a result.

"People [at Jefferson] were questioning all the time what was happening politically or socially. I've certainly become less strident over time," Dave Roberts says. "You recognize that some questions you're just never going to answer."

Or maybe we're just busier. "When you're younger, you have more enthusiasm to debate things," classmate Eric Cryan says. "You have a lot more hours to talk about things then, where now you have to work all that time."

As for who won all those debates, it's hard to say. Maybe it's some hybrid of liberalism and conservatism that came the closest to victory, where the meatheads have stopped saying "fag" and the progressives have stopped trying to teach them why this was good. "I'm not as absolute about things as I used to be," Karen Taggart says about the sort of things we once debated. "Things don't seem so black-and-white anymore." So we talk instead about ourselves, because at twenty-eight years old, we can.

9 Chris Sununu

CHRIS SUNUNU: *"There was a period where every time I'd go to school, [the media] were just outside the driveway with telescopic lenses."*

WES BLACK: "We had kind of a similar background, having grown up around politics. My dad [longtime Republican strategist Charlie Black] knew his dad. We were friends, but we weren't super tight. The first time I met him, freshman year, I was like, 'Hey, my dad knows your dad.' And he had his guard up—he goes, 'You're full of shit!'

"Friends of ours would come up to him and spread their arms like an airplane, make airplane noises. He'd get pissed off. He was probably a little embarrassed about the whole [scandal involving his father]. I think that hurt him. He was a good person."

REBECCA (GRAY) LAMEY: "I went head-to-head with Chris constantly. Usually what ended up happening was, he always had all the guys on his side, and I always had all the girls on my side. Something about him—there were a lot of guys laughing and applauding him that wouldn't have normally. One argument I remember was about the differences between the sexes. He and I ended up getting pretty heated. He was going on about how if he took a woman to prom, and rented a limo, and bought her dinner, he'd better get *reimbursed* for it at the end of the night. I said, 'You'd expect her to put out just because you spent money on her?' And he said, 'Yes, definitely.'

"He was one of those people actively speaking out against the change in the handbook [forbidding harassment of fellow students because of sexual orientation]. I heard him saying something about how that [clause] was stupid. . . . I always thought he was a rich, preppie, snotty asshole. It never occurred to him that things could be any way other than the way he thought. When we'd argue, he'd never concede a single thing."

WAYNE STEWARD: "He was your typical straight guy—a guy's guy. Our lockers were near each other. We disagreed on stuff, but at no point did I ever have a really nasty interaction with him. At no point did he ever come up to me and say something overtly prejudiced. Then again, I was already out, you know? What, you're going to walk down the hall and call me faggot? I'd just turn around and say, 'I *know!*'"

VANYA (SEAMAN) WRIGHT: "Freshman year I went to Karen Taggart's birthday party—everyone was invited. It was at a mall, and we were trying to get seated at a restaurant there and we couldn't get in. We walked around and around for forty-five minutes. Then Chris mumbled, 'I never have to wait for a table when I'm with my dad.' We went back and changed the name to Sununu and got right in—though maybe they were going to let us in then anyway."

JOHN HELMANTOLER: "I really liked Chris. He was a great guy. He was friendly. At the same time, I wouldn't say he was closed off, but he definitely had a core, smaller set of friends. The one time I ever saw him cut loose, it was the end of the night at this party at Wes's. Sununu and I were the last men standing—everyone else was passed out—and we were on the back porch smoking cigars. We were like, 'Ooh, let's break shit!' We grabbed a bunch of bottles and ran through the neighborhood smashing them. It was a good connection.

"Politically, his reputation was that of a Rush Limbaugh/Fox News type. That was definitely an accurate portrayal of him. He was definitely of that 'intolerant' camp—I suppose I was, too—though it's a bad word. He was of that party line—'What the hell's going on? We're making these people heroes and martyrs for coming out of the closet!' In our defense, we hadn't seen this before. It's usually not until college that you start seeing this stuff, and for us it was happening in high school.

"One other thing: He was very loyal. I remember running into him on a ski trip and he was with his girlfriend, who was not a world-class skier. [My friends and I] went down the easy slopes a few times with them, but then we tried to get him to ditch the girl for a while and do the black diamonds. But he wouldn't even consider it. He was a nice, nice guy."

■

To tell the story of Chris Sununu's life since high school graduation—the life of a tall, gregarious engineer, with a soft, handsome face and twinkly eyes—fairly or unfairly, one must begin with Chris's father.

Yes, *that* Sununu.

Elected governor of New Hampshire in 1983, John Sununu was named chief of staff to the first President Bush six years later, after proving instrumental in the 1988 primaries. Under Bush, Sununu was known for his fabled intellect—as the *Atlantic Monthly* once reported, his IQ rose from 170 to 176 to 180 as the fable grew over the years—and for his conviction that global warming was a myth, and for his long list of enemies; half of all references to the man contain "abrasive" at least once in the sentence.

But what made Sununu famous changed overnight in April 1991, our sophomore year of high school, when it surfaced that he had been making inappropriate use of government aircraft during his time at the White House. The apparent extravagance ultimately cost taxpayers over a half million dollars: It was widely reported that Sununu flew to two dental appointments, a stamp convention, and a ski resort; still, he claimed seventy-three of the seventy-seven flights were official or political business. Sununu ultimately reimbursed the government $47,044, with help from the Republican Party, according to the Associated Press.

"Air Sununu" had Americans far and near shaking their heads over the temerity of their president's chief of staff. For weeks it was not uncommon to see Sununu on the front page of the *Washington Post.* Critics complained later that the paper had it in for him, but as far as the chief of staff's son was concerned, the damage was done.

Now, at a café in Oakland, Chris mentions the gaggle of journalists who once camped out in front of his family's house. "I remember I had this piece-of-junk car that my brother had had in Boston when he went to school there. [He'd kept it] in his back lot, and he came out one day and there was a bullet hole in it. Anyway, years later, I now own this car in Virginia. Finally, my mom started telling me to park my car sideways so they wouldn't have pictures of bullet holes and get the wrong idea! It was a mess. At first it was interesting, then it was really annoying. [The media spotlight] lasted a good year. The cameras outside the house were only there for maybe a month, six weeks."

School offered Chris no protection from harassment—an ironic predicament for someone remembered as an opponent of our famous anti-harassment clause. Charlotte Opal recalls a local radio station playing a parody song, to the tune of the old Steve Miller Band hit "Fly Like an Eagle," called "Fly Like Sununu." ("I want to fly like Sununu, to the sea / Fly like Sununu, let the Air Force carry me.") She can't confirm the rumor that another student sang the song to Chris in chemistry class and reduced him to tears. John Helmantoler remembers John Doyle (Chapter 19) asking Chris if he could spare any airplane peanuts. According to the Center for Media and Public Affairs, John Sununu was the subject of seventy-six late-night talk-show jokes in 1991, edging out Clarence Thomas (seventy-two) and Ted Kennedy (seventy). Only Bush Senior, Saddam Hussein, and Dan Quayle got more laughs that year. "I won't say he flew a lot," Senator Bob Dole allegedly remarked at one point, "but he won't start a cabinet meeting until the seat backs and tray tables are locked into the upright position."

In December 1991, Sununu was asked to resign. (For years the story had it that the president sent his son, George W., in with the hatchet. The *New York Times* reported later that W. only reprimanded him.) According to the *Colorado Springs Independent*, Vice President Quayle noted his departure with an incontrovertible assertion: "This isn't a man who is leaving with his head between his legs."

"That was a different time," Chris says now with a casual flick of the wrist. "That's what kind of put this whole shell on me. I kind of closed up."

CHRIS SUNUNU, CONTRARY to his high school reputation, is a sweetheart. Our first meeting is an unambiguously lovely time. It starts in daylight and we part ways after dark—and then only because I'm out of tape. He has a frequent and easygoing smile. He has a friendly and endearingly high voice. He does not, despite what some tell me, say "faggot" at any point.

Because of his father or not, Chris's is a name that comes up in a lot of conversations with my high school classmates—no small feat in a group of more than 400. Almost unanimously among them, he is remembered as a ferocious conservative, one who opposed gay rights legislation, who raged at the mildest environmentalist notions, and who was not to be gotten started on feminism. If tolerance became the issue du jour for us, jour after jour, Chris is recalled as its most stalwart antagonist.

This doesn't make it so. Sununu, as many called him, was two things: a living, breathing student—argumentative, quiet, friendly, obnoxious, confident, or shy, depending on who's describing him— and a vigorous but inanimate legend. The legend of Chris reflected not his own personality but the one bystanders constructed for him. ("Why did they think I would say that?" is a common refrain of his upon hearing words rumored to have come from his mouth. "I never said anything like that!") To be misunderstood is hardly rare in high school, but seldom is the condition amplified via telephoto lens.

Those who knew Chris liked him; those who knew only his reputation, or who tangled with him from afar—these people kept their distance over the years. Distance is a passive arrangement in high school. The gods of adolescence divide their dominion according to social, political, and cultural calculations that are beyond us. We students simply *receive* the grid. The grid, in return, keeps things simple. Cocky Republicans don't mingle with pretentious liberals, and vice versa, and so forth.

After the disclaimer that he is, in fact, very fond of the first George Bush ("I'm partly biased. My dad worked for him, I had a little bit of a personal connection with him. But I think he did a great job"), Chris tells me a story that illustrates the corner he often occupied at Jefferson.

"We were going through this whole [election] thing senior year, in our government class, and someone had to get up there and pretend they were George Bush and debate these issues. And everyone said, 'Okay, Chris, you do it.' And I said, 'No! I'm not doing this!' And they said, 'Yeah, yeah, you have to.' And in the end I got railroaded! And I felt like, *Why me*?! This stupid stigma! I didn't have a passion for politics—I had grown pretty cold to it. I read and listened and took everything in, but I tried to keep most of it inside. Because I kept feeling like I had to keep fighting that impression people had of me."

Years of fighting seems to have tenderized him, if anything. He's low-key, gentle—nowhere near abrasive, certainly. Only very politely does he inquire, a couple beers into our first conversation, how, per chance, one might have found his number. The son of a former White House chief of staff and New Hampshire governor—and now the younger brother of a New Hampshire senator—he tries to keep his general accessibility limited. The Internet, I tell him. Chris nods and sips his beer and smiles gently like a man who knows he will always, always, be tracked. If it's not reporters, it's friends. If in high school he was something of a pet store mynah bird—everyone who walked by tried to make him talk—the pestering continued even after he flew the coop.

The double ghosts of pigeonholing and misattribution, real or imagined, still haunt Chris. When we first sit down to talk, I get the sense I'm lucky he responded to my calls—just a few months earlier, he played possum to at least one interview request during his brother John's 2002 Senate campaign.

"Sure enough, my brother called me a couple days into it and said, 'Hey, I talked to [this woman] from the *Concord Monitor*, she said you didn't return her call.' I said, 'No, of course not, why would I?' 'Well, they were doing this whole piece about me—it was a great piece, you should read it!'

"I grew very callous to that type of media in high school. My dad was all over the newspapers for a while, and I learned, 'I gotta grow a hard shell and not let this bother me—I don't give a rat's ass what they say.'"

Chris concedes that his suspicion of the media might be "a bit unwarranted," but this is more a reflection of his own rhetorical generosity than any faith in the journalistic arts. Even Chris's most reviled enemies are patiently praised for their few virtues when he talks about them, and it's not grudging praise. "Clinton was an excellent statesman . . . and brilliant," he says, thoughtfully, of the president he just finished calling sleazy and despicable. California, a fickle and tree-huggy state whose fiscal disasters are "unbelievable," is also recognized as the one with the potential to be "the greatest in the union." This sounds a bit like moral relativism at first—worthy of Clinton himself, actually—but over time it becomes clear that Chris is in no way a waffler. No, he's something else, every bit as elaborate: the son of a famously inflexible politician, and then the son of a man forced—railroaded—out of Washington by an equally inflexible media. Somewhere along the way, Chris began looking at things from more than one angle.

Other strategies took hold. Escape from the shadow of his father, and from his own reputation—whatever it was—began in twelfth grade, soon after his mandatory Bush channeling. Chris's interests began shifting away from national politics and more toward foreign affairs, particularly the Palestinian-Israeli crisis. Chris himself is of Palestinian and Lebanese descent, but the more immediate draw for him seems to be the complexity of the region. "Lebanon, Syria . . . I find that whole area really interesting, because I feel I'll never understand it," he says.

After TJ, Chris buried himself in abstruseness even further, majoring in environmental engineering at MIT (which his father had attended and where he had later earned his Ph.D. in mechanical engineering). "I didn't know what kind of engineering to get into," Chris says, "so I did what my roommate was doing. It sounded like fun. I liked being outdoors." He graduated after four and a half years. ("I wasn't the best student in the world," he offers by way of explanation. "I'd say I enjoyed Boston.")

College was also when he met his wife, Valerie, who attended a small women's school nearby ("not Wellesley" is her description). She began noticing Chris from afar after she met friends of his at fraternity parties.

"My first impression of him was that he was unapproachable and intimidating," she recalls. (Valerie herself is not these things, incidentally. She is warm and inviting and not unreceptive to such abstract conversations as *what makes your husband tick.* Answer: "I don't know. What makes anyone tick? Loyalty, maybe?") Over time, and still from afar, Valerie deduced a little more about her crush. "Amidst all these schmoozy player types, Chris was different. At [fraternity parties] he couldn't stand drunk girls. He wouldn't talk to them."

It was a summer day in one of the frat houses when Valerie walked in on Chris doing a very un-Sununu thing, at least as far as his high school reputation went: He was painting. Sort of. If I understand Valerie's description, he had a projector set up and was throwing images of different classic rock albums up against a wall, which he would then trace over with a brush. It was a pure and quiet moment of homage, and that was when she knew.

Chris, for his part, remembers one of the first things that touched him about Valerie: "After we started seeing each other, she was like, 'What does your dad do?' And I thought that was great. Thank goodness. I don't *want* you to know! Not that politics is a bad thing, but . . ."

CHRIS GRADUATED WITH an engineering degree and a firm commitment to not being an engineer. He went to film school at NYU—for two months. He didn't want to pursue the lifestyle many of his classmates there seemed destined for. ("Bumming around from film project to film project with no real focus" is how he describes it.) Anyhow, Chris didn't like the art-house movies NYU leaned on its students to make. He now occupied an uncomfortable position. He called his best friend Steve and commenced Plan B.

On a summer day, Chris and Steve caught a bus from Massachusetts to Bangor, Maine, and then hitched rides to Mount Katahdin and climbed out of the car. Then, with some difficulty, they walked to the state of Georgia. The Appalachian Trail is more than 2,200 miles long, and Chris and Steve spent five months covering it. Chris calls it his life-changing event.

The planning alone lasted months. They carried a pot, two cups, a burner, a stove, a pan, dry clothes, water, and food for the whole trip. They packed no tent, just slept in lean-tos or wrapped themselves in a tarp. They learned about misery via hip problems and shin splints and blisters and loneliness and mice. The mice scurried around the lean-tos and scared Chris, who's afraid of them. Ten percent of those who begin the trek don't make it. A good many relationships and marriages dissolve. "Fuck you," Chris and Steve told each other periodically. Chris's most irritating habit if you're walking next to him for five months? "I'm a little parental. Cautious. I give too much advice probably." But they knew how to maintain their friendship: "People have to be as accepting of each other as possible," he explains. In keeping with the long-held tradition of trading one's real name for a trail name, Chris, fresh out of film school, became Fade Out. "When you're out there, you're not part of your old life," he says. "It's a separation from the rest of the world. It's a new life."

Chris had begun dating Valerie, so now they dated remotely. He sent postcards and made calls from pay phones. He kept a daily journal. "Don't ever do this again," he wrote in a number of places. Why did he walk 2,200 miles, never accept a ride along the way, do the thing backwards (most hikers go south to north), and resist the constant urge to quit? "It was a way to get my head straight in terms of what I want to do," he says. By Georgia he knew. He didn't want to become an "eighty-hour-a-week worker, like so many people our age," but he also didn't want to become "a floater, a two-bit guy without a steady job"—a common inclination among those who complete the hike and want more and more adventures. What Chris wanted was a life in the middle.

Chris came back to Valerie. He'd decided he wanted a life with her, too. They packed their bags and drove to San Francisco for an adventure of their own. Soon they were married. Valerie took a job as a teacher in Marin County, and Chris began work as an environmental engineer for an Oakland firm. "It gets me outside," he says—specifically, it gets him wading in sewage, tapping toxic plumes, or sampling groundwater, wondering idly whether hepatitis is afoot. His task at these venues is to devise affordable cleanup solutions. "I never would've pegged you for an environmentalist," I say. "Oh no," Chris replies, waving a finger. "Don't use that word."

But even without that word, it's clear that his life since high school—film school, the Appalachian Trail, California, engineering—constitutes a tremendous migration from the Chris Sununu people thought they knew at Jefferson. "It's not permanent," he says of this life he's made in San Francisco—the Sununus will return to New England—but for now it's a respite.

WHAT TO MAKE of this nice person, this nonmonster? Could Chris really have stood for bigotry years ago as so many classmates tell me? Nothing in his current behavior lends itself even remotely to that idea. Not because friendliness and passionate conservatism are mutually exclusive, but because Chris's particular brand of openness gives the distinct impression of acceptance. He explains it this way: That bigot never existed in the first place.

"I was fairly conservative, but I always thought I got a bad rap. A lot of times it was very mean-spirited—things I didn't want to be associated with. Like that gay guy who came out, Wayne, I didn't know him from a hole in the wall. And I immediately got associated with this group of people that didn't like Wayne Steward and couldn't believe he was gay. And I remember being in high school thinking, 'What do I care that he's gay?' And I knew Wayne didn't like me—I found out down the road. I heard different stories, that people didn't like me, and people were really offended by me, and I thought, *I never said anything. I never did anything*—they just associated me with that."

Because of my dad—that's the part of the sentence always left unsaid. Chris refers only obliquely to his father, or at least his father the politician. Same for the *other* John Sununu in his life—his brother—who's now in the position of sending more indirect fire Chris's way. The National Stonewall Democrats claim "Sununu opposes all non-discrimination and hate crime laws that include sexual orientation. He has continually refused to sign a pledge that states he will not fire his own staff based on their sexual orientation." The League of Conservation Voters, meanwhile, blasted the former congressman as having one of the worst voting records in Congress when it comes to clean air and water. Sununu's spokeswoman, Barbara Riley, replied that her boss had been misrepresented; a pattern begins to take shape in this family.

And indeed Chris does still catch hell: "Valerie took my name, and all of a sudden people were like 'Do you know who you married?! Do you know what his father does?! Do you know what his father did?! Do you know his brother's in the Senate?! They're *really* Republican! You're *married* to a Republican!'"

Ugliness happens when 1,600 people are crammed into a building, and when a single person is crammed into adolescence. Later, the ugliness must be either processed or disinherited—the choice, I suspect, determines the course of one's high school reunion. It's perhaps no surprise that Chris recalls nothing beyond innocent, if heated, in-class debates when I press him about high school. Did he do anything that people might have construed as homophobic? *No.* When I mention Lesley, who claims to have been his archrival, and to have often gone head-to-head with him, he just barely recalls her. "She had a baby in high school? I don't think I forgot, I just don't think I knew her that well."

I'm aware of two scenarios in which an adult may deny unpleasant stories about his or her past. In the first, the unpleasant stories present some inconvenience—perhaps the adult has since matured, or else the society around him has matured and left him in the cold. ("Everything's different now," classmate John Helmantoler says, illustrating the latter in his own case. "I may have a vice president at my office who's gay, but I'm not going to walk into his office and call him a fag.") In the second scenario, the unpleasant stories were never true in the first place.

This is what I'm learning: American high school is an unsorted heap. American high school reunions are a rooting around in the heap. The nature of my class's ongoing quarry is ideological, owing I suppose to our idiosyncrasies and to the decade around us. We search out unseemly ideas, either because unseemly ideas are taking the world in the wrong direction or because they substitute for relationships we'd rather not pursue. *Fag*, certain people hissed in high school, and sometimes other types of slur were insinuated, too. *Bigot*, certain people hiss now. Lesley looks back and accuses Chris and other Republicans of homophobia. Brian looks back and accuses an entire class of misrepresenting him. Lorraine looks back and accuses me and other whites of racism. I look back and essentially write a book's worth of accusations, albeit couched as journalism. All this digging around for the hidden truth—is this the maintenance of an open society or the stirrings of its closure? I don't know the answer, and so with Chris, as with every other classmate I find, I decide the best that can be done is the thing we never did in high school: hang out.

———

DESSERT PARTY, CHEZ Sununu. In a fit of hayseed paranoia, my girlfriend Amy and I Google "dessert party" in advance—is this some traditional Republican sacrifice we hadn't heard about? Turns out "dessert party" is a party where guests bring dessert. Still, the tendrils of young American conservatism promise to be illuminating. It's one thing for a scion of power to put on a show for an interview, I decide, and quite another to keep the façade up for the duration of multiple strudels.

The tendrils prove limited on this particular Saturday night. Just half a dozen of us show up, and the stereo never gets louder than elevator music. We mill around in what will soon be Chris's ex-apartment, in San Francisco's tony Pacific Heights neighborhood. Chris and Valerie put in two good years on the left coast and in April they will head back to New England, where all New Englanders eventually return. This is something of a warm-up for the good-bye party.

The circle of friends here—all couples—have a distinct generationless look about them, which is to say they're dressed conspicuously *normally*. As with Chris, their outward appearances betray no particular culture: neither military, skater, hippy, geek, jock, freak, nor frat. They are casually preppy and friendly, just as likely to know about thread count as German motors, not afraid to call a good beer "a tasty beverage." The men of Chris's orbit are firm-handshakers yet not macho, the women fairly reserved but not submissive. Amy and I make small talk about vacations until the chocolate liqueur kicks in.

"I think Chris is one of the most complex guys I've ever met," a friendly architect named Noah tells me once I've explained my high school reunion project. Chris himself is just a few feet away, and I watch for the pricking up of ears, but they don't budge. Noah continues. "To have a past like that and to never mention it, even to keep it at arm's length, that's got to mean something"—here Noah makes a face that says *don't ask* me *what it means*—"we'll be playing basketball and it'll come out that he's hung out with Magic Johnson, or Madonna. And he just seems unfazed by it."

I don't know. People who seem unfazed seem to be the first ones you find mumbling under the overpass a couple years later. Then again, Chris really does seem to have things sorted out. I think of Lesley, whose dynamism and idealism has sometimes taken a backseat to bad luck. Chris, by comparison, appears to be just plain happy, and surrounded by an amiable cadre of dessert eaters. Of course, he didn't raise a son at sixteen, injure his back, or receive a creepy call luring him off to a dead-end street. But he also went to great lengths distancing himself from the person so many people thought they understood a decade ago.

There is an unwritten letter in Chris's head, he tells me in one of our conversations. I have a version of this letter in my own, and I suspect it's not entirely uncommon. Chris's, were it ever to reach paper, would go out to just a few people he's known in his life, "mostly from college, some from high school." "'Hey, sorry about all that!'" Chris says, reading from the imaginary missive. "'Hope that's all under the carpet now.' I just don't want to go to my grave with people thinking I'm a dick."

The dessert party fades out before too late (though not before I'm promised the blue ribbon for my key lime pie, I should point out). By 10:30 we're watching photos of Chris and Valerie's recent Hawaii trip pop up on a computer screen and then cycle away. The photos are generic vacation photos—a romantic one here, a nature shot there, here a funny face—and by rights we should be bored. But the documents of someone's private life keep a fellow nailed to his seat when the private life is so hard-won. "I could never go into politics—no privacy," Chris told me at one point, but of course he *is* in politics, and has never had a choice. But he also has a trail name he can answer to, and can wander off into Appalachia with his wife whenever he likes.

BEN KIM: *"[I was] insecure. Not that I'm not now. The hardest thing was, I didn't know who my friends were. I guess I was popular, I knew a lot of people. High school was not easy. I didn't quite figure out why I wasn't getting straight A's. I ended up with a 3.7 or something, and I'd thought that was bad. Maybe it's because I was Korean. . . . Not just Koreans, but Asians in general . . . think that there is a perfect path. They want you to fit a certain mold—lawyer, doctor, whatever—or make a shitload of money, and gain status that way. It's called 'honor.' But what is honor?"*

SETH BLEIWEIS: "We got to be friends at the very beginning of high school. We rode the same bus, and played football together, and were in band together. The first thing I think of with Ben is that big, shit-eating grin of his. He was always laughing out loud at people's jokes. Everyone always liked him. He had a broad circle of friends.

"He was taking care of his little sister all the time, always looking out for her, driving her places—a good big brother. Also, he was always the gadget guy—he was like that with his saxophone, and even now he'll tell you all about the stereo system he got for his dad, with all the bells and whistles."

RICH VUDUC: "He always struck me as incredibly diligent. [At college] he did applied physics, which is theoretically the hardest discipline. He was also very involved in his sax playing. I remember us once having a conversation where he spent a lot of time talking about high school and all the people he'd met there. He had enormous respect for people who had accomplished a lot."

SUSIE LEE: "We've been friends since freshman year. . . . Even if he achieves everything he thinks he's supposed to, it won't be enough. He's never satisfied. Which actually rings bells for our whole generation, in a way. Then again, maybe every generation goes through that."

BRIAN MCCONNELL: "He was that fast little Asian dude on the [football] team."

■

We aren't the first ambitious generation, but we might be the *most* ambitious, "slacker" be darned. In 1999, Yale University Press published a major study of ambition in American teenagers—specifically, those teenagers moving through high school on pace with my own class. In *The Ambitious Generation,* Barbara Schneider and David Stevenson reported that, in the late '90s, 90 percent of high school seniors expected to attend college, compared to 55 percent in the late '50s. At that time, 42 percent expected to wind up with professional jobs, compared to 70 percent forty years later.

The number relevant to Ben Kim right now is 20,000. That's how many dollars he stands to receive should he win the Collegiate Inventors Competition, which looms before him when we first get in touch. It wasn't the Boom that put Ben in this spot, but the Boom would no doubt approve if it were with us today. What comes next—a whopping check or a goose egg—will do so on the merits of his ingenuity alone, a Boom trope if ever there was one. And like any good dot-commer, Ben favors impressive schemes and daydreams over the gradual climb toward success (though he's ever adaptable to any program that will get him there). Without launching a single Internet start-up, Ben has come to embody our class's mothlike fluttering to the flame of professional achievement: It makes him miserable, and he can't help it.

Walking through Georgetown in Washington, D.C., one night, and then finally settling down for a few beers, Ben and I review the facts. From nearly 200 entries, he's been selected as one of sixteen finalists in the contest, which is sponsored by the National Inventors' Hall of Fame. In two weeks he will go to New York to compete for one of six grand prizes. Does he have a shot? Ben is humble—more humble, for sadder reasons, than a twenty-seven-year-old inventor ought to be—but humble has its limits. What he has submitted is a torpedo-noise-control algorithm that has the U.S. Navy throwing its caps in the air at ports all over the world. A shot? The contest, Ben tells me, is in the bag.

Ben is a Nice Guy. Everyone I've talked to who went to high school and then got ten years older is, without exception, nicer than they were before. But this was always Ben's condition—he's a smiler and an out-loud guffawer, a fellow who instinctively touches your arm when a good idea occurs to him, so that it may occur to you too. Lots of ideas occur to him. He is fixated on success—at times he craves it, other times despises its allure; it's the Korean-American curse, he says. But he doesn't wring his hands over curses. He has realer things to worry about, but more on that later.

At TJ, Ben was a star football player—his teammates turned "Benjamin" into "Ben Jammin'" on account of his speed—but senior year, his father made him quit the team. Ben's SAT scores could be better, he decreed, and his free time would be spent preparing for the test. Ben's father had come to America with $150 of borrowed cash in his pocket. He found a job as a gas station attendant and gradually learned auto repair along the way. Eventually, he'd saved enough that he could begin buying and managing his own gas stations. That Exxon at the foot of the Key Bridge in Washington—you can see it briefly in *The Exorcist*—belongs to the Kims. "We're Korean," Ben says about his father's concern over the SATs; it's a refrain.

Ben did quit the team, though it's hard to say he went on to resuscitate his academic career; it had been suscitated all along by most standards. Ben got into Cornell and graduated from TJ with a 3.7 GPA. I ask if Ben resented his father's order. Ben, who has an endearing way of sighing about life, and whose kind eyes are perpetually framed by laugh lines, doesn't seem to know the meaning of "resent." What he'll allow is that he didn't use his liberated hours to study. Where there was once football practice, he simply practiced saxophone instead.

He'd been playing sax since fifth grade and had gotten good. Actually, he'd gotten to be one of the best in the country. "Junior year, he got way into it, practiced a couple hours a day, easily. He became better than anyone else," Seth Bleiweis says. Around the time Ben got into Cornell, he got into the prestigious Michigan State University Saxophone Studio too—one of three people in the country to do so. It was Ben's dream to become a professional saxophonist, but his father forbade him from going.

That May, having already agreed to attend Cornell, Ben played one last time. It was the Woodwind and Brass Solo Competition, sponsored by the Fairfax County Band Directors' Association. Coincidentally, the other two students admitted to Michigan were also in the competition. Ben went home with first place.

"I'll never forget it. My mom had already left—she didn't wait till the awards were announced—and my dad and I were walking back to the car. And he goes, 'You know what, maybe you do have talent.'"

ALONG THE COUNTRY'S various tech corridors, American capitalism at the end of the twentieth century meant not having to explain. Faster, quieter, smaller, bigger—these justified the latest upgrade, and the technology didn't need to be broke in order to be fixed. In the far-reaching corners of the private sector, pay phones were going dusty with the rise of cellular, a cloned sheep appeared from nothing, and Kasparov fell muttering before Deep Blue. But miles from the tasteful, satisfied beeps of our New Economy gadgets, a classified number of leagues under the sea, a decades-long problem persisted for national security: Torpedoes were making too much racket. Ben set about changing this, joining that special subset of engineers focused on helping the military catch up with the larger tech explosion.

In movies, torpedoes run as quiet as goldfish; in real life they grind and rattle and groan their way through the water. This is fine for most of us but bad for the Navy, which prefers for enemy submarines to hear nothing but a mellow *swoosh* right up till the last moment. The Navy prefers this to the tune of many millions of dollars, poured year after year into acoustics research. Active noise control, or anti-noise, would silence the grinding and rattling and groaning essentially by creating the mirror image of the noise within the torpedo—picture a sound wave overlaid with its precise opposite. Problem is, no one has ever been able to make it work.

Ben enrolled at Penn State for grad school and found the anti-noise field already marked with a single giant footprint. In 1989, a Penn State Ph.D. candidate had devised an algorithm that more or less crowned him the king of noise control. The king went into acoustics textbooks, as well as a professorship at Princeton. The textbooks still touted this algorithm when Ben began his work. It not being in his temperament to leave a celebrity algorithm unturned, Ben built a model, ran a test, and noticed something alarming: It didn't work—the noise wouldn't actually cancel out consistently.

Once he determined the incumbent noise control emperor lacked crucial clothes, Ben concluded that the only honorable thing to do was actually solve the problem himself. The next period of his life resembles that of Thomas Edison's famous search for a lightbulb filament. The search nearly drove Edison mad, and Ben's research had the same effect. Anti-noise was the noise keeping him up at night.

"I was depressed for a long time. I seriously thought I wasn't going to get a Ph.D. Bright people all over the world have been doing this for how long? And no one was getting anywhere. Navy commanders had to approve these control systems to be put in subs, and they wouldn't go for it. What happens if it goes unstable when you're supposed to be in stealth mode?"

Like countless inventors before him, Ben was sitting on the toilet (insert anti-noise joke here) when the first breakthrough came.

"I didn't have any reading material with me, so I'm sitting there and I'm bored, and I'm thinking back to other things I had read before, while I was in that same stall. It just so happens that I [had been] reading about the technology behind CD audio. They have this thing called dithering. Three words came to mind: Make a change."

Restroom epiphanies notwithstanding, inventing is a gradual, sputtering affair. Ben got off the toilet and mulled. He drove to a wedding that weekend and mulled all the way to New Jersey. On his way home, on Sunday, he also mulled. He called his mother that night to tell her he'd gotten home safe. As they talked, he did the Ben Kim version of doodling: scribbling equations. By the end of the conversation, he'd scribbled "something really solid." (It's impossible for normal people to follow the specifics of these heroic moments. Here is a typical Ben Kim epiphany: "If you have a complex fraction and you multiply by the complex conjugate of the denominator, you get a scalar product in the denominator, and you can actually do it! And I'm like, *God, this is it!*")

Ben was getting close, but not close enough.

"At night I'd come up with something, the next day I'd try it, and by the end of the day, I'm like, *Oh my God, I was totally going in the wrong direction.* It was like a roller-coaster ride. You get so emotional about it, and you get depressed, then excited, then depressed. Then the last week of August—it was a Tuesday—I was like, *Fuck this. This is not going to work.*"

It was nothing less than starting over the night Ben grabbed every relevant paper he could find and headed out the door; the plan was to forget everything and begin researching again from scratch. He remembers the details of the evening like it was his wedding night. He went to Chili's and got a burger for $4.95. He took out the papers and read and then put them back. At ten, he got to the library. He took out the papers, but this time he interrupted himself. "Not more than three seconds into reading, I saw myself pulling out a scrap piece of paper from my book bag and I started writing stuff down. It was like—it *was* the hand of God writing."

BEN IS THE new king. Since his discovery, he's been too busy developing additional algorithms to write everything up; once he does, the textbooks will be rewritten. The Navy is ecstatic, he has patents pending, and every day seems to bring a new job prospect. Presumably these are the kind of credentials that would appease even the most ambitious of Korean parents. (Actually, "Why do you keep playing that saxophone?" is what his mother asks.) Ben does take pride in his achievements over the past year, but lately a new voice has begun to mitigate that. "So what if I invented an algorithm?" he asks. "That's not the most important thing in life."

Ben isn't being glib. A few years back, while he was in college, doctors delivered startling news. His father had Parkinson's disease. Parkinson's symptoms can be mild—a tremor here, some stiffness there. They are not mild in Ben's father.

Ben drives home from Penn State every three weekends, three hours and fifteen minutes each way—damn the torpedoes—to hold his family together as one might a handful of sand. With a sister in college and a brother recently discharged from the Army, Ben says he's the sibling saddled with the majority of the care. On a given visit home he'll clean up after his father, change his diapers, wait at the table when meals stretch over an hour, and try to convince him that the family hasn't been trying to strangle him in his sleep.

"It's heartbreaking," Ben says. "He was a truly able man, and now he can barely talk, eat his food. It's unimaginable."

The worst has been the dementia. "He's a shell. He's not the same person anymore. I lost him." Ben remembers his parents arguing over a car they were planning to buy. His mother wanted it to be wine-colored, and his father refused. Suddenly, he was pointing a gun at her. The police have come to the house so often, "they know us by name," Ben says.

"One day they just said, 'He has to come with us.'" They put his father in a psychiatric ward for two weeks—around the time Ben was preparing for his thesis defense. "The worst moment came when I saw my father trying to get a nurse to give him a urine test. He thought someone had been slipping him drugs. That night in bed, I bawled and bawled."

There are times Ben longs for the day his father will be delivered from his misery. Other times not at all, like the day he heard him singing along to music in his headphones. "Moments like that are why it's worth it."

There's double meaning in "worth it"—the Parkinson's has nearly wiped out the Kims financially. It would take years to dissect the algorithm that describes Ben's strange relationship to money these days. On one hand, he could care less about the stuff—if he's learned anything, he says, it's that achievement, paycheck, and status mean nothing next to family. On the other hand, he's also learned that a family with Parkinson's needs cash badly. Ben's mother and older brother run the gas station now, and though it's a money-maker, it scarcely keeps the family afloat. (This is the same station that, in November 2001, sold a Powerball ticket to a taxi driver named Ihsan Khan. The ticket was worth $55 million. Ben doesn't mention this story—I read about it on my own—and neither do I.) The net result is that Ben can speak with heartrending candor about "what truly matters," and two minutes later can reach out, touch your arm, and say, *I want to win that fucking contest money.*

THERE'S SOMETHING AMERICAN about an inventors contest, something proud and provincial and hopeful, with the flicker of profit down the road—apple pie and the Manhattan Project whipped together. In November 2002, it comes time for Ben and the fifteen other finalists to convene in New York for the judging. Ben's mother goes, so does Susie Lee, his old friend from high school—I glean what I can from Susie and Ben after the fact. Nick Clooney (George's father) emcees the event, the *New York Times*'s gadget reviewer speaks, and several celebrity brains circulate—the inventors of the diabetes test kit, the electron microscope, dynamic RAM technology, and others, Ben reports.

Ben himself gets the celebrity treatment, he says. The CEO of the Inventors Hall of Fame—himself a musician—invites Ben to a lavish dinner, then to a jazz club, where they stay until 5 A.M. Lawyers from "one of the biggest and baddest" intellectual property law firms tell Ben he'll have a job with them if he goes to law school. The head of public affairs for the U.S. Patent and Trademark Office says to give a call if he wants work. The coup de grâce: James West, inventor of the electret microphone and onetime president of the Acoustical Society of America, tells Ben he wants his help on his next "pie-in-the-sky project."

All of which sounds like almost enough to overshadow the contest itself. Almost. Six winners are picked in the end, and Ben isn't one of them. He sends me a letter some days later:

"I'm thinking this competition did some damage somehow. The

CEO of the National Inventors Hall of Fame made it a point from day one that we were all 'winners.' [But] if I'm a winner then how come I feel like I've lost? I used to scoff at those kids on [the show] 'Popstars' who would cry when told that they didn't make it to the next level. I used to think that those girls had lost their grip on life. I think I just may have myself."

Doubtful. It is no easier for Ben to lose his grip than it is for a man to let go of the live wire he's grabbed by mistake. Sure enough, Ben has rallied himself by the end of the very same letter:

"If anything, this 'loss' has lit a fire under my ass, as has every loss I've ever experienced in my life. I feel as if I need to compensate for it by doing more work (call me crazy). I guess that's what's driven me all my life: the unwillingness to experience losing in whatever form it may come in. Actually, that's not a guess, it's what I know now."

He also knows something else. Ten years after his father kept him out of music school, Ben's put the saxophone back into his future, where he'd always wanted it. He tells me he just might have what it takes to make it as a musician.

"What I wanted to do back in high school was become a famous saxophone player and move to Korea and become famous over there. I'd still like to do that one day—just play in clubs. People start talking about you if you're good enough."

Last year, while defending his thesis and tending to the family, he applied to the Berklee College of Music and was accepted. Even with all his academic accomplishments, though, Ben says his family's vision of success still has no room for jazz hornery.

"I'm not of the Korean mind-set. There are so many things I've seen that aren't that good about Korean culture—and not just Koreans, but Asians in general. They think that there is a perfect path. They want you to fit a certain mold—lawyer, doctor, whatever—or make a shitload of money, and gain status that way. It's called 'honor.' What is honor?"

For a guy rejecting Korean expectations, Ben still holds on to a lot of them. Even as the Berklee plan began to shape up, he started thinking law school might be more practical. For the record, his wall would hold a B.A., a Ph.D., a law degree, and a Berklee certificate. "Occupying free time is my drug," he tells me at one point, with a smile meant to convince me it's okay, he's joking.

"We Can Totally Do This"

I f high school gave us arguing material—our political causes, our taste in music, whatever else lends teenagers their friction—the years immediately afterward didn't exactly mellow everyone out. The mid-'90s saw a broader discord, what with Whitewater, militias, the Unabomber, the Oklahoma City bombing, the burning of several southern black churches, and the initial rumblings about some White House intern in a black beret. In short, our hot-button years at TJ gave way to more of the same in the real world.

But then money fell from the sky on top of us. It hit us on the head, and we forgot our bickering. We took Internet jobs instead, or jobs that sprung up around the Internet, or jobs nowhere near the Internet but downstream from Internet trickle nonetheless. A small percentage of us actually got rich, but mainly we got busy, and busy people stop being upset—you can't talk about abortion rights *and* stock options in the same breath. Even after the economy crashed, we'd been sufficiently transported, and previously insurmountable barriers seemed to remain largely unreconstructed. At a planning meeting for our ten-year reunion, I watched former incompatibles mingle freely over such concerns as golf and Cisco stock. We are no doubt someone's vision of larger hostility doused: Get those protesters off the streets and into Aeron chairs.

The mythologizing and exaggerating inspired by the Boom has been well-recorded. What's been recorded slightly less is how this period went to work on a specific generation. Those of us who graduated from high school in 1993 enjoy a special relationship to the Boom years. *No one told us about them at first.* Whereas younger graduating classes came of age expecting New Economy opportunities, ours first had to dangle in professional uncertainty, if only for a couple years. Upon delivery from our whimpering and searching, the feeling was that of having benefited from an error: Finally, a faulty ATM was spitting out hundreds at us. Me, I took a salaried and wonderful editing job at the age of twenty-three. There had been no ladder; from a bike messenger job, a waiting job, a string of temp gigs, and just a little freelance writing, I went to work full-time at an online magazine. My job, like so many I heard about—loose, lively, engaging—was the sort of thing a person would do for free. Ha ha, everyone thought on Friday afternoons, all friends, finally happy, changing capitalism, drunk on the cosmopolitans someone had mixed in the office kitchen. All over, uncomplicated entrepreneurialism trumped business school and profitability and standard accounting practices—a good idea was all you needed, and my generation appeared to have no shortage of those. We'd wanted to *fix everything,* my classmate Rebecca Lamey had said of our class. Now a different sort of idea was in play.

Adam Rice's experience of the Internet economy was not atypical, though it's the sort often overlooked in the obituaries of the era. Adam never got rich, never lost a lot of money, never named any of his children eLaine or Dot Org, and in the end never rubbed up against corporate malfeasance. What he did—like me and thousands of others—was get a job he neither expected nor deserved, at least as far as traditional ladder-climbing went. The dot-com explosion put wannabe artists, writers, animators, musicians, and armchair philosophers into the inconceivable position of getting paid. Where creative types once muttered away their twenties at café and temp gigs, they now sat in ergonomic chairs and spent the day *brainstorming*.

Or else quitting. The New Economy supported that, too. Job drifting, once a shameful indicator of aimlessness, became almost institutionalized—from their first days of school, young people are now reminded that the average person switches careers seven times. Adam's first job, at NewYorkOnline, lasted just over half a year. From there he moved on to a series of short-term Web jobs and so far has been able to support his family this way—on skills he learned in spite of college, rather than because of it. "As a generation, we have the luxury of jumping around from place to place or job to job," classmate Liz King says.

The Boom was a moment of young people not just inheriting unexpected opportunity but devising theories about that opportunity too. We could afford the luxury. My classmate Stacy McMahon, an IT consultant, wrote this on an online discussion board I set up for my classmates this past year: "Up until the late '80s clerical work took a staff of many people to support every one decision-maker or technician. But by 1998 in the office I worked for, it was literally the other way around—every three lobbyists or researchers were supported by one admin assistant. It worked because with the software tools available, they could keep up with three bosses. Now the association could spend more on the lobbyists and policy analysts that are their raison d'etre, and less on the office overhead. That's huge. And now that the dot coms have turned into dot bombs, a lot of people seem to think that the revolution failed—once again the real success story is getting overlooked."

Classmate Sebastian Fonss tells me he "got rather bored with college" and left before he had his degree. "I got a sucky job doing computer support for a military contract, and got them to pay for my Microsoft certification. Then I promptly left them for a company offering over twice my salary."

In high school, Rich Vuduc went by the nickname Ween and wore a long ponytail and studied computer science. He studied computer science at Cornell, too. Ten years later, he's still studying computer science, though Ween and the ponytail are gone. He will soon graduate from Berkeley with his Ph.D. Becoming a computer science professor has long been the plan; the Boom, for Rich, was a funny, brief distraction, and a couple hours or so where becoming a millionaire instead actually seemed feasible.

Snailgram.com was to be the vehicle, and Rich managed its technical side. It was an online paper greeting card company that kept track of customers' various dates—birthdays, graduations, anniversaries—and sent actual cards out at the appropriate time. "The idea was that electronic greetings are really cheesy. People want real paper, but everyone's a procrastinator. We'd even handwrite it if that's what you really wanted.

"This was your classic naive dot-commer view of the universe: *Yeah, this is doable!* Well, we worked really hard, and it survived for about two years on no money. I would spend my entire day on campus, then maybe I'd eat something, and then I'd go over to their apartment in this sketchy Berkeley neighborhood. We set up some servers in one guy's bedroom. At the peak we were getting fifty to a hundred orders a day. I think at some point we actually broke even, although it depends on how you do the accounting.

"I definitely felt that there was a democratic element to [the dot-com revolution] at the time—just a bunch of kids saying, 'Oh, we can totally do this.' But that seems incredibly naive in retrospect. One of the reasons Snailgram fell apart was that there were a lot of aspects of business we really didn't understand."

Rich returned his undivided attention to school and its host of nonvirtual stresses; the Boom was a strange blip of optimism. Looking back, he's hard pressed to say how that optimism managed to be so contagious. Statistically speaking, it was still unlikely that the average grad student would hit the jackpot. There were certainly a number of enticing jobs—those office pool tables did exist—but people never stayed at them long anyway. Maybe we were buoyed by something else in the air—Clinton and his silly saxophone, possibly—or maybe it's simply that the clouds of war and terror were elsewhere awhile. Whatever it was, we felt free, sort of. We approached our careers differently, yes, but we also felt a general encouragement. We cooked up harebrained schemes that had nothing to do with the Internet; we put diaries online, converted warehouses, tried new drugs, and generally scratched out heartfelt new theories of being. People made comparisons not just to the Gold Rush but to the Renaissance. *A bit much*, we might have thought, but then again some kind of rebirth was surely afoot.

When the correction finally came, it was as irrationally exuberant as the Boom itself. A great many decent babies went out with the bathwater. For every half-baked Internet start-up that scoffed at the old economy's interest in, say, profit, there was another little company that labored earnestly to make work a more pleasant and creative prospect than we'd grown up thinking possible. Those who worked at these places seem to have scattered into those odd crannies of underemployment that they'd managed to skip over immediately after college.

Classmate Chris Dwan graduated from college in 1996 with a degree in computer science. "Everyone but me went west, into start-ups," he recalls. "And almost every single person I know who went west has had a dot-com fold under them. My old drinking buddy had three go out from under him. Now he's teaching swordplay in Germany."

The correction didn't just lose people money; it was also a correction of bad information—some people never made that money in the first place. The percentage of Americans living below the poverty line did decrease from 13.1 percent in 1989 to 12.4 percent in 1999, according to Census 2000 figures, and the median household income rose from $39,008 to $41,994, adjusting for inflation. But the prosperity was most concentrated among Americans who were already fairly prosperous. Industrial suburbs throughout the country, rural pockets of the South and Midwest, and even Los Angeles and Queens, New York, saw increases in poverty. The economic consequence of the decade wasn't just greater wealth in America, of course, but greater disparity, too.

My classmate Amanda Rieder managed to live in the Bay Area through the entire dot-com bubble without making a dot-com dime:

"[During the Boom] the money was definitely visible. My friends would be like, 'Hey, let's go down to Mexico for a couple days!' And I'd say, 'Um, how about we go out for a drink instead?' I was never hurting, but I'd rather have been doing the kind of work I like—investigative work—than bartending. Of course, now that everyone's broke, I'm making tons of money, because people drink when they're unhappy."

Anne Farbman saw the boom and bust pass right through Austin, Texas. "There's so much talk here of the Intel building, which has become this symbol of the '90s," she says. "Intel built its headquarters here, but they only put up the piers and slabs for the first four floors, then pulled out. The city gave them hundreds of thousands of dollars. It's just sitting there—it looks like a parking garage with no walls. It's become a symbol here of that kind of hubris. But you can't have hubris without having so much self-confidence and so much self-esteem that good things don't actually come out of it. . . . I definitely don't think the bubble was just an economic bubble. *I* had no money. It was very much a combination of capabilities and confidence."

Classmate Missy Melberger began working at AOL in 2000. After Enron, WorldCom, and other accounting scandals, she noticed a dramatic change in the way business was conducted around her. When federal auditors came through her own department in its investigation of AOL's accounting practices, Missy was forced to surrender the entire contents of her office—twenty-seven boxes—for inspection. "We weren't allowed to delete anything from our computers, either. I had e-mails from my boyfriend there. Suddenly, there's no such thing as your office anymore."

In high school we'd been told of a new order. The world was our oyster, beaming career counselors swooned at us, and if the oyster was no good, a new one would be genetically engineered any day. With the Wonka-like promise of the New Economy, here was the evidence. And so from angst we were delivered a flitting vision of success—a thing infinitely more stirring than success itself, for it's entirely openended. Only later, in both our public and personal affairs, would life reveal open-ended to be a risky venture, occasionally even a *cash-flow-negative* type of proposition, as for a short while we learned to say.

12 David Garber

DAVID GARBER: *"I just didn't know what to do around people. I said 'hello,' I was as friendly as I knew how to be, and I dunno, that's about as far as my conversations with people usually got. . . . I started kinda thinking like I was worthless, like I was just of no value to anyone. I was even almost suicidal at times, really."*

MATT PROBST: "I knew him since we were babies, through our religious congregation. He was raised with strong Mormon beliefs, and in general he's a person of deep conviction. He never really fit into any of the social groups per se. He's not the type of person who follows a crowd—this was partly because of his religion. He wouldn't watch rated-R movies, for example. Or if conversations turned toward joking about things like drugs or sex, he certainly wouldn't go along with that. It would catch him off guard. He's very pure-hearted and innocent.

143

"He could have decent conversations about things he knew, but he also had his limits, and those conversations had bounds. Going outside of those would cause him to take a step back, get quiet. And it was very, very different if a girl was involved. With girls there was just a mental block that caused him to become incredibly nervous, almost to the point where he was shaking and could not speak.

"We talked a lot about ways he might have an easier time fitting in. People did go out of their way to include him, but he wasn't always flexible. For example, he refused to listen to any kind of music that he didn't already like—classical and show tunes. Same for movies and books and other things that might be of interest to other teenagers. He had his world, and stepping out of it was very difficult. Anything outside the norm he couldn't deal with. Later, after high school, he couldn't even step out of the house. I remember when we were young, there was a long time when he refused to drink water. He only drank milk. One day I suggested to him, 'Hey, why don't you try this out?' and he just said, 'Well, I like milk!'

"But he's got a wonderful, wonderful heart. He would go out of his way to do something for a friend."

SAM ZEITLIN: "We had choir together and our mothers were friends. He didn't talk that much. He was not part of the social aspect of choir. You always got the impression he was uncomfortable. But he worked really hard and was always enthusiastic. And as I recall, he was a pretty decent singer."

■

To the New Economist's mind, Ben Kim works Harder Not Smarter, and knows the Upside, grasps Scalability, and most definitely Thinks Outside the Box. His loss at the inventors contest is but a setback, a brief dip in his stock; he need only reapply himself and his achievement habit will prevail soon enough. But what of those less suited to the era's requirements for success, professional or otherwise?

"I had glasses and braces and I was really chubby, and I had allergies" is how David Garber recalls his younger self, and it's true that he stood out in this respect. But as a science school, TJ had no shortage of odd-shaped computer whizzes and funny-looking physics prodigies. There was indeed an upper echelon that tended to close ranks around the fabulous—the senior lounge, with its happy blue benches, was romping zone to the cheerful and well-adjusted—but the rest of the student body remained fairly nerd-indifferent. This might have had something to do with the free tuition and the entrance exam. As an ostensible meritocracy, we cherished the idea of disregarding traditional social hierarchies. So it was something else that kept David apart from his fellow students. More than that—for my class boasted plenty of contented loners—it turns out something kept him miserable.

I rarely crossed paths with David at TJ, but we said hello now and then. His was a misery draped in relentless, awkward cheer. "Hi there!" he'd say with a big smile, sometimes even a full wave, but even a stranger could see the enthusiasm was manufactured. In one of our yearbook photos he celebrates something called "Red, White and Blue Day" in full regalia. The photo was a surprise to me—I'd been unaware any students actually observed the faux holiday, much less wore American flags in their caps. This was David: eager to join the fun, never briefed on how.

Exaggerated sunnyness is far preferable to posturing in the other direction—never did David affect such high school deceptions as coolness, assurance, or indifference. Classmate and longtime childhood friend Matt Probst attributes this to David's "wonderful heart" and describes a lost soul both guileless and breathtakingly sincere. It was a wonder he'd been raised in the same era that produced "Piss Christ," 2 Live Crew, and other late-twentieth-century vulgarities. I remember speaking slowly with David, as I might with someone from another country; it wasn't that *he* was slow—no doubt he was a better student than I was—but that I feared profaning the exchange with some accidental slang that hadn't yet reached his very Mormon ears. I don't say this pityingly; the impression I got from David was that he moved in a different orbit, probably a holier one, and preferred it this way. When I phone ten years after our last stiff hello, I come to see this was indeed so—for a moment. I ask him how he remembers high school, and his initial response is a mixture of canned gusto and implausible chuckles.

"I really enjoyed my time there," he gushes at first, chipper as a car salesman. He almost seems to be reading from a script: "I sure learned an awful lot. For example, the first three physics classes I took [at college], we pretty much covered everything I learned in my one physics class at Thomas Jefferson! I learned a lot, and I really enjoyed it, too. I had a lot of good experiences not just in science and technology, but in some of the other stuff I was involved in. Like I was very heavily involved in the choral program at TJ, and I just loved that. Ms. Clark was just a fantastic instructor for that, and she was almost kind of like a second mom to us, in a way. She was great. I had a blast in that."

When I reply that my memories of high school are much more ambivalent—that I flat out disliked it often enough—David switches personas instantly.

"Well, actually I did too," he says, and what follows is a kind of unraveling. "I spent a lot of high school just feeling really, really, really lonely, and really depressed. . . . I just didn't really have any friends, didn't really seem to fit in anywhere, and I was just really lonely all the time. . . . Time continued to pass and I still [didn't] have any friends. And well, my freshman year ended, and I went to summer vacation, came back my sophomore year and still just didn't have any friends, and I just started feeling really, really lonely. It's a tough time when you don't have anyone you can share things with, you know? It was really rough on me.

"Academics never caused me a whole lot of anxiety. It's been mainly social. Social anxiety disorder. And just a lot of depression, mainly related to the social problems, just making friends, getting to know people. I just wanted to talk to people, but I just didn't really know how. I didn't know how to get started, I didn't really know what to say or do, or whatever. I just sort of scratched my head and went, 'What do I do? I wanna talk to these people, I wanna get to know them, what do I do, what do I do?!' All I could do was just sit there and scratch my head. Unless they actually came over and made an effort to talk with me or include me, I'd often just sort of finally give up. . . . [In addition to the choral program] the other thing that really helped a lot was my church. If it hadn't been for that, I might have gone ahead and blown my brains out or something."

David and I have several lengthy phone conversations about what he calls his "many challenges." Indeed, if I sound even remotely comfortable describing him as some kind of outsider at TJ, it's only because he himself is uninterested in anything but candor. The portrait he paints is that of a young man thoroughly out of place in his school, yes, but also in his time. For all their purported inclusiveness—one pictures Clinton here, arms outstretched—those ten years were hard ones to keep apace of, particularly for a teenager devoid of colloquialism and informality. If the '70s have gone into the books as a muddled and frumpish decade, the '90s seem slick and irreverent in hindsight. Technology was snappy, car commercials ironic, world leaders oversexed—a person had to spend a number of sunny days in the Theory section of the bookstore just to keep up. And that's what my generation did, one way or another. Grow up through the thickets of MTV, infotainment, and virtual reality, and a homespun theory of contemporary survival becomes essential. But every now and then one of us slipped through the cracks and made it to adulthood without learning the cynical-making ropes of modern life. The rest of us may spend our lives aspiring to this kind of purity, but in high school it's simply ill-preparedness, and it brought David considerable pain.

IF ONE MODERNISM did make its way into David's bones, it's his lack of hesitation in talking about his life and his unhappiness. Some time into one of our conversations, I ask him why he's decided to be so candid with me. "I've always been straightforward about things," he replies, a little taken aback, as though there could be no other way. "Sometimes it's embarrassing, but for the most part I like to tell it the way it is. The church teaches you it's right to be honest."

Honest he is, but dispassionately so. When he mentions suffering from social anxiety disorder and "a lot of depression," he sounds more perplexed than disturbed, as if he'd just removed a curious stone from his shoe. Possibly this is because he's been removing curious stones for years. When David goes back to the period he calls "a pretty happy childhood," he goes back all the way to third grade. "I was involved in Scouts, I did all sorts of things. I had a pretty good life back then. I'd always make friends wherever I went. I'm not sure exactly how I did it, it's not like I had any technique or anything. It just sorta, kinda happened," he says. Two decades later, he's developed something of a scientific approach to his challenges. It's nothing short of biology when he isolates and identifies the partition that kept him and his classmates apart:

"If I had been more understanding with how to conduct small talk with people, I think I could've done a lot better. I could've walked into a crowd of people and just started talking with them, struck up a conversation. And I think that would've made a big difference in my high school life, and into my college years as well. I would've been a lot more skilled, socially."

It's not a crazy idea—one can imagine the chart correlating happiness with small-talk-ability—but in truth David had his introduction to unhappiness long before chitchat became valuable. He was in fourth grade, and it seemed like nothing at first: One day he noticed himself clearing his throat every few seconds. "I just had to do it," he recalls. "If I didn't, it's sort of like holding your breath. It just builds up and builds up, and finally you just gotta do it."

From there, twitches in his arms and his eyes. Then he was throwing up after meals. Neither he nor his parents had any idea what the problem was—"I just knew something weird was happening."

Finally David went to a doctor, who diagnosed him with Tourette's syndrome. It wasn't the Tourette's one usually thinks of. "Some people have trouble with shouting out expletives without being able to control themselves. I never had that particular problem, fortunately," he says.

If anyone could have used a huge, loud, and well-timed expletive, it was David. His medication, Haldol, made things "almost as bad as the disease itself. That's why I had a tremendous weight gain [going into high school]. That was probably the worst symptom, actually." As for the original Tourette's symptoms, the Haldol diminished them, but only somewhat. Meanwhile, middle school was hell. "I had . . . these weird nervous twitches from Tourette's, so I was a big hit in junior high! I got teased just constantly, all the time."

"Could you talk to your parents about these things?" I ask.

"In some ways my parents and I weren't really all that close," he replies. "We kinda lived in the same house, but for some reason I guess we never really talked all that much, especially about that kind of stuff. I never really tried all that hard to talk with them, and they sensed things were wrong, and they seemed really concerned about it, but we just never really discussed it much. I'm still not sure why that is, but boy was I lonely."

One day, as mysteriously as it had appeared, the Tourette's vanished. It had disappeared just in time for high school. "I think usually when you get it, you got it, but in my case, no, it just sorta went into remission and . . . good riddance!"

David never looked back. "I never really read a lot of the literature or anything. My mom did a lot more with that than I did. I guess I was never really interested in it much. I knew all that I really wanted to about it."

As far as I can tell, David encountered good luck precisely once in high school. It happened his freshman year, with the discovery of TJ's choral program. It turns out David, a baritone, sings beautifully.

"It was one of the few things I had going on in my life that was a really positive thing," he says. "I started my freshman year—I think it was called the 'Symphonic Chorale.' And I picked that because I couldn't get into some other elective I wanted. It was like my last choice or something. And I just had a wonderful time. I was in every after-school group I could get myself into from then on—men's chorus, show choir. We performed at different places, like nursing homes, and we had concerts a few times a year. I remember we went caroling every December in different malls and stuff. And that was a blast. I always looked forward to that every year."

David says it was choir that got him through high school, but church was always his fundamental rescue. Every summer he attended a program for Mormons called EFY—Especially For Youth. "They'd have all sorts of classes and gospel subjects, and then they'd have activities and dances, and a service activity, and all sorts of games, and it was a blast, I loved it," he recalls. "Everyone there was sort of new, so we were all sort of trying to reach out and get to know each other. And I think it was easier there." When it finally came time to leave high school for college, there was no question where David would go.

Brigham Young University was founded in 1875 as the Brigham Young Academy, a high school, and named for the then-president of the Church of Latter-day Saints. To the Academy principal Karl G. Maeser, Young declared this: "Brother Maeser, I want you to remember that you ought not to teach even the alphabet or the multiplication tables without the Spirit of God."

At the twentieth-century version of BYU, David found students who shared his faith, but his social problems failed to disappear. In fact, they intensified. By the end of his first year, it was clear that David couldn't focus on his studies, even when he easily grasped the material itself. In August 1996, instead of beginning his sophomore year, he left Utah for Michigan. David would devote the next two years to converting strangers to Mormonism.

Again, he's sunny at first in his account of missionary life. "The days seemed like weeks, they were just so jam-packed full of everything. But then the weeks seemed like days, they just went by so fast. Kinda weird."

David describes an actual day in the life:

"You get up at 6:30 in the morning, and then you have a time to study and get ready for the day. You take your shower, read your Scriptures, you have a personal study. . . . Somewhere around 9 A.M. you start hitting the pavement, going around knocking on doors. Sometimes people call, ask for free videos, or free Books of Mormon, or free whatever, and we go deliver those to people. We go talk with members, we make calls from the telephone, we call back people we've talked with before, and schedule appointments, and we go and visit people. It's quite a variety of stuff we do, really."

David loved going door-to-door, and even though most people weren't interested ("Okay!" he'd say, and move on), he claims that "one of the great things about missionary is all the people you meet." It was also during this period that he befriended a fellow Mormon named Shane, now a chef back in Utah. David even made a little headway in his own troubles. He speaks of coming to see certain "false beliefs" he began nurturing about himself in high school. "I just started kinda thinking like I was worthless, like I was just of no value to anyone. I was even almost suicidal at times, really."

I ask David what stopped him.

"Well, I decided pretty early on that suicide was never going to be an option for me. . . . I wouldn't be satisfied with myself. I'm here for a purpose, and even though things might be kind of dark right now, there's still hope that I can change and that I can get over these problems that I'm having. And I just don't want to give up and call it quits, I want to just keep plugging along and stick it out, and eventually we'll get through this, this dark cloud, and find the silver lining out there and things are just gonna get better. If I just keep trying and praying and doing whatever I can, things are eventually going to work out.

"[Growing up] I'd always believed that the Church was true, and it always seemed right to me. Everything I learned, it made sense. But I got to the Missionary Center and . . . I was thinking, 'If I'm gonna go out here for two years, I need to know. . . . And so one day, I just knelt down and I prayed, and I prayed really hard. And I just wanted to know if all this was true, even if I didn't understand it fully—if this Church was, indeed, God's true Church on this earth. And, boy, did I pray hard. I really wanted to know. And, in fact, if I didn't get an answer 'yes,' I was actually thinking about going home, because I didn't think I could continue there unless I was sure.

"And at that point, I just had a feeling that I'd never felt before, exactly, and I don't think I've ever felt since. Well, not that strongly; I *have* felt it since. But it just came with an incredible power and just came all over me. It was just a calm, peaceful, comforting, enlightening, invigorating, just amazing feeling that came all over me. And somehow, in the middle of all that, I just *knew* it was true. I can't exactly explain it, but I just knew."

After that moment, David never again doubted his place at the mission, and grew even more eager to "start talking to people." Sometimes he would describe the moment to strangers, and he says sometimes they were actually convinced—"at least half a dozen times," he guesses. According to my calculations, that's 120 days of walking, biking, and driving through Michigan for every conversion. Suddenly, the years of insistent, relentless cheerfulness at high school make sense: David doesn't quit.

When we first talk, it's not yet a year since 9/11; there is much talk of religious devotion in the air. Inevitably, our conversation turns to the politics of David's own faith. He acknowledges that a good deal of violence has happened in the name of God, Christianity most certainly included. He's no Crusader—he has a reflexive dislike of violence—but the matter of reconciling multiple unyielding faiths proves tricky.

"What do you do about somebody who believes in his heart that he is following God's orders?" I ask.

"If they're not willing to consider the possibility that they might be wrong, then there's nothing much you can do. You can try to talk to them, persuade them, change their minds or whatever."

"Would someone be able to persuade you that you're wrong?"

"Well, I'm not sure how they could at this point!" he says with a chuckle. "I'm pretty much satisfied that I've found the Truth in my life. Someone's welcome to try, but don't expect anything to change."

"What if you have an Islamic fundamentalist who says roughly the same thing—'I'm convinced this is true'?"

"Obviously one person's wrong!" He laughs. And then, out of a new understanding of getting along, or out of fundamental decency, or perhaps out of both, David tacks on an afterthought: "But he's welcome to believe that if he wants to. We all gotta get along in this world."

NO MATTER HOW much truth he finds, a fellow can only be a missionary in Michigan so long. After the standard two years, David returned to BYU.

"I really learned and grew a lot, and I kind of wanted to keep on doing that. But at the same time, I just felt like it was time to move on. It was time to get going with the other aspects of my life, my career, college."

It proved harder than David had planned on. He describes a period even tougher than his first year at school:

"Toward the end of '98 I was feeling really down about the course of my life, and was so depressed that I'd get up and go to class, then come home and toss myself into bed and just cry. I'd never been so depressed, and so lonely. The guys in the dorms were nice, and they wouldn't mind my being around or anything, but I didn't get all that close to anyone."

Brigham Young suspended him for a year on account of his grades. David sought counseling, and even tried antidepressants, but found no relief. David's childhood and high school friend Matt Probst— himself a BYU graduate, and now a father and grad student at the University of Utah—kept in touch with David on and off around this time. He recalls encountering a persistent stubbornness in his friend, even when it was painfully clear that something had to change this time.

"I remember at one point in college finding out that he'd started a DVD collection, which seemed strange because his family was having a hard time financially," Matt says. "Finally, one day I asked him why he was buying all these things—he had a pretty decent collection by then—when he didn't even own a DVD player. He just said, 'Well, eventually I'll have one!'"

When I first began getting in touch with my classmates, I sent out a group e-mail to as many addresses as I could find. David, in a prompt and friendly response, wrote this:

"I have been majoring in Honors Applied Physics: Computer Science Emphasis. I have not found the coursework especially difficult; however, I have suffered off and on from social anxiety and depression and various related problems, which have caused me to flunk quite a number of classes over the years. As a result, I have yet to graduate. I have one year's worth of classes left to complete, at present, which is what I had one year ago. Right now, I have taken some time away from school to work and to get some more counseling."

Uncharacteristically for David, the encapsulation of his life had a huge omission, and it's not until we've had several extensive conversations that he gives me the awful account. It was Christmas Eve of his first year back at school, and David and his parents had been driving to his grandmother's house when they stopped at a gas station. "My dad was filling up the tank, and then something just . . . something wasn't right with him. He went into the station and was breathing in and out of a bag. We figured we had to get him help. We got him in the car and started heading toward a hospital, but all of a sudden he just collapsed, drooling. There was this ambulance in front of us at a stoplight, and I started honking and honking like crazy. My mom ran out to get their attention, but I guess they didn't see her, because the light changed and they drove away. So we ran into a business that was nearby, and told the guy there to call 911. The paramedics came and picked him up, and we followed them back to the hospital. We were praying so hard. And then they came out and told us. He'd had a stroke. He died."

There had been no warning, not so much as a sniffle. David describes the following months as "the worst ever," and he leaves it at that. He returned to school once his academic suspension ended. Not long after my first conversation with him in 2002, he was suspended again.

"It's been a difficult road for me these last ten years or so," he wrote to me in an e-mail, "but I think that I may finally be about over a lot of these problems, most of which had their origins during my high-school days. I wish that I could say that I graduated with honors a few years ago and was now well on my way through graduate school toward my goal of becoming a university professor of physics, but it just was not to be. Perhaps in another ten years . . . ? And maybe I'll be married then too, although that may take a miracle, considering my history."

———

IT WOULD BE hard to find a soul with more perseverance and determination. In July 2002, David returned to the stage. In spite of a ghastly-sounding illness the day of auditions—David is ever generous with details—he won the part of Joseph Hewes, "the delegate from North Carolina," in a local production of the musical *1776*. (As reviewer Eric D. Snider noted in the *Daily Herald*, the production was somewhat Utah-ified. In the original, it's "hot as hell" in Philadelphia. In the Provo version, it's "hot and smells.")

"It's a pretty small part," David explains with a chuckle in one of our later conversations. "Mostly what he does is just respectfully yield to South Carolina. He disappears in all the congressional scenes, and has a few speaking lines once in a while. It's a pretty small part, but it was fun anyway."

I ask David if he gives free renditions, and he obliges me with an impeccable accent:

"'Mr. Jefferson, nowhere do you mention deep-sea fishin' rights! We in North Carolina . . .' and everyone's like, 'Ohhh, fishing rights! Ohhh! How long is this piddling going to go on?!'"

True to form, things took a turn for the worse soon enough. Since his father's death, David and his mother had been living on savings—a supply that was now dwindling. In April 2003, David tells me that he's been officially cut off. "My mom just can't afford to pay for both of us anymore," he says. He now spends almost all his energy looking for ways to make ends meet.

"Without a college degree, I just can't find work that pays enough," he says. "Jobs in Virginia that would pay $13 an hour only pay $7 here."

His mother wants him to move back to Virginia—through connections at the church, she might be able to help find him work. But David isn't anxious to leave Utah, a decision he equates with giving up on his dream of being a physics professor one day. Just a year's worth of classes stand between David and his diploma. Under his current suspension, these classes have to be postponed yet again, but one BYU physics professor has reached out to David recently, and is allowing him to participate in a class of his, albeit unofficially. For all his forays into therapy, David says, "what's helped me most has been having friends, like Shane and now this professor."

In our final conversation, David tells me there's a new plan. He will soon begin making a living buying liquidated merchandise and selling it on eBay. Or perhaps more significantly, he'll be making a living from the privacy of his apartment.

"I don't know," he replies merrily when I ask what he'll sell. "Different items. Depends on what's available, and what folks are interested in buying. We'll see!"

"We'll see" is somehow both worrisome and encouraging. If the outside world often ends up surprising David, the surprise is ever mitigated by his faith. Since returning from Michigan, he tells me he's learned to superimpose new ideas over the false beliefs he held in high school. It's religion, he says quite plainly, that kept the darkest thoughts out of his mind. "There's more to life than just this life," he says. "There is a God who loves me and who wants to help me, and I can turn to Him and seek His help. There's a lot of strength and comfort in that."

RYAN BECKWITH: *"I was always kind of a loudmouth, and [halfway through high school] I tried to talk less, be a lot more mindful of how I was acting. I used to write lists for myself: 'Don't be critical of other people,' 'Don't overanalyze other people's motives,' 'Let it flow,' things like that. Every morning I'd read this list—I was pretty motivated—and then I would try to go as long as I could throughout the day acting on these principles. And it worked, actually. After maybe six months, I looked back and it was like, whoa."*

JOHN HELMANTOLER: "He rowed crew, but he wasn't exactly a crew geek. He'd go to parties and get *shithoused*. He was always stumbling around at those parties—which was cool, because he wasn't really part of that clique. He was the kind of guy doing Denny's runs at 6 A.M. He was always like, 'Dude, I got two hours of sleep in the last five days!' He always had that weird edge about him."

ERIC CRYAN: "He was a freethinker. Didn't look for a lot of social acceptance. I met him freshman year. We hit it off, and he invited me to go boating with him and his dad. I remember he was into this new thing called 'skurfing,' where everyone else was just doing water-skiing. Later in high school, we'd skip class and go bowling. He was less reserved junior and senior years. Let people know his opinions."

DAVE ROBERTS: "We were friends since I met him on the crew team. He was a little keyed-up, not calm. Very smart, not self-effacing about it—some people at our school were shy about how smart they were. I always felt like Ryan was the opposite of that.

"He was always questioning things. Everything. I remember sitting next to him on a bus ride, going up to a regatta. He was talking to me the whole time about all this philosophy and religion that he was reading, and I remember he kept calling it 'philosophical bullshit.' He was saying, *I'm trying to understand the world*, but he called it bullshit because he knew it was a futile effort. He became less cocky over the years in high school."

F ire Mountain Great Vow doesn't say a word as he opens the door to the house in the woods where he's reworking everything. Off go my shoes, and we tiptoe out of the foyer. "Gorgeous up here," I whisper, unclear on what's sayable in a place like this. Fire Mountain smiles in a distant kind of way—not because it's gorgeous up here, more like he's lost in the reverie of human voice.

Fire Mountain hasn't heard or made a peep for four days. The silence was meant as a kind of warm-up to the sesshin, or Zen retreat, he's beginning here at the dark, creaky No Abode Hermitage, fifteen miles north of San Francisco. The sesshin, involving just two other monks and one nun, will last several months. Except for days off and occasional errands, those practicing here shall not leave the premises.

Fire Mountain—a translation from the Japanese *Enzan Daigan*—has torn up more than any other classmate I encounter. He has not had a job or an apartment in a very long time. He does not have a car, or a stereo, or a romantic interest, or a favorite bar, or a magazine subscription, or just about any of the other things most twenty-seven-year-olds acquire along the way. He calls himself a dharma bum; try dharma *slut*, joke his friends when he crashes on whatever couch is free. Dharma slut it is, he shrugs. He shrugs a lot these days.

Enzan Daigan, Fire Mountain—in high school we just called him Ryan. He was quiet then, with short blond hair, handsome blue eyes, and no visible signs of dharma. He liked biology, knew before college he'd go pre-med. He rowed crew out on the Occoquan Reservoir, gray and blustery, second home to other strong, lanky types like himself. Not unlike Zen, crew was for the committed, a world of deep concentration and earnest self-discipline aphorisms.

Some classmates remember two Ryans, as they remembered two Tim Yeringtons, for instance—the adolescent cleft is not uncommon, I'm discovering. Until the summer after our sophomore year, Ryan was more or less a mild-mannered teenager. When he returned next fall, he was entirely different, with an earring or two and spiky hair. It was the hip skaters he now associated with, and late-night parties he went to. He wore T-shirts for bands heard only on the alternative radio station. He continued to earn exceptional grades, but did so while cutting class to play pool. It was with quiet intensity that he did these things. His eyes did not drift lazily from one thing to another like summer flies, or like teenagers themselves, but rather locked on to something far off in the distance, as if he were just back from war. Or the pool hall. His was a rare and unmistakable focus, the object of which was beyond us. He might well have been described as smoldering.

Over a decade later, after getting reacquainted at various bars and restaurants around San Francisco, I've come to Ryan's temple for twenty-four hours worth of sesshin. Ryan lives here now, it's as much a home as he can lay claim to. His quarters are a mat on the floor—the two other men here occupy far corners of the same floor—and the only sign of a prior life is the small photo above his mat: a teenage Ryan with an arm around his father, a kind-looking man in flannel. In the picture Ryan beams with affection, and with the confidence and good luck of a young man ready to do something big.

Once there had been a plan—it involved confidence and good luck, plus med school, a medical practice, and eventually a white picket fence—but the plan has changed. After December he'll leave No Abode for even greater solitude, perhaps to study one-on-one with a teacher in India. He will train thusly for years to come, temple to temple, teacher to teacher, until he himself is qualified to teach. Then he will train and teach, and do this for the rest of his life. Med school? He laughs at the thought. The term just barely exists nowadays, certainly not as a neutral descriptor, but there's no two ways about it: Ryan is a dropout.

I'VE ARRIVED DURING a short break in the intensive meditation regimen here. The next twenty minutes are the closest No Abode comes to unregulated ordinariness, with people reading books, perusing the mail, stretching limbs, tidying up, and generally living in mute normalcy. Ryan uses the time to prep me on certain Zen forms—how and when to bow, sit, breathe, and so on—and to show me around the place.

The temple is actually a regular suburban house, a pretty one donated by a friend of the San Francisco Zen Center. The interior has been reincarnated as a fully functional Zen monastery. Paper screens cover windows, straw mats cover the wood floors, spare Zen proverbs dangle unobtrusively from the ceiling, and through a drift of incense haze, likenesses of friendly-looking roshis hang just about everywhere. "We bow whenever we pass this one," Ryan says—his silent period is over—indicating a photo of The Great Teacher, Shogaku Shunryo. We pass Shogaku Shunryo all the time.

No Abode exists in a region already rich in solitude and alternate living arrangements. San Quentin prison is nearby, beyond that Alcatraz. To the north lies dramatic and seal-flecked Point Reyes, the otherworldly Muir redwoods, and the foggy-then-dazzling Stinson Beach. This is Marin, one of the wealthiest spots in the United States and home to all manner of dropouts. It's here that New Age hot-tub cokers famously traded their excess for exercise in the '80s and '90s—mountain biking was invented here, right on the side of Mount Tam—but legends of old Marin decadence are still dusted off periodically. John Walker Lindh, the "American Taliban," spent his formative years here, and to a swarm of tickled moralists, the only surprise was that this dissolute's mecca hadn't spawned a traitor sooner.

The fire mountain showing me around is dormant these days—the occasional eruption of temper is one of the things he's learning to shrug off. He wasn't always this peaceful. Before moving to Virginia for junior high, Ryan lived in Pennsylvania and was something of an elementary-school thug there. "I was kind of a popular kid," he'd told me some months earlier, pre-hermitage, at a café in San Francisco. "And I was a bully, too. I used to bully kids. It was kind of an unconscious thing. Then in middle school I got the other end of the stick.

"Middle school for me was absolute psychological hell. I was being fucked with, bullied, picked on. I wasn't overly nerdy, but I wasn't hip and stylish. I didn't wear the cool clothes, I didn't peg my pants. I didn't have very cool glasses, and I was always on top of my classes and stuff. I remember having sixteen-year-old rednecks in the eighth grade bullying me—kids kicking your feet as you walk down the hall, kids flicking your ears constantly.

"I would go home and think about suicide almost every day. I would lie on my bed and stare at the ceiling and meditate in the dark for hours, daily, and think about death. It was really hard for [my parents]. They didn't really know what I was going through at all. I used to call my mom a fucking bitch. It was really hard for them. I was like 'fuck you, fuck you, fuck you.'"

Ryan applied to TJ not so much for the academics—"I liked science fine"—but to get away from the kids from his middle school. It worked, too. But Ryan started slipping into his old self.

"I was still kind of a dick. I [had] made a resolution with myself before I went to TJ—I wanted to totally change how I was, my mode of being in the world. I felt like I was selfish, cruel—I felt like I was having this new start. [But] freshman year at TJ, I kind of reverted to my old self [from] before I got tormented. I remember a couple times saying some cruel things to people. One time I punched [classmate] Chris Tom. I got mad at him and punched him in the arm.

"Freshman year went by and I felt like I had friends, and I was in a more popular group of people, [but] after that I felt like I hadn't really changed. I got really pissed at myself. I was like, 'I made this resolution, and I basically didn't do shit.' So I got more and more intro-spective, especially during my sophomore year."

It was here that Ryan made his lists of self-improvements—"Don't be critical of other people," "Don't overanalyze other people's motives"—and he reports that they actually did the trick.

Not that he was immune to the occasional lapse. Senior year he dated a vegetarian and couldn't resist picking at her philosophy. "I would ridicule it and be like, 'It's not going to do anything—cows are still get-ting slaughtered.' I was horrible, absolutely no consciousness or respect," he says. "Of course, I've been a vegetarian now for almost four years."

Lapses aside, Ryan approaches self-improvement with a savantlike intensity.

"I think the psychologists would say I was pretty self-actualized. I felt like I'd become the person I wanted to be."

WHEN RYAN TALKS about Buddhism's calming effects, he's referring partly to his now-resting political self—there was a time not long ago when he was a firecracker. On a few of our meetings outside No Abode, I catch a glimpse of it. In a drafty old bar Ryan tells me about globalization horrors. And secret radiation experiments. And capitalism.

Ryan is a monk, but he's also an angry, earnest, zealous, actually-he's-onto-something conspiracy theorist. Over several conversations, he segues impossibly from the CIA's spread of crack cocaine, to insti-tutional racism, to the Church Committee of the '70s, to the medical establishment, to the Kyoto Protocol, to Zbigniew Brzezinski, and so forth—to witness this fury ten years after our high school graduation is to witness the crowning fury of the stymied and paranoid-sounding left in the era of George W. Bush. And, of course, some of his kookiest theories are well documented, as with the CIA's secret LSD experiments and other government mind-control adventures. At first, he'll only discuss his research into this last subject off the record. "Look at what came out of the Earth First! trial in Oakland," he says, explaining his reluctance to speak publicly. "Basically every single person who called Judy Bari or Darryl Cherney [got] their own FBI file, and I guarantee they were being put under some level of surveillance."

Eventually he agrees to talk about the latest in government mind control—if the authorities wanted onto him, he decides, they'd have been onto him long ago.

"I've done a fair amount of research on mind-control technologies, and using electromagnetic waves to influence human behavior. It's been a black area of government research now for forty years. What researchers have found is that the brain is both a chemical and an electrical system, and you can influence the brain remotely with pulses of electromagnetic waves. You can actually train certain brain states, and certain rhythms of brains."

The world, in Ryan's telling, is a crumbling and misled place; back in high school, before he kept a file on CIA mind-control advances, Ryan possessed none of these ideas. He did not have notions, didn't talk about "the Big Lie." If he ever spoke of The Man, he probably meant Mr. Johnson, our biology teacher. But with his spiritual awakening came a political one. The Buddhism and the radical dissent are responses to the same larger spiritual dysfunctionality. Ryan's credo would seem to be something like this: Within and without, a sickness has spread, requiring treatment at multiple levels. That which leads to global injustice also creates suffering in the seeker himself, and that suffering must be addressed first; Ryan's response to Bush, racism, and the military-industrial complex begins with a cleansed soul.

————

WE THE TJ class of 1993 spent a remarkable portion of our child-
hoods preparing for a drug-addled high school experience that never
materialized. It was we who learned to just say no, to D.A.R.E. to keep
ourselves off drugs, and most of all to beware the stubbly teen who
lurks in the high school parking lot: The Ziploc in his pocket would
be our undoing. High school was billed as a place of vulturous,
depraved dealers, jonesing for nothing less than our unsuspecting
souls—which might or might not be dosed against their will.

When my class got to TJ, it turned out our souls faced no danger;
the drug war, in our tiny, nerdy world, had largely succeeded. There
were no stubbly teens forcing us to say no—there weren't even many
stubbly teens. The only people lurking in the parking lot were us, and
we were just looking for our after-school study groups.

So we did our drugs in college for the most part. Ryan found pot at
UVA and smoked a lot of it. Sophomore year was when he began to
be "stoned all the time," he says, something that happened "pretty
much every day for most of eight years." He dropped a lot of acid, too.
Pot indeed was a gateway drug of sorts. Ask what led him to his current spirituality and he's not ashamed to say it was marijuana and
marijuana culture.

"Actually, *High Times* magazine—people mock it, but they have a
lot of articles on Earth First! and what's going on with the redwoods,
et cetera. I was planning on going to northern California and joining
Earth First! when I was twenty or twenty-one," Ryan says, recalling his
first exposure to radical ideology. "I knew no Earth Firsters at the
time, I knew no radical environmentalists, I knew nothing—it was
my own angst about how fucked up this whole system of society was,
and wanting to actually do something physically about it."

Ultimately he rejected the Earth First! philosophy—"It's primi-
tivism," he says. But marijuana turned out to be just the first in a

series of steps toward an entirely new path for Ryan. Not long after discovering radical environmentalism, he began reading the work of the respected New Age philosopher Ken Wilber, a disciple of Deepak Chopra and a cartographer of human consciousness. Wilber's work led to "a totally different orientation" for Ryan.

About this time, Ryan started having doubts about medicine.

"I majored in biology because I really liked high school biology, I loved nature, I loved animals. I got to college and it's all biotech-focused, all molecular-focused. That's where the money is, that's where they funnel people," he says. "It's a pretty fascinating field, in terms of genetic engineering and everything else, but I just was not interested in that. To me, looking at the state of the world, the last thing I thought we should be devoting our energies to is prolonging the human life span. It's a joke. There are already eight billion people, and they're already destroying the planet. For me, seeing all these smart, talented people devoting their energies to furthering what's already a gross imbalance—it's suicide."

But the erosion of Ryan's faith in medicine would not be his greatest shock in college. Sophomore year, without warning, his father suffered a massive heart attack and died. He was forty-eight.

"After he died, I had something like a nervous breakdown. I had panic attacks. I didn't want to see friends of mine, I'd hide in my house, I wouldn't want to go out. I remember having a panic attack in this crowded hall, my heart pounding, and thinking, *Oh my God, I'm going to die right here.* I was living with a guy who was diagnosed as bipolar and was taken to a psych ward for many months. I was thinking, 'That's going to happen to me.'

"Even before my dad died, life was getting very mentally difficult. The first girl I was ever in love with, freshman year—she broke up with me, and later I found out she'd cheated on me for the whole time. My dad died six months after that. It felt like the people I loved were leaving me."

Ryan transferred to George Mason University, in northern Virginia, to live at home with his mother for a semester. When he returned to UVA, he spent a lot of time in his apartment. "I'd smoke bud, hang out with my dogs, hang out with my friends. A lot of my classes, I never went except to take the tests. . . . I was just trying to graduate at that point."

He did graduate, with a 2.8 GPA. As for the panic attacks, it would take longer for them to disappear. "With time, things slowly got better," he says. "I had no confidence, I didn't want to be around people. It took like four years to get back to being around people, crowds again." After graduation, Ryan and his then-girlfriend got in the car and sped west.

THE FOUR BUDDHISTS who roam the vast No Abode house enlarge it further with their silence, bringing to mind a mansion patrolled by ghosts. Residents drift from room to room in elaborate robes, footsteps mere poofs on the wood floor. A summer camp–like focus on The Schedule permeates life here. Do we rest now? Does this discussion last fifteen minutes or twenty? When does cleanup end today? The hours are divided into zazen sessions, chores, meals (informal and formal), study time, discussion period, chanting (in Japanese, no less), rest, and the occasional supplication excursion. The day I visit, Ryan and company had trekked into town to beg outside an upscale supermarket. No Abode is one of only two temples in the United States to implement this aspect of Japanese Zen, Ryan tells me. "Faggot!" some teens have been known to holler at the berobed and behatted monks on their way to town, but by and large the beggars are met with relaxation, as Ryan would say. Once they even received steaks, which they promptly donated elsewhere.

Zazen time is signaled by a bell at No Abode; the sitters and I gather quietly in what used to be the living room. Where another household might have built a fire, this one convenes a collection of statuettes and other ceremonial objects. If there can be degrees of silence, this one is in the red zone. We bend at the waist toward the fireplace Buddha, then turn to the small, dimly lit room on our right. This is the meditation room, and we bow our way in. I try my best to be mindful. What happens in here is more or less that for which Ryan has forsaken all else in this life.

In the meditation room, we make our way through the incense to the round black cushions that await us on our mats. The cushions resemble cheese wheels. Very, very, very slowly, each of us bows toward our cheese wheel and then away, and eventually ease onto it more or less lotus-style. Clockwise—always clockwise—we rotate on our butts until each of us faces the wall. A candle flickers, throwing shadows of ourselves up on the ceiling. Great adjustment ensues, robes rifled and sorted and smoothed until what's left is a hazy room full of silent cloth mounds.

The idea is openness. In our laps our hands meet in something of an O, for openness. Back go the shoulders, causing similar openness in the chest. What is openness? Ryan resists defining it; I've decided it's a portal through which Nothing may enter and attachment may exit. Attachment to desire, attachment to frustration, attachment to Buddhism. "I like some of my attachments," I'd told Ryan when he was prepping me. "That's fine," he said with a smile. "Just don't get attached to them."

Form follows nothing in the meditation room; we do everything just so. I'm not sure whether my eyes are supposed to be open or closed but decide to detach from that worry. A minute passes, barely. Ten minutes later, another. From branches in a breeze outside, more shadows move around on the wall. They brush over to the left and bow a bit. Then they brush over to the right some. The incense comes and goes. Ahead, inconceivably, lies thirty minutes of uninterrupted nothingness. This is the world of Ryan Beckwith in 2002. No e-mail, or radio, or talking. No fiddling with the shirt buttons or chewing on a pen. No hovering at the refrigerator or reading horoscopes in the back of the magazine. No horsing around with the girlfriend and no girlfriend and no horsing.

Among those who mock it, meditation is a leisure pursuit taken up by the doughy and soft of heart. In truth, sitting at the No Abode proves incredibly difficult—scary too, in a "Yellow Wallpaper" kind of way. The brain, usually a benign and quiet organ, starts to pound. The silence and focus and nothingness of the meditation room just might be the closest a law-abider can come to solitary confinement. One realizes the true value of the loud, flashy consumer society beyond the temple doors: It's a distraction. Remove the distraction and what's left are the exposed beams of our sanity; meditation assumes the uncomfortable dimensions of a termite inspection.

How long has this been? After twenty minutes, or perhaps just five, Ryan appears focused and open, his back rigid like an arrow. My own spine has begun to curve in on itself, like one hand preparing to clap. Lines are de-sharpening at this point. I reflect on the texture of the wall. Is reflect the word? Could I pass through the wall? The place between sleep and awake stretches out. Images of salamanders and trees and bent grass visit me. I snap out of it, wonder if I'm getting There, think better of it, just sit. Meet everything with relaxation, Ryan advised me before this. At temples, as at all religious outposts, you never know who's talking when someone's talking. A master? An ancient text? A self-help guide? I meet this thought with relaxation, but it's too late; I've lost my focus. "Once you start thinking about the end, you're gone," one of the other monks tells me later.

RYAN AND MAYA, his girlfriend, didn't have a plan when they reached the West Coast. It was 1997 and many thousands of fellow young people were arriving in California at the same time, from Virginia, New York, Idaho, India, and everywhere else. Like so many of these people, Ryan and Maya had great luck.

"We met a Methodist minister on the beach, and she invited us to stay with her for two weeks, rent-free. I met another guy on the beach with a dog. He let us stay with him for a month."

In the great tearing-up that was the '90s employment scene, it wasn't uncommon to find academics who'd ditched the nonpromise of scroungy university work for the Internet, which was actually paying cash to big thinkers. Ryan and Maya were not these academics; for them, the Internet was a distant eddy too far across the water. Not long after settling in, both took old-economy jobs at UCSF and, unlike everyone else in the Bay Area, were doing precisely what they'd long trained to do.

Ryan hated it. He was a technician in a biology lab, and the work was mindless. (Still, his mother misses the UCSF days, Ryan laughs. "'You're too smart to be doing this,' she tells me [about being a monk]. She liked it better when I had that terrible lab tech job, because then she could brag to people that her son worked at UCSF.")

What happened next was further disassembly of Ryan's life. It's a well-worn process on the West Coast—northern California isn't just a great hatchery of new lives, after all, it's a vast littering of old ones: some burdensome Judeo-Christian values here, a forsaken squareness there, et cetera. In Ryan's case, it was an impressive university job, a longtime girlfriend, an apartment, and eventually a beloved pet that fell away. Just a couple of years out of college, he was a streamlined spiritual unit, and the San Francisco Zen Center he'd been visiting was now home.

Plenty of weekend Buddhists dabble at the Zen Center and never feel the need to escalate; Ryan couldn't dabble in anything if his life, or lives, depended on it. He's machinelike when there's a devotion at hand, and there's always a devotion at hand. In high school it had been crew. Then biology. At college, there came the triumvirate of pot, Ken Wilber, and consciousness. At the lab in Berkeley came sub-version: There's only so much to do while the centrifuge is spinning, and Ryan spent the time getting a radical's education over the Internet. There was chess—"I got way into that for a while, but got tired of it." Finally there was Buddhism and ever more burrowing into the world of northern California Zen practitioners.

Single-mindedness isn't unheard of in our generation, but far more common is a bevy of interests and professional aspirations. Ben Kim can't immerse himself in algorithms unless there's also a saxo-phone nearby, and even then he's thinking law school. Brenda McEl-downey won't stick to acting when there's singing and dancing to be done, too. Lesley Cook finds herself paralyzed at the architecture/art/law enforcement/theater fork in the road. With most of us, our passions rarely amount to a vertical mass; more often they just fan out laterally, cards spilling across a tabletop.

FOR THE SAKE of historical and karmic context, I should reveal that my visit to the No Abode happens in October 2002, just before Chechen rebels took hostage an entire Moscow theater, after Pennsylvania convicted '60s consciousness guru Ira Einhorn of murder (silencing his claims of a CIA mind-control plot), and the same day the Washington, D.C., snipers gunned down an FBI employee in a Home Depot parking lot. After our first meditation session, we take seats in the reading/dinner room at foot-high tables and have something like a current-events discussion. It's the first real conversation I've seen here.

"Oh," says Luminous Owl, an uncompromisingly moony monk and one of two priests here. He looks dreamily in my general direction. "What is . . . happening . . . with Iraq?"

I proceed to tell him the details of the recent House and Senate votes authorizing the president's use of force in Iraq, throwing in a few choice quotes from certain members.

Owl cocks his head at such an angle as to suggest a child's beatific bafflement at the world. "So . . . we're not . . . at war?" he finally asks.

Ryan has dropped out, but he remains tuned in—he calls friends on days off for news and, yes, box scores—and even maintains his own theories on certain news items.

"CIA mind-control experiment gone wrong," he tells us when the subject of the Washington sniper arises.

"Sniper?" Owl asks a few seconds later.

Following our current events conversation and a brief Zen reading afterward, we suffer through a light gruel dinner, then kitchen cleanup. Doing dishes at No Abode is literally a system of bowing and scraping. Everyone faces the center of the kitchen and bends at the waist, then proceeds to fork their food scraps into the compost bucket. There's a Zen way and a wrong way. "Um, we like to use the sponge like this," Luminous Owl tells me as I scrub. "No, more like this. Also, don't rinse. Put the unrinsed bowls over on this side, and somebody else rinses. Okay?" Attention to detail, I observe, can be tense business here. Later, Owl describes to me a kind of greenhouse effect that can build at monasteries like No Abode. "Someone can be pouring your soup, and you're wanting them to give you not just broth but the chunks of food, and if they don't, you think about it for days and days."

Eventually, we all retire for the night. Sleep happens without a lot of fanfare—no reading in bed, no end-of-day wrap-up, just a silent joining of body and sleeping bag until wake-up call. At ten till four, an hour at which dropping out of society starts feeling highly *un*enlightened, we begin again.

Day two is much like day one—a similar combination of meditation, chores, meditation, chanting, eating, and, later, more meditation. Around noon, Ryan takes me aside to prepare me for oryami, the formal lunch ceremony you can find at any Zen retreat. It's the last time I'll see him alone for several months, and I ask, finally, why he's doing this. Chanting about compassion doesn't create compassion in the world, I tell Ryan, the CIA is still preparing to magnetize our brains into jelly, presumably, and the 3:50 wake-up is a pain in the ass.

Ryan answers loosely—this is a training ground, the compassion will be carried out into the world later, the discipline pries us loose from our desires—but it's not until the end of our conversation that he gives me a satisfyingly personal response.

"One day some shitty-ass thing's going to happen to you," he says, putting the oryami setup aside for the moment. "You drop dead, or your girlfriend gets shot in the parking lot of Home Depot—you'd better be prepared."

Some months after my stay at No Abode, Ryan calls to say he's finished his study there. We visit once, and then he flies to Florida to see his mother and two sisters. From there he will travel to Europe, and then on to India. We have one last conversation before he leaves the country. Fire Mountain Great Vow has just returned from an alligator farm when I call.

"It was tough the first couple weeks, seeing my old patterns come back," Ryan says about being home. "I'd be grouchy, lose my patience. At one point my mom said, 'What about all that meditation you've been doing? Where'd that go?'

"But things are good now," he continues. "It's been great to spend time with my mom and my little sister, who's sixteen. I've been teaching her how to drive." And here he chuckles—at what can only be the notion of a would-be doctor-turned-hermit talking about turn signals in Florida. We agree to keep in touch, although it seems understood that our paths might not cross again for quite some time. It's with relaxation that we meet this possibility.

14 "We're Overwhelmed"

W hat really happened to the class of '93? In high school
simple politics consumed us, then Nasdaq-begotten
giddiness did. In every direction lay potential. We were
young people bewildered at the strange turn of the strange century
around us—bewildered at the apparent explosion of consumer culture, at the titillating absurdity of O.J. and everything else that suddenly seemed O.J.-ish. Bewilderment was a reasonable response to life
at the peaceful, self-conscious end of history. It helped that the stakes
in America were low. Y2K was the biggest danger we could drum up,
and when that failed to destroy us, we had one more wry chuckle at
millennial quirkiness. This was postmodernism, a fragmented, decen-
tralized realm, and it promised to deliver us from the lie that truth
ever existed in the first place. It was fun.

And then it wasn't. From all I can gather, we got older—gradually
we became no longer pleasantly bewildered but *overwhelmed*. We

weren't overwhelmed in an overworked sense, or even in a moral, William Bennett vs. Times Square sense, but something broader: a multidisciplinary overwhelming, where the sheer amount of information, commerce, latte options, Armageddon scenarios, chat rooms, Barbie accessories, career possibilities, and theories regarding the above collude in a jumbled assault on clarity.

Regarding the general state of everything, classmate Richard Scalzo, now working on his astrophysics Ph.D. at the University of Chicago, rattles off a soliloquy of ambivalence: "Modern society has become so complex that it's a complete headfuck to figure out what's connected to what, what attempts at a solution will result in what effects on other things, and so forth. I look around me and see things that appall me, like the class stratification of our society and the number of homeless people on the streets, the marginalization of women and various minority groups and the battles they've had to fight to get recognition, the crass commercialism, the difficulty in getting interesting content through mass media, human rights abuses abroad and in America, workmen on Arctic oil rigs eating baby seals for breakfast, et cetera. But each of these problems seems to be one head of a hundred-headed hydra, and if you cut off one head, two grow back in its place. There are plenty of smart people that don't know how to solve these problems, and if they do, they are voices crying in the wilderness."

Chris Miller, who played in our class's revered heavy-metal band Citadel, perceives a more general disorder-at-large, which he tries to keep at arm's length: "I go out less and less. I find it easier to stay at home and away from all the noise than to adventure out into the world and having my mind and emotions pulled in fifty different directions all the while trying to see what is actual and what is false. I see and feel so little cohesion between people today in our society...."

Mike Janssen, who in high school founded the Coalition for the

Righteous Application of Plants (C.R.A.P.), is now a journalist cover-ing the public radio industry, and seems to find American irony a lit-tle less . . . ironic now. He describes our overwhelming in political terms:

"I was at NPR last week interviewing various folks, and several journalists commented on something that, to me, certainly seems true. We are in an environment in which the major news events that used to happen every decade now happen every year. The presidential election of 2000, 9/11, the ensuing war in Afghanistan, war in Iraq, and now possibly war against Syria. . . . It all adds up to a deeply com-plicated web of sorrow, violence, and confusion that I think few of us could say we fully understand. I didn't really become politically cog-nizant until the end of college, but even I could agree that the years of the late '90s were hardly as populated by so many 'significant' events."

Ryan Beckwith, one of my few classmates who literally headed for the hills, puts it this way: "We're constantly being bombarded with bullshit."

DID OUR CLASS actually grow up into an especially confounding era? Perhaps twenty-eight-year-olds always feel bombarded, and always with bullshit—young Athenians probably felt a primitive post-modern dread even as the Great Golden Age was upon them. But the debunking of the myth of "simpler times" is overdue for a debunking itself, my classmates seem to suggest. Technological improvements in the last decade changed the pace of our lives, and in so doing changed the content. The "strange disease of modern life," as Matthew Arnold put it, now infects with such constancy, over so many channels, that it no longer even registers as sickness; through sheer proliferation, the bullshit bombardment gets reified into the norm.

Many classmates I spoke with refer, in one way or another, to this feeling. The terms are hazy—*bombarded, overwhelmed, headfuck*—but they seem to flick at a similar experience. What I gather from more paranoid comments is a collective suspicion that we've passed through the looking glass, that the formula governing reality itself—from politics to art to popular media—is much closer to something Lewis Carroll dreamed up than anything that resembles sense. If every generation is assigned some existential preoccupation or other, this might be ours. Where once it was possible to look at the length of someone's hair and understand his position on the Vietnam War, it's now possible, if the lighting's just right, to look into someone's eyes and know whether he or she feels lost amid the growing, dizzying din.

"I constantly am asking myself if we are actually ready for this amount of information, this constant bombardment of different messages on all levels," Chris Miller says. "Turn the clock back fifty years and people [were] bombarded by information on a much lower level. Less outlets of information equal people talking about more of the same things. That's why . . . there is more 'white noise' than ever before. Many more people on many more levels are thinking and feeling differently on many more subjects and reacting in more ways than ever before. So where is the truth in the chaos?"

My classmates and I came of age at the moment of a fundamental shift. American culture has veered from peculiar but generally intelligible—say, a televangelist caught with a prostitute—to painstakingly, comprehensively absurd. How else to describe the interlocking series of disconnects that passes for modern, daily history? How else to explain dimpled chads and Freedom Fries; antimaterialist rhetoric showing up on Citibank billboards; a 2002 *Washington Post* survey showing 69 percent of Americans believe Saddam Hussein was connected to 9/11; the Stones' "Start Me Up" signifying no longer sex but a Microsoft ad? On their own, these examples are discreet and sufferable phenomena—co-optation, selling out, hyperreality, et cetera. But as part of a system, their sum total is surreal, jarring. What we have in response are vague impressions, intermittently paranoid: a growing noise, a general quickening, a cacophony of choices, a hulking, cross-platform illogic.

My classmates may not behave the way they do because their TVs carry too many cable channels, but invariably their life choices reflect some measure of the absurdity afoot. David Garber headed for the seclusion of Utah, and in so doing pushed modern, secular, towering America to a gaudy twinkle on the horizon. Lesley Cook found her own seclusion, but without the input of organized religion, and therefore with a little indecision—torn between art, tattooing, antiques, an English degree, and forensics. Tim Yerington keeps things as simple as possible, fleeing grad school for a nine-to-five job that turns him loose now and then for walks on the beach. Brian McConnell builds cannons.

Of course, we're not a population of Luddites, victimized by and distinct from all manner of progress. Our generation is very much involved with the machinery mediating and shaping reality, from VW commercials to books about former high school students. As a Web producer at Playboy.com ("Yes, that does include airbrushing breasts"), Chris Miller has his nose right up in the absurdity.

Nor are we so priggish that we can't abide quirkiness. America's reckonings with absurdity have often been America at its finest—from Twain to Mencken to *The Simpsons*, the country's best has often coincided with systemic decadence, hypocrisy, and madness. But those phenomena no longer seem exceptional, and therefore there can be no pleasure in excavating them. The offending institutions, from ad agencies to politicians, have perfected the art of accommodating criticism and dissent. As Gary Kamiya described it in his

Salon.com review of Thomas Frank: "You can't fight the system because the system won't fight back. You scream and scream, and at the end of the day you're a celebrated Angry Young Man and rising literary star, interviewed in *Details*." The sort of institutional falseness that Twain found so teasable is now everywhere, always, on too many networks and too slippery to keep under one's thumb. Sporadic, breakable ridiculousness is fun, and fun to shatter; constant and spongy ridiculousness only absorbs our critiques and ultimately folds us into its dirty crannies. "Things aren't *light and fluffy* anymore," as classmate Eric Cryan puts it.

WHAT'S ALL THE FUSS? earlier generations ask. *Are young people really being gobbled up by the system? Is it so bad? Can't you just turn off the tube?* I suspect my classmates and I are still too young to know the answers to these questions. Maybe all the flawed modernity we perceive is none other than life. Maybe adults have always known the world to be absurd, and we just need to get used to it.

Dave Roberts says he does feel overwhelmed—when he leaves Vermont, where he lives with his wife and works as a transportation planner. "I'm a little cut off up here," he tells me. "We just have a slower pace. It helps keep me sane."

"Have things *ever* really been in control?" David Garber asks me, and certainly the idea of *white noise*, of *constantly being bombarded by bullshit*, probably sounds like some obscure, urban, intellectual boogeyman—which, in fact, it might be.

Tu Tran and I dated in high school, and she always had a sanguine outlook on things. Now, as a master's candidate in the Interdisciplinary Computer Science program at Mills College in California, she maintains that simplicity is still possible. "Life is complicated these days, but I think it's probably just as complicated as it was for people before us—our parents, grandparents, and beyond. [And] I think life is as complicated as you make it. . . . Sometimes when things seem to be spinning out of control, you have to step back, say, 'Things are okay,' and list all the good things in your life. I have housing, I have my health, family, my dogs, friends, plants, memories of vacations, et cetera."

Then there's the position that overwhelmed is good for us. The vast noise that engulfs us is not just Jerry Springer coarseness, but also a better understanding of trade implications in New Guinea, of influenza trends in China. With the maddening quickened pace and labyrinth of ideas and possibilities has come a useful broadening of horizons, Charlotte Opal points out.

Classmate Anne Barnhill simply chooses to embrace the chaos. It's why she lives in New York, she says. "The world is saturated. I like being immersed in something that's really huge and out of my control. I *always* feel overwhelmed."

15 Karen Taggart

KAREN TAGGART: *"Each year I tried something new. Freshman year I remember being angst-ridden and punk rock—you know,* hate everybody. *Sophomore year I decided to try on the popular-girl style and buy my clothes at The Limited and have a normal hairdo. That didn't work so well. By the end of sophomore year I was the girl from [the band] Dee-Lite—beehives and '70s dresses and all that. In chemistry my hair was so big I had to modify my safety goggles. Junior year I went back to the punk rock freak thing, but also got into the jock role, with lacrosse. Then I did the drama geek thing, wrote a couple columns for the newspaper. I tried every single club. Senior year I was an activist."*

ERICA KRUGER: "She was always a very vivid person—comfortable in her own skin, and willing to assert her opinions and feelings about a given topic, regardless of whether or not those

185

thoughts would be well received by her audience. . . . Her talent at improv was enhanced by these characteristics—she was not afraid of what others would think about her—and so she was always willing to put herself out there, give her whole energy to a project and then see what happens. She surrounded herself with similar people—genuine souls, trying to be themselves over 'fitting in.'"

JOE GIASSON: "I wrote a song about Karen. We went out for two months, freshman year. Karen's the type of person that, no matter what she does, she's always going to have a cause, and she's always going to fight for it. I had my little sister meet her when she was growing up, just so she could see someone like that."

K aren is a happy, loud redhead who has been cheerfully dissatisfied with almost everything at one point or another. She has been dissatisfied with certain political developments, certain social norms, certain high schools, certain colleges, certain jobs, and most consistently, her own self. She does not complain. She puts on funny clothes and extreme lipstick and sets out correcting the problem at hand. What's interesting about Karen isn't her need to fix everything—perfectionism, the neurotic cousin of ambition, doesn't particularly stand out in our overachieving high school class. What's interesting about Karen are two recent and oddly commingled outgrowths of the perfectionism: (1) She's left her white world largely for a black one. (2) In the face of that overwhelming, zazen-inducing noise, Karen has eschewed mountain retreats for diving in headfirst.

Karen resembles a bulldog. She is squat, cute, part Irish, unbudgeable, and doesn't know when a fight is bigger than her. "Free South

Africa!" she would exclaim at various times in high school. "AIDS needs to be stopped and we have the power to do it," an article in one of our yearbooks quotes her as declaring. Even on the subject of school dances she strained against her leash: "They did a good job with homecoming," she allowed in that same yearbook, "but [student] government needs to get more in touch with the students."

Before visiting her in Washington, D.C., I spoke with Karen on the phone several times, and she sketched out her bumpy high school trajectory. She began at TJ with the hangover of a conservative Catholic upbringing. In junior high the idea of gay people frightened her, and she longed to attend pro-life rallies (her parents forbade it). She speaks in terms of a truer self wanting to emerge in high school; in fact, so many selves emerged there that she had to cycle through them like a person trying on clothes. Throughout each identity—the punk, the diva, the jock, the activist—she remained opinionated, outrageous, and prone to kitsch. We had every reason to believe she would end up on the moon, or on a polka-dotted stage of some sort, or at the helm of a movement.

On paper Karen has a good deal in common with Lesley Cook. Both were noisy, antiestablishment, chronically thwarted lefties, both from conservative homes, both proud kooks. And yet a fundamental difference separated the two: Karen couldn't have spent a minute in Lesley's ceiling redoubt, couldn't have devoted a second to driving a baby to daycare. For all her assaults on conformity, she took her schooling more seriously than anyone else I knew—including the kids too busy for political causes. Ask her a test score from fourth grade and I'm sure she'll remember it. Education was her first priority, and she developed an ulcer to prove it; I knew of no other classmates in high school with Rolaids in their lockers. Once she tore the binding out of her calculus book when she couldn't solve a particular problem. "I wish I could say my parents were forcing me, or that I wanted to be better than my brother, but it was me," she says. "[As a girl] I played violin, and had to be the best. In fifth grade I had to be the spelling champion. Whatever was the hardest thing for me to do, I just had to do it."

The education obsession could not be moderated, but it could be directed. Junior year she read *Walden,* and it opened her eyes to the shallowness of traditional public schooling. "I realized I was prepping to take a test that would prep me to take another test that would help me answer multiple choice. . . . It just was not real." But *Walden* didn't mellow her preoccupation with learning; if anything, it only encouraged her to pursue education in its purest form, like an alcoholic who eventually goes straight for the ethyl. Intent on finding "the anti-Jefferson," Karen enrolled at Hampshire College in Massachusetts, the same test-free school where Lorraine and Adam Rice went. There the preoccupation only reshuffled.

"At Jefferson I knew when to stop. You stop when you get to 94," she says, referring to the cutoff between a B+ and an A. "At Hampshire no one told me when to stop. You're supposed to stop when you've learned, when you're satisfied. No one had ever taught me how to know if I was satisfied. My first semester I had all my final papers done two weeks early. My professors were like, 'Chill.' I was like, 'What could I do to improve it? OK, I'll get you a draft tomorrow.'"

KAREN DOESN'T MENTION it when she rattles off her list of high school personalities, but one identity has been a part of her for years. As long as I've known her, she seems to have identified with a race other than her own. *Sister,* this pale white suburbanite, owner of 114 freckles, would call a fellow pale white suburbanite. It wasn't a matter of, say, liking black music. To the outsider's eye, she seemed to experience a profound connection to a group of people that, on the surface, had very little in common with her. But if this was an unsupportable limb she'd ventured out upon, she gave little indication she cared—which might be why it held her.

"I feel like I exist in two worlds," she says with a casual shrug. "I'm not sure when that started. I remember junior year [of high school] we all had to read a coming-of-age book. Everyone chose *The Catcher in the Rye*, and I chose *The Autobiography of Malcolm X*. And I don't know why—I just picked it off a bookshelf. Some things just happen for a reason. I read that book and was crying the whole way through. Same for watching *Eyes on the Prize*. [And] the Civil Rights movement—for some reason I always felt like I was there."

Karen isn't so naive as to think she *was* there, in any sense of the word. And she understands that her empathy could earn her a reputation as a fetishist or worse. But she's not the sort to get paralyzed by the complexity of contemporary race relations, nor is she the sort to silence whatever inner black woman might be lurking. ("I remember her yelling 'Free South Africa!' at our football games," Vanya Wright recalls. "How exactly were we supposed to do that?") And so it was that, in the fall of 1996, Karen found herself in Birmingham, Alabama, studying black voting rights.

Karen had carved out a concentration (Hampshirese for major) that was part American studies, part political theory. She says she liked theory ("I was a big Hobbes-head") because real-life politics fell too short of excellence and therefore depressed her. Eventually, she discovered a cause both theoretically rich and meaningful beyond academia: proportional representation. PR, as its advocates call it, is nonmajoritarian voting. Karen describes it this way: "If your party gets 30 percent of the votes, you should get 30 percent of the seats. It's what every other major democracy in the world uses but us. Here if you get 49 percent of the vote, you get none of the seats."

In the fall of 1996, Karen traveled to Birmingham to watch Ed Still work. Still is one of the founders of the Center for Voting and Democracy in Washington, a former teacher of activist Lani Guinier, and a prominent voting rights attorney from Alabama. She nearly hyperventilates when she describes the experience: "I got to interview John Lewis, I got to meet Constance Baker Motley, I got to meet Fred Gray, one of King's attorneys. I got to go to all these meetings where I wasn't the only white person in the room, because Ed was with me, but I was definitely the only woman. I got to see Angela Davis at the 16th Street Baptist Church. I got to go to Kelly Ingram Park, and I went to Selma, and I walked across the [Edmund Pettus] bridge.

"I got more and more into looking at [things] from a black perspective," she tells me, recalling her time in Birmingham. Again this strikes me as a foray into murky race territory—either just the right thing to say or just the wrong thing. I ask her if, while trying on the black perspective as a college student, she ever irritated anyone who'd actually been born with it.

"Black people really didn't give a shit. Some [would] ask out of curiosity, not hatred, 'How did you come to discover this? Why are you here?' I don't want to be so arrogant as to say, 'No, everyone was totally cool with me,' but they never [complained] to my face. Maybe it's because I was always escorted in by the right people."

If migrating across the race line ever caused any tension, Karen says, it was mainly with other white people. When she moved into a white part of town and told a neighbor where she'd be working, the neighbor looked at her funny. "She was like, 'Oh that's on the other side of the tracks, don't go North Side.' I was like, 'Why don't I go North Side?' And she said, 'You know, honey. You know why you don't go North Side.'"

———

PARTLY IT'S JUST Karen's disposition that keeps her from hesitating on the subject of race—she's not the self-conscious sort. And partly it's an active blurring of traditional lines: For the past four and a half years she has been in an interracial relationship. Recently she picked out her wedding dress.

The story of Karen's love life begins at the beginning of college, when a funny thing happened: Everyone thought she was gay. The fact that she had a steady, long-term boyfriend—she'd begun dating him at the end of high school—did little to convince people. Maybe it was because she had lots of gay friends, or because she decided to arrive at Hampshire with a shaved head, or because she was active in the AIDS community. Maybe it was that suspicious quote in the *Washington Post* about teen sexuality, following TJ's harassment-clause hubbub: "'Everyone is bisexual, if you ask me,' said Karen Taggart, eighteen, who is heterosexual and just graduated from Thomas Jefferson. 'Most people are somewhere on the line. You choose to love whomever you choose to love.'" Karen recalls her precollege orientation trip, on which she became friends with a girl who'd just come out. At the end of the orientation, the leader of the trip sat Karen down and said, "I really want to thank you, it was so good that you were there for Beth. It's important for Beth to see someone who's out like you are." Karen responded with the first of many protests. "I was like, 'I'm not gay!' And I wasn't! My whole first year I had all these girls hitting on me, and I was like, 'I'm not gay! I'm not gay! I'm *not gay!*'" From a dramatic standpoint, what happened next was inevitable. She announced that she was gay.

It was after college, through a friend of a friend, that Karen met the woman who would bring her into the fold of domestic, monogamous bliss. Her name's Salua—she was raised as a Black Muslim—and after four and a half years Karen still squeals when she describes the relationship. "We're *both* five feet one and three-quarters! She likes pancakes, I like to make pancakes!"

But this is not to say there haven't been issues, including the race kind. I tell Karen about my discussions with Lorraine, my ex-girlfriend, and she tells me about the ones she's had with Salua. Some are gentle. ("I discover assumptions I have—not racism but little cultural things. Like, she uses a lot of lotion! White girls are never taught to use lotion. I have a new appreciation for lotion!") Others are thornier, and here Karen is quick to agree with Lorraine: White people are fundamentally racist. "Yeah, absolutely we are. '*Prejudice plus power*,'" she rattles off.

For all her consciousness, though, it's hard to know how race actually registers for Karen. She speaks in slogans sometimes ("'Love knows no color?' I think love *knows* color, and it's wonderful!") and occasionally has an insider's glibness on the subject, suggesting black-white relationships can be as straightforward as her pancake equation. And maybe they can—but before long we've strayed into stickiness.

"Certain people have a preference," she tells me. "If you're Jewish and you want to date a Jewish person, that's cool. The last three people I dated were all black—what does that mean? Do I have a preference for black people? Yes, I do!"

Karen concedes that this position is precarious. Earlier in her relationship with Salua—"when I was still earning my wings"—a few black friends sounded the fetish alarm. Her response was that, well, she likes dating black people. "Maybe this is stereotypical, but the black women I've met are much more outspoken, and willing to take risks, and are just sure of who they are, and [have] stronger relationships with their families. There are exceptions to that—it just happens to be the people I've met."

Karen's parents have accepted Salua as family. (When Karen and

Salua finally told the Taggarts of their engagement over dinner one night, a brief pause passed. Karen's mother looked at Karen's father, who said, "So, where are you going to be registered?") Karen's grandparents, however, don't even know that Karen's gay. As with Adam and Lorraine Rice, Karen says, it just doesn't make sense to apprise earlier generations of everything. (When I remind her that she's being interviewed for a book, she says she's not too worried.)

All things didn't fall into place as neatly as her love life, though. Back in Alabama—pre-Salua, this is—Karen had polished a strategy for maximizing the amount of change she could effect in one lifetime. When she got back to Hampshire she laid out her plan. She would finish college, attend UVA for five years, graduate with a law degree and a master's in public policy, and go to work at the Justice Department. From there, there would be no stopping her. When she was selected to apply for the prestigious Truman scholarship for public policy study—and then when she made finalist—it looked like the plan was right on schedule.

The thing here is momentum. Karen had been on an activist's roll so long—since junior high, wanting to stop abortion—that she didn't even slow down when she didn't get the Truman. She would go to law school anyway, find a way to pay. Karen is the dramatic sort, and it would take something bigger to derail her plans.

The day of the LSAT arrived. She showed up, took her seat, and prepared to leap the final hurdle between her and the future for which she'd startled teachers and hoarded Rolaids all these years. What happened next still lacks a gratifying explanation: She rose from her seat, canceled her test scores, ran to the bathroom, and vomited.

"It was the first time in my entire life I didn't know what I was going to do after college," Karen says. "I was scared shitless, but also really happy at the same time."

WASHINGTON, D.C., 2002. Karen's eighth-graders—Ms. Taggart's eighth-graders—file into the ice-cold classroom, jumping and dancing and chewing an unbelievable amount of gum. "Gum," Ms. Taggart says, and several pieces relocate forlornly into a piece of paper in her hand. "Gum," she adds a couple minutes later, and more gum goes in the hand. The kids, students at a hopeful experiment called the Hyde Leadership Public Charter School, settle into their seats after a long, noisy while. Maybe "settle" isn't the word—more like *coil*. It's a Monday morning, and as a way of wrapping up a unit on Jim Crow laws, the class will be discussing race in America today. A juicy bubble, Gonzo Grape, I think, pops defiantly. "Chardonnay," Ms. Taggart says without even looking, and Chardonnay reaches into her mouth and walks to the trash can.

Aside from me, Karen is the only white person in the classroom. Lily-white, to be specific, red hair cropped short. She was a finger-snapping, diva-ish marvel in high school; now the bright lipstick's gone, the plastic cockroach-covered cap is gone, and she's a marvel for her stark whiteness. In the part of D.C. where most of her students live, white people are scarce—seldom more than nervous drivers quickly exiting the neighborhood, the kids tell me. So it's with both love and curiosity that they regard their strange young history teacher, this flamboyant activist/thespian/lesbian/fireball-turned-inner-city marm. She's treated as somewhere between black and white—a place she's found partially by accident, but also one she's actively cultivated. The kids themselves say they act different with black teachers, that black teachers put up with less, but Karen isn't treated as an interloper, either. "She's my favorite teacher," a girl with a lisp tells me in the doorway. "She's nice, and she's funny when she tries to get us to pay attention."

It's true, she's funny. Karen, like Ryan Beckwith, is an idealistic person and generally has only the loosest understanding of why she's not being consulted on most world affairs. As with Ryan, it's not one central problem on the planet that worries Karen so much as a thousand lateral ones—it's that hundred-headed hydra classmate Richard Scalzo mentions. The thing about Karen is, she's chopping off one of the heads anyway. As a first-year history teacher in a poor and violent Washington neighborhood, Karen has chosen to make a career out of baby steps—a battle over chewing gum here, an argument over homework due dates there—where once she spent every moment urging our generation to make giant leaps. The condition of our age group may be *overwhelmed*, and Ms. Taggart is surely more overwhelmed each day than most of us in a year. But rather than collapse or make a beeline for the closest hermitage, she forges ahead, gum hand outstretched. "Overwhelmed? Yeah, but I'm sitting here with ninety lives in my hands," she says to me.

The half-decade or so that began in front of the toilet at the LSAT testing center was unlike any other period in Karen's life, for she did something she'd never done: She bounced around aimlessly. She took a fundraising job at Public Citizen, the public-interest group founded by Ralph Nader. Then she went to People for the American Way. Then she went to a marketing agency to do direct mail for nonprofits— Planned Parenthood, the DNC, Al Gore, and the like. ("Do you think that's a good idea?" they asked when, before the 2000 election, she put up a Nader sign. She did, so she left it up.) Then she enrolled at a George Washington University program on museum education. Then she decided she didn't want to do museum education. Then an internship brought her over to Hyde and, quite plainly, she fell in love with teaching. Was Hyde hiring? No. She asked later: Was Hyde hiring? No. Was Hyde hiring? No. And then it was.

I've picked a freezing November day to sit in on her classes, and the eighty-year-old schoolhouse on T Street is a meat locker. Her kids wear their winter coats over their mandatory khakis and white dress shirts—it might be worth noting that the purpose of the dress code is defeated here if so many purposes weren't defeated so frequently in D.C. public schools. They are among the worst in the country. In 1997, the *Washington Post* published an extensive report on them, and the condition of the buildings alone was stunning. They leak, violate fire code, and ooze asbestos. Sometimes there's no toilet paper, and sometimes no teachers. Violence is rampant, of course. SAT scores in 2002 averaged 799 out of 1,600; the national average is 1,020. Most staggering of all is the simple conclusion drawn by a 1996 report from the D.C. Financial Control Board: The longer students spend in D.C. schools, the less likely they are to succeed.

And so the charter school has arisen as a promising alternative for Washington kids. Hyde was founded in 1999 on the premise of a "character-based curriculum." Students agree to take their schooling seriously, and their parents do too. Family participation is a requirement for enrollment. In exchange, the school promises not only to help kids "discover a deeper purpose in their lives" but to develop "citizens who will renew the American experiment in democracy."

Of course, things don't always go as planned.

"Let's get out our homework, people," Karen calls now from the front of the classroom. A worrisome lack of shuffling follows.

"You guys—you're kidding," she moans. The class, without exception, looks down at the floor. Not a single person has done the assignment. The assignment was to bring to class a newspaper article that might be relevant to a discussion of Jim Crow laws.

"I feel extremely disrespected," Karen says, touching a special nerve here at Hyde. Respect—along with curiosity, concern, destiny, humility, and a few other prescribed virtues—is what keeps Hyde above the water as so many other Washington public schools gurgle to the bottom. Hyde students agree to these precepts when they come here, or they don't come here. "I did *my* part," Karen says. "You couldn't take five minutes to do yours?"

If vomiting away one's law school plans teaches a person anything, it's the necessity of improvisation. What Karen improvises now is a new lesson plan, as she's done a thousand times before. Sure, she spent all weekend preparing the original plan, but there isn't time for grousing—by anyone's guess she'll have thirty to forty-five seconds' worth of collective guilt to exploit before the classroom devolves into chaos. Anyhow, the stakes are too high to get hung up on daily defeats. "Every two or three weeks a student has a father or uncle shot or stabbed or sent to prison," Karen tells me later. I ask her what she expects will happen to these kids. "Some will be lawyers, some will be dead."

Within moments, Plan B has sprung into effect. Plan B is the same as Plan B's throughout educational history: an in-class discussion. "In what ways does Jim Crow affect our lives today?" Karen asks as the class shoves its desks into a circle.

Silence. For nearly a minute it looks like this isn't going to work. Karen crosses her arms. Finally, one boy raises his hand. "It, um, I don't think it affects people because, um, we don't got segregation no more."

"What about Hyde?" Karen asks. "Is Hyde segregated?"

A girl answers this time. "It's not segregated, but everyone's black."

"There's white *teachers*, though," another student adds.

"Why they didn't hire more black teachers this year?" someone else asks, and finally the group is on a roll.

Jump-starting a lively conversation about race in America may not be the hardest trick to pull off in a history class—I'd hate to see the nineteenth-century tariff policy discussion—but it's a victory nonethe-less. Karen hits her stride, and a few minutes into the conversation, even a bit of silliness becomes a teachable moment. In a tangent worthy of Jerry Lewis, one of the many class clowns breaks out a mock-Chinese accent. Over raucous laughter Karen intervenes, guiding the incident back into the lesson.

"That's extremely disrespectful, Jimmy. You're not in trouble, but let's talk about stereotypes," she says. "What if I said all black women only care about their hair, and all black men are lazy and end up in jail?" Her students holler back instantly: "But that's true! That's true!"

"Stereotypes are when you think something about someone but don't know anything," one girl speaks quietly. The class settles down at this and nods solemnly. The seriousness lasts until Karen asks for examples of stereotypes about white people. At this the classroom re-erupts, then rattles off a list as familiar to them as the days of the week: "They got flat butts!" "They ugly!" "They smell like mayonnaise!"

Class breaks on a high note—it must mean something that her kids leave the room smiling more than when they first arrived. It's hit or miss, she tells me over lunch later in the day. This morning she accepts hugs from a few kids on their way out; last week, she broke up a fight and caught a punch in the face. "She's funny," a student tells me at one point, visibly enamored. "She's *weird!*" a boy corrects her with a quick flick of the ear.

Some weeks after my visit to her classroom, I phone Karen and ask if she ever has second thoughts about the career she stumbled into.

Teachers, possibly more than anyone else in the world, know the value of a good answer. Karen pauses after my question and then goes to get something she's filed away. By way of a response, she reads a piece of writing one of her eighth-graders handed her recently. Her voice breaks only slightly:

"It is one thing to be a good person, you have to be smart, sensitive, successful and reliable. But it's another thing to be an excellent person and an excellent teacher. You are not a failure, you are an inspiration. You are not a teacher, you're our motivation. You are not just Karen, you are Ms. Taggart too. And as much as you love us, we love you two times [more than] you've given us social time detention. You are so Ms. Taggart and Karen, but you are something more. You are Karen Taggart, the motivator we adore."

There isn't much else to say after this, so we say goodnight and hang up. Anyway, it's almost 9:30 and Karen is exhausted.

16 Becky Earle

BECKY EARLE: *"If I spent half the time on homework that I spent thinking about boys or talking to friends about boys—I would've been a straight-A student."*

JOHN DOYLE: "You hear stuff about somebody, you see a person in action, and then later on, you get to know them better and you learn 'Wow, you can't always judge a book by its cover.' I would say that perhaps that reputation [of Becky's] was unfounded to begin with. . . . I think it was perhaps a few things that occurred that were blown way out of proportion and then turned into the truth."

CINDY NEUNERT: "I remember us just going out and laughing and having so much fun. We'd have slumber parties, and stay up late. . . . I'd say we were maybe the wild children. [We] liked to go out and party and have a good time.

"Becky was always the most political among us. While the rest of us sat in the back of A.P. Government making Fluffernutter sandwiches, Becky seemed really interested in that stuff.... She's always loved English, and writing, and had strong political views.... She has that banter that it seems like you'd need in Washington."

MIKE JANSSEN: "I remember her as being always quite composed—made up and with her hair looking like she had spent a long time on it. And she struck me as, well, not necessarily a goody-goody, but I guess I deduced from her appearance that she liked having things in order and being organized, or something."

S ome of my classmates seem to look in the mirror at twenty-seven or twenty-eight and find life has carried them through a series of odd and remarkable changes, like a twig on a stream. Other classmates appear to have carried *themselves* through these changes—less twig, more motorboat. Becky Earle, as far as I can tell, gunned the engine straight out of our graduation ceremonies and didn't pause until she reached the sea.

Which, in her case, happened to lie just across the Potomac. If America is the country where people go to remake their lives, Washington, D.C., might be the city where Americans go to remake the remake. Most everyone has left something behind in order to go there, it's said, and the tacit agreement among new arrivals seems to be that the past shall be forgotten. Even when unpleasant histories are dredged up, Washington has an uncanny ability to absorb and forget; where else could Marion Barry, Oliver North, and the Comeback Kid himself, Bill Clinton, find love after what would have been career-wrecking stumbles? As every Beltway born-again knows, hard work and a fierce patina offer the perpetual promise of safe delivery from ancient whispers—escaping the echoes of high school prattle, then, must be a breeze.

For five years Becky worked in the office of Virginia congressman Frank Wolf, moving up from opening mail, answering phones, and general grunt work to campaign manager and legislative assistant. Becky struck me as someone who might provide a rare glimpse of the inner workings and not-workings of American politics—the Senate Majority Leader drafting his remarks in the nude, the Speaker of the House making prank calls to freshman members of Congress, and so on. And though once or twice she pulled back the curtains a few inches—"Mr. Wolf would never be in a car with just a woman, he would never be in a room with just a woman," she said in a conversation about general Gary Condit fallout—ultimately Becky wants to continue eating lunch in this town. Only later did it dawn on me that Becky would sooner burn a flag than resort to gossiping, for in some ways it's gossip she fled.

Becky was a flirt, to use her language (and the language of our sophomore-year superlatives contest—"Biggest Flirt" was her official fifteen minutes of fame). Some classmates I talked with favor the term "party girl." She was many other things too, of course: a senior-class senator, an organizer of graduation activities, a clarinetist in the marching band, and utility infielder for the softball team one year. But yes, she went to parties, too, even a couple college parties, and there her eyelashes batted. At one gathering, she recalls, she drank a six-pack and started to pull her shirt up; a friend stopped her. The nap she took later was on the bathroom floor.

"Probably making some halfway racy double entendre—I don't even remember that much," she says, describing her flirtation habits to me on the phone one evening. "Of course, the flip side of that is that I didn't really have any boyfriends, per se, in high school. I dated guys, and there were a couple people here and there who'd probably fall into that category if I thought hard enough, but not really. I either had short-term crushes or long-term obsessions with people. If I have one regret, it's that I didn't spend more time focussing on the stuff that needed to be done then—like school. It seems like a waste.

"Flirting's not a bad thing—it just took a while to understand it. It's appropriate at times and inappropriate at other times. If a guy is going out with another girl, it's inappropriate to flirt with them. It took me a little while to put that piece together. But that's what high school's for.

"Boys paid attention, and I didn't quite know what to do about it. I just took it and ran. Honestly, if you asked half the guys I would've known at Jefferson, 'Did Becky Earle ever flirt with you?' they'd probably say yeah. I either flirted with every single person who halfway caught my eye, or kissed a third of those. It was a way of getting attention."

High school students can certainly be counted on to deliver attention where it's sought, but they're always mixing up the order. Becky's plan backfired when rumors got out of hand.

"I heard some horrible things said about me freshman and sophomore years," she says. "I remember running for office, I think it was sophomore year, and a couple of guys hanging out near my locker made some crude comment about 'Oh, you'll swap people a *whatever* for a vote.' Which was so not right."

As Becky explains it, the genesis of the flirty phase was innocent enough. "In junior high, I'd been the dorky kid with . . . really short, close-cut curly hair, big glasses that took up half of my face. I came to Jefferson and I didn't look like a tool anymore. I think it took me a year or two into high school to shake that that's what I looked like, even though I then had contacts."

The modern superhero genre generally allows for an episode in which the hero, having discovered his or her exciting new powers, tests their limits. To the outside observer, Becky's newly naked eyes could be made to twinkle at will.

"Then, around junior year, two lines converged," she says. "I kind of figured myself out some more, as far as, 'All right, Becky, you don't need to be kissing a different guy every week,' and people also started becoming more comfortable with their sexuality. And I think things just kind of leveled off then."

So it was mainly the first two years of school that generated the material of her reputation. But in the late-twentieth-century language of Web commerce, fables of Becky's exploits had stickiness. The task became damage control, a sealing of perimeters. When Becky gets to recalling the years that followed, a motif of transformation overlies much of her recollection. People who have her respect, for instance, are those who'd grasped "how much I changed in high school."

BECKY IS THE only person from our class who went into national politics, as far as I know. It began with the whiff she got early in college, when she interned briefly on Capitol Hill. The whiff was good, or at least hallucinogenic, and later when her classmates began lining up jobs before graduation—this is how leaving is done at Mary Washington College, no wandering off into the fog—Becky applied for work as staff assistant to various members of Congress. The day after commencement, she had her job with Congressman Frank Wolf.

Half a decade of work in a congressman's office is closer to half a century in Hill years. Becky stayed because she was happy. "He's just a wonderful man . . . a man of conviction," she says of the Virginia Republican. First elected in 1980, Wolf was chairman of the House Transportation Appropriations Subcommittee for several years, and he's currently a member of the House Appropriations Committee. Wolf is widely hailed for his human rights concerns—he serves as cochairman of the congressional Human Rights Caucus—and is outspoken on the destructiveness of gambling. He has also "worked tirelessly to preserve the essence of the American family," as his Congressional biography blurb reads—a *family values* man. Indeed, his is a conservative's record. He's voted to deny federal recognition of gay marriages, bar desecration of the American flag, and he was a cosponsor of President Bush's controversial education-reform package in early 2001, which reduced funding to schools yielding lower test scores.

Mostly Washington is a combination of strange and boring. Since Becky has worked there, though, the birthplace of the filibuster could actually be considered exciting from time to time. In the ten years that followed our graduation, government activity surpassed normal levels of scandal and morass and proceeded right on into surrealism. Becky was there during Monica, through the Gore/Bush election mess, the antiglobalization protests, Whitewater, Elián González, Chandra Levy, Enron and WorldCom, and finally 9/11 and the contortions that followed. Becky presents herself as little more than a bystander to all the commotion, but Washington politics are diffuse enough that almost anyone involved can claim this. When people are close enough to the blast zone, I ask her, don't they *become* the blast zone?

Becky maintains a dedicated nonchalance about her work in "this little microcosm" and her proximity to history-making activity. She concedes that she's been around for some "interesting" moments— "the [2000 Bush/Gore] election was fascinating"—but maintains that most of her experience of Washington has been of political minutiae. Becky knows about committees and subcommittees the way regular people know their own phone numbers. She knows what's on the floor, and what's nearing the floor, and how so-and-so will likely vote on it. If you're a sitting congressman from Virginia, she knows how to get you reelected, and if you're a defeated opponent from the same state, she knows how to make you sound graceful and insignificant. Still, every now and then she can be coerced into a little Big Picture reflection. "Damn, for five years I talked to a congressman almost every day. It's just neat to be that close, to be able to pick up the phone and get pretty much any piece of information you need," she says. "There's a lot of power that goes with saying, 'I'm Becky Earle from Congressman Wolf's office.'"

Becky is five feet two, with straight brown hair and fine posture and a not-quite southern accent. She has the composure of a woman twenty years her senior. She is polished like glass, or a CEO. "Her dermatologist wishes she would run for office," her father, Steve, jokes to me one day over the phone. People she knows are "wonderful." She maintains fine manners, even when dealing with a fellow young person. "Excuse me one moment," she tells me on the phone, not "Hang on."

In general, *excuse me one moment* is the rule in the adult life of Becky, an immaculate and politic universe that appears remarkably free of bad manners and other disorder. "Please give _____ my best when you see her," she says to me at one point, and it was the first time I'd ever heard a fellow young person say such a thing. Hers is a total, unrelieved cordiality, to the point of opacity. She gives nothing away, even after a couple of drinks. A decade after the detours and convolutions of high school, Becky is a cipher, with no signs of her former self. She is put-together and seamless, a perfect, miraculous egg. I do my best to coax a small crack, this being what messy non-eggs do, but she's been a Washingtonian far too long. "I've been talk-ing and talking!" she'll say just when the light might start to shine through. "How are *you*?"

Becky allows that she grew up in Manassas, Virginia, where the Confederate army won two major battles, where Thomas J. Jackson became Stonewall Jackson, and which, in 1993, Disney tried to rein-vent as a vast historic theme park. Becky is American in that *American* sense, which is to say hardworking and guarded and decent; she knows the name of the church where her parents met. Her mother and I exchange a couple of e-mails at one point—along with a phone conversation with both parents, it's a pleasant but fruitless effort on my part to catch an unfettered glimpse of Becky's *core self*—and hers end with the words of the National Anthem's last verse.

My sense, particularly after talking with the Ryan Beckwiths and the Karen Taggarts of our class, is that the Becky Earles among us are the ones behind our country's gentle, persistent tug to the right, to God, to that vague place indicated by words like "values" and "tradi-tional." She'd deny it. She's genuinely easygoing, and would say she's not tugging anyone anywhere. "It's not for me to decide how anybody should live their life," she says. She means God will decide, or at least even it all up subsequently. This position happens to double as a buffer against certain aspects of conservatism—she says she'll always be a Republican, but that there's no need to march in lockstep.

"One of my best friends from college, she considers herself a fiscally conservative Democrat, and I consider myself a socially mod-erate-liberal/progressive Republican. But if you sit down and talk to us about fifty issues, there may be two or three that we deviate on. It's amazing what those labels do."

It's understandable why Becky might be eager to distance herself from elements of her party. Wolf remained moderate, mostly, during the time she worked for him—a human rights champion, an outspoken critic of religious persecution—but the so-called "extra-chromosome" conservatives (as George Bush Sr. and his late strategist Lee Atwater called them) had already gained prominence in the GOP. The various smear campaigns against Clinton are well documented by now—rumors peddled, journalists paid to dig up dirt, Richard Mellon Scaife and John Fund and Bill Kristol and Ted Olson—and as a result, some fracturing did occur within the party. But in spite of years of proximity to this kind of ruckus, and to ruckus on the left as well, Becky maintains a dedicated equanimity on the subject of national politics.

"I really don't think we're [Democrats and Republicans] all that different. Do you want people spending your tax dollars indiscriminately? No. Do I want somebody telling me how I should live my life? No. So how far apart are we really, when you look at it in that respect? But some people are so entrenched in that dichotomy."

True to her word, Becky withholds judgment on homosexuality, has lost faith in the death penalty's deterrent value, and, despite her work with Wolf—who regularly voted against access to abortion—says it's not for her to decide whether a woman can have an abortion. But there are moments when Becky is a plain old conservative.

"But who's saying that?" she shoots back at me when I slip the gentle phrase "massive environmental degradation" into one of our conversations. "Are we talking about clean water? Are we talking about clean air? Are we talking about natural resources? Do you not think that it's much better than it was thirty years ago, as far as industrial pollution and corporate responsibility on those issues? I do. For some people, it'll never be enough."

And here we get into it. We get into it because I want to pick the brain of a person who voluntarily enters politics in this day and age.

Coming from a school with such a vocal, if not vast, liberal move-ment, Becky is one of the seemingly few conservatives who don't claim to have gotten softer, as our formerly conservative classmate Justin Romberg put it. In the time we were in high school and college, America seemed to become a place just slightly colder to the values of her party—culturally if not politically. This coldness materialized in the form of pop secular humanism, evacuating vestiges of Judeo-Christian thought from public discourse here and there; it material-ized as the prudery of earlier generations becoming campy satire in Hollywood movies. It materialized as recreational drug use, premari-tal sex, and homosexuality edging toward acceptability in corporate-owned mass media; as everyday political rhetoric assimilating the values of "multiculturalism," however indistinct. It materialized as aspects of radical '60s culture filtering into mainstream '90s culture, however diluted. For a twenty-seven-year-old to emerge quietly from this superficial liberalization, conservatism intact, heels had to have dug in deep.

Today, Becky's brand of conservatism—at least what's directed at me, whom I'm sure she remembers as a liberal—is the chastened kind, the kind that knows better than to say anything remotely sug-gestive of Jesse Helms, of Strom Thurmond. On global warming "there's no empirical evidence in that respect that's it's as bad as everyone's making it out to be," but still it's "an issue." She opposes legislation that would require carmakers to improve fuel efficiency in SUVs, minivans, and light trucks. She thinks the need for campaign finance reform has been overstated: "I don't think people give money expecting X or Y—I think it goes toward building a relationship." She's enthusiastic about Bush's faith-based initiative strategy, and per-haps feels uncomfortable with how church attendance was "standing room only" after 9/11 but later dropped again.

Becky's general restraint on hot-button issues makes exception for Clinton's adultery. For her, though, the issue was basic honesty.

"It wasn't about whether or not he'd had an affair with the intern, even though that was deplorable," she says. "There was a preponderance of evidence that he had lied under oath. . . . I don't even remember exactly what the lie was, I'd have to go back and look it up, but basically he lied under oath, and it was in regard to the Lewinsky affair."

Becky had been on the Hill about a year and a half when the Lewinsky story really broke into a gallop. The ensuing gridlock seeped everywhere. Becky herself was kept busy noting constituents' outrage, whichever side it fell on. Wolf's office received 200 to 300 letters and calls a day at the peak of the scandal.

"A lot of people's opinion on it—because that's how the media spun it—was 'It's his sex life, it's none of our business, even if it was a little bit twisted.' But he is the president of the United States. The part that was ridiculous was that there was major news going on involving the leader of our country, and parents couldn't let their elementary-school kids watch it. Hell, some parents had to have stuff explained to them," she says. Later she adds: "I met Ken Starr's wife and his daughter at an event once, and they're just the nicest people. I think he was just doing his duty the best he could."

MUCH OF WHAT occupies Becky's time these days began one night at a party shortly after college. Becky had met a friend of a friend there named Dennis. Two years later, she had an extra ticket and invited Dennis to a Baltimore Orioles game. He didn't make it to the game—by the time he got back to her, she'd given the ticket to someone else—but a few days later, he asked her to a happy hour with some friends of his.

"We're doing the more traditional 200-person, sit-down-dinner kind of thing," Becky said about their upcoming wedding. The ceremony had been in the works, more or less, since a golf game between Dennis and Becky's father some time back. As Becky understands it, the two had finished and were loading the car when Dennis turned to Becky's father. "Dennis just said, 'Mr. Earle, you know I love Becky very much, and I just wanted to know your feelings if I were to ask her to be my wife'—something along those lines," Becky says. "Of course, my dad was doing cartwheels, since he just thinks Dennis is great."

When Becky and I cross the Capitol steps in August 2002, preparations are almost complete. The invitations, the limo, the flowers, and the tuxes have all been taken care of, as has Becky's conversion from Methodism to Catholicism ("I knew that my husband, and hopefully our children, were all going to be Catholic, so I figured I'd learn about it. And the more I learned, it really synced up with where I am. I like it," she says). Aside from a few last arrangements, the only thing left to do is move in together. The plan is to move into a condo a few weeks before the wedding, and then eventually find a place to buy.

Having already tried Becky's parents, I decide Dennis might be the one to provide another view of Becky's core self, which after hours of interviewing I still find impenetrable. We talk on the phone. Dennis is a friendly database manager and amateur political junkie with a likably ornate habit of saying "and such." He is vastly admiring of all things Becky, but he goes to town on the subject of her intelligence.

"[She's] not only book smart, but [she has] unbelievable people and common-sense skills. She's intelligent about everything. She just knows how to read people in situations," he says. "I've dated a lot of girls, and almost nobody was as bright as I am. But she's every bit as bright as I am, if not brighter."

Becky and Dennis overlap on a great many opinions and convictions—"most of those things are just politics, but it's [also] life in general, [our] values and such"—and what's more, she's a fellow sports nut. "She actually enjoys it. Basketball, baseball, golf even."

As with Becky, one of the first impressions Dennis gives off is that of being awfully electable. He's positive and clean-cut. His days of hitting the town with his "single buddies, looking for women and such," have been sagely traded for domestic bliss. "Just enjoying each other's company, watching our children and possibly grandchildren being grown up" is how he describes their future.

Dennis won't entirely rule out a run for office one day; for her part, Becky says, "No way."

"I enjoyed being on the inside, being involved with the process, but I like having control of my life," she says.

Becky's out of politics—for now, anyway. She'd been with Representative Wolf five years when the lobbying firm Rhoads|Weber Shandwick approached her. ("They said, 'Have you ever considered leaving the Hill?' and I said, 'I always keep my options open. . . .'") The job started in 2002. Becky is quick with her fondness for Wolf, but working in the private sector means certain perks—an office with a door, for instance. The rest of the job she describes only in general terms.

"We devise strategies for [our clients] to communicate and push initiatives with Congress, and we use our relationships with people we know—most of us from years on the Hill or from around town— to facilitate communication and try to get stuff done."

Having spent time on both sides of the lobby fence did little to shake her faith in the system. Though she acknowledges that Beltway business is "based on relationship," she says the idea of money buying influence is "overblown." Campaign contributions aren't about "expecting something," but rather "supporting someone who supports what you're for."

In recent years, a guiding principle has emerged for Becky, something to help navigate Washington and all its entanglements—she calls it personal responsibility.

"The shirking of individual responsibility [is] probably my biggest concern, and I think we're all guilty of it to a degree," she says. "It's about blaming somebody besides yourself. It's Marion Barry—'The bitch set me up.' And Bill Clinton—'Depends on what your definition of 'is' is.' People are way too good at making excuses, myself included. It's something you see every day, in so many ways. . . . It's [about] how somebody could say, 'Oh, well, I'm flipping burgers at McDonald's, but if I'd gone to Jefferson, I'd be president of a company.'

"It's about always having an excuse for why you're not better," she continues. "[It] then ties back into the media and mass market [supposedly] making us all feel inferior. 'I'm too short' or 'My hair is purple instead of blond,' or whatever. You hear it every day—someone gets pulled over on the highway and they say, 'Well, my dog died, so I had to speed.'"

All of which has long been a mantra of the right, of course, a prefix in many cases to entreaties on limiting the size and purview of government. It's not without critics in our own TJ class.

"All that Republican 'personal responsibility,' 'rugged individualist' stuff—I'd like them to talk with some of the mothers of students I have, who work three jobs but still can't make it," Karen Taggart has said to me. "Or [talk to] my girlfriend, who's black and—it's a cliché, but it's true—can't catch a cab. How does rugged individualism work when certain individuals can't even get a taxi to pull over for them?"

But Becky, whose new employer is owned by a group that's represented controversial clients from the tobacco industry to the Japanese

Whaling Commission, has an answer to questions like these. In fact, it might be an answer to other questions, too.

"Luck, chance, and situation does play into it, but it's personal determination [that matters]," she says. "I could say my life will never be right because I'm not going to be a Victoria's Secret model, because I'm not five-ten and voluptuous. There are always a thousand good reasons why you *aren't* something—it's more about being who you are."

Matt Farbman

MATT FARBMAN: *"I think I was an asshole. I think I was pretty clueless. I didn't even have enough of a sense of myself to know what sort of things I should inquire within myself about. So I was just kind of hopeless."*

KAREN TAGGART: "I always thought: stringy-haired computer geek! Tall, lanky, awkward. I don't mind saying so, because that's pretty much the exact opposite of now."

VANYA (SEAMAN) WRIGHT: "He was very clever, a little nerdy. My biology teacher warned me to stay away from him. And in chemistry I was the only person who'd be his [lab] partner. The teacher couldn't believe anyone would want to be his partner—he was different, and different-looking—so she'd stand over us to see if I was just trying to cheat off him. I get the impression he didn't

217

have as good grades as [teachers] thought he should have, based on how he looked. He was a smart guy—I guess he had other things to think about.

"Before Humanities class, often he'd get into the class early and write puns on the board. Just a long list of them. Once there was a school assembly and we were all gathered up to watch some video. The rumor was that he'd switched the video with a cheap porn tape. I never got verification on that, but I do seem to remember watching a few seconds of something strange before they switched the tape."

ANNE BARNHILL: "He had long scraggly hair and a weird beard—not even a beard, a strange pattern of facial hair. I think he wore jeans pulled up too high, and weird T-shirts. Definitely his mannerisms were weird. He would say outrageous things—he's a running-commentary kind of guy, and that came with a kind of global irony.

"We were friends, in a way. He was a freak. I really liked him, because I like freaks. We were in the same gym class and the same French class. He said a really great thing to me once: 'You aren't the kind of person you appear to be.' It was an interesting thing for him to say, in retrospect—apparently that's how he felt about himself.

"I thought he was really genuine. He was really smart, smart in every way. He was really interpersonally smart—not that that did him much good. He was pretty weird by most people's lights.

"Somehow he was not cutting corners. He was tuned in. I don't want to make it out like he was some kind of prophet. I had a lot of respect for him, but he did seem human, and fallible, and authentic. A person owning up to life. He clearly had his own perspective. It was very important to him to be different. I got the impression he thought most people were doing things the easy way and he didn't want to do that."

■

The cop eased the squad car over to the two youths, who were in the wrong neighborhood at the wrong hour. It so happened that one of them—the tall, lanky one, my classmate—represented all that may evolve in a human being over just ten years, perhaps represented human potential itself in this way, certainly represented the most dramatic transformation among the Thomas Jefferson High School Class of '93. This was not apparent or of interest to the cop. He arrested them.

Or rather, he had another cop arrest them—they often do it this way, my classmate explains to me a few years later, having a certain but classified familiarity with such things. This was one of Minneapolis's controversial Code Four sweeps, a system of periodic neighborhood purges designed to get criminals off the streets awhile or to repress systematically the underclass, depending on which side of the argument you're on. "I had a flashlight—all punk kids carry flashlights—so [later] he said I had 'burglary implements,' so I must have been planning on breaking in somewhere." (Later, the official charge became "lurking." My classmate, a lover of words, delights in "lurking," and briefly considered getting a "Lurking Class Hero" T-shirt made.)

Before he could have them arrested, the first officer had to ask the two what they were doing. What they were doing was walking toward a Dumpster, which they hoped to liberate of some free clothes. They kept this information to themselves.

"I don't talk to police in that situation—there's no point," my classmate says. "Their job in that situation is to incriminate you. They're not trying to find out what's going on—that's the job of the D.A.'s office, the job of the judge, the job of a jury, technically. The only responsibility the police have is to elicit evidence from you, and any question they ask you has that aim. What I generally say is 'Any information that you need from me is going to be on my I.D., here's my I.D.'"

And this is where it starts—where it always starts—my classmate says. The officer takes one look at the I.D. and snorts. Later, at the jailhouse, more snickering.

"They've got me in the search room, and of course they have to have a male or female officer, whatever's appropriate. And they kept [saying], 'This one's one of yours.' 'No, no, I think this is one of yours.' 'No, I think . . .'"

My classmate was Matt Farbman in high school. Now she is Anne. The people at the jail threw up their hands finally, put her in a solitary cell.

BECAUSE SHE'S EERILY brilliant, because these days her mind is more or less a supercomputer in the process of decorrupting its own files, reality is an electric thing when you finally track down a current number for Anne and get her on the phone; just stabilizing the *terms* of the conversation is like grabbing hold of a fish.

I will start with the information Anne calls irrelevant, that Anne used to be Matt.

Even this is debatable. *To be?* Was she truly, in any meaningful sense, Matt? Her driver's license said so, her parents said so—even she said so. But she said a lot of things when she was he, and life since then has been a brutal reckoning.

He? She? Neither of these questions is worth a moment's time, according to Anne. First of all, pronouns are just pronouns—a hackneyed bit of formality for unthoughtful people to get hung up on, a way to linger near the surface of gender and identity. Second of all, certain facts are irrelevant, and besides, what's a fact? According to what authority? Who made that authority an authority? And so forth. For the record, and surely to someone's frustration, I've decided to use "he" when describing Anne's pre-hormone-treatment self, and "she" afterward.

Certain facts are irrelevant, Anne says, and she means that her anatomy doesn't define her gender, and likewise her gender doesn't define her self. Early on, because I hadn't yet learned transsexual/transgender community protocol, or because at some level I'd decided not to tiptoe, I asked Anne point-blank if she'd had a sex-change operation. "I don't want to talk about that," she answered, and recalled being interviewed by a *Washington Post* reporter at a tranny event in Michigan. The way Anne tells it, the reporter asked amiably what she did for a living, where she was from, and then, out of the blue, what Anne's genitals looked like. ("Her biological status is 'irrelevant,'" the reporter ended up writing about this "young Texas writer with a tall, rangy frame and ponytail peeking out from under her kerchief.")

"Everybody thinks it's their business," Anne tells me. "It's not."

When I first phone her at the house where she rents a room in Austin, Texas, she's content enough to describe adventures like her lurking arrest in Michigan. "I shouldn't tell you this," she'll begin, and in no time I'm hearing another great, albeit off-the-record, account of a run-in with the law. What shuts her up instantly is my broaching the aspect of her life story that I suspect the average person would find most extraordinary: her gender.

"It's not the most interesting thing about me," she answers slowly when I ask why the subject makes her cagey.

"I don't only ask people about their most interesting things," I reply. "Anyway."

"Anyway" is a staple of Anne's vocabulary, and not just as a tool for avoiding touchy subjects. Because she thinks so quickly, and in such fragments, she requires a stable of maneuvering devices. In the most casual conversation Anne will launch a tangent, add at least three parentheticals, and then double back and cross the whole thing out before she's finished a sentence. The effect is a thousand half-starts, each splintering into a thousand more, all gathered periodically under Anne's corrective *never mind, never mind.* It's the sound of a person reminding herself to simplify.

Certain facts are irrelevant, Anne says, and though it's an attempt to correct an autocratic notion of gender, she herself sounds a little dogmatic here—damming the flow of information and all. But contradiction is hardly news for Anne Tagonist, to use her cyber-handle (she's answered to Angry Annie too). This is not just because she possesses an arguer's heart; quite thoughtfully she rejects rules and boundaries that do not suit her, including the apparently bourgeois assumption of rhetorical consistency. Unlike other classmates of ours who might take umbrage at this idea or that, Anne is a radical. Since high school she's severed ties to much of what society expects: the law, college, professional aspiration, fixed shelter, conventional hygiene, and of course her God-given biology.

"Isn't it—exhausting," I ask at one point, "being . . . underground all the time?"

"Underground," she repeats, and chews on the word, and then laughs. "Well . . . never mind."

IRONICALLY, IT'S MATT'S outside that our former classmates remember most vividly.

"I have very specific memories of what he looked like then, but after that it gets blurry," Sam Zeitlin wrote to me. "I remember what he looked like holding his books against his hip, his very long legs."

"Tall, skinny, long hair, a little unkempt—you'd expect to see him behind a computer," Vanya Wright recalls.

Anne herself remembers little of Matt, or at least she chooses to remember little, or at least she says she chooses to remember little. Anne preaches fluidity of sexuality, fluidity of gender, but when it comes to the line between Anne and Matt, she's a bit rigid. "I don't know," she fires back to most questions about her past. And this: "I don't really feel like I had any sense of self at all in high school."

Over a series of conversations—vast swaths of them theoretical, inheritances of Lacan, or Judith Butler, I suppose—we manage to isolate a few concrete facts about the high school student known as Matt: He conducted role-playing games with friends. He attended summer school, by choice. He didn't fit in and didn't particularly care to. "I was completely socially dysfunctional. I am to this day. I'm horrible at faking it, and I don't say that with punk-rock pride."

"I know that if I'd gone to my base school [instead of a magnet school] I would have killed myself. I was horribly depressed. I was horribly depressed all through school, but it became much better when I went to Jefferson. I have no idea what the difference was. I think there was a much lower yahoo factor. I know that even now, I get kind of homesick when I don't have incredibly smart people around to listen to. My mental metabolism functions fast—and that's a horribly elitist thing to say. But is Jefferson the model of the role of the intellectual that I support now? Absolutely not. . . . You can't ignore the fact that the school was created in northern Virginia, under the Reagan administration, and funded by the defense industry. Jefferson represented a particular futuristic vision of the interrelation between government and science and industry, and the role of the intellectual in that."

Here, as often happens, the conversation retreats from the personal to the theoretical. It would be wrong to dismiss this as evasion. Anne is clearly most alive—and most functional, to use a word of hers—when she's about sixty leagues above literal. Perhaps it's not incidental that her bad high school memories aren't of bullies stealing her lunch money but of the Frankfurt School not making it into our English homework. For Anne, whose very identity seems to be an abstraction, the theoretical *is* personal.

"The concept of Jefferson was [to provide] an extremely high-level adult education to high school students. We were doing the same projects being done in major universities—the big hole was cultural theory. There was no critical thinking in the sense of social analysis. . . . The idea of an academy in which the intellectual was separated and trained in all these 'hard sciences'—purified of the socially disruptive, dangerous thought of critical theory—that was the conservative vision of higher education. That was the wet dream. Good education without Foucault."

Matt didn't entirely reject the Jefferson way of life. He even applied for one of the D.C. area's coveted Department of Defense internships—though he attached to his application a letter stating he wouldn't work on any military project. He was rejected.

"I don't know what the hell I was thinking," Anne says. "That's the contradiction I was in at the time: I had neither the backbone to just refuse and work at a bagel shop, nor did I have the wherewithal to just go through with the [DOD] experience."

"Why apply to the DOD in the first place?" I ask.

"Because it's what you're supposed to do. I felt that pressure. The same way I felt going to college as pressure."

Here, again, we get too—too what? Too uncritically biographical? The subject is changed before I can ask more about the pressure she describes.

"You don't like to talk about when you were younger," I say before the end of the conversation. There's a pause, then Anne says this:

"It was just really, really bad. Being there was really, really bad. It was kind of like one of those things where you'd wake up each day and you wouldn't have a point, and you'd just kind of do a few things, and go to sleep, and there wouldn't be a point. And you wouldn't really know where you were going, and you wouldn't know what was going to happen, and you wouldn't really care."

SENIOR YEAR, MATT was accepted at the University of Chicago. Anne's recollection of college, like all her recollections of life as Matt, is brief: first a math student, then linguistics, and anyhow out of the closet within months. "I hardly knew I was queer in high school. I *kind of* knew, and it scared the hell out of me," she says. Midway through sophomore year, he dropped out of school. "My reason for being in college was that it was what came after high school. That was not enough to dedicate my life to it."

It was in September 1996—what would have been the beginning of his junior year—that Matt changed his name legally to Anne, but friends had been using that name for much longer. Earlier, to little effect, Matt had begun taking what he'd heard were herbal supplements to the sex-change process. Next, he'd gotten his hands on illegal drugs. Finally, he decided to do everything legally. Anne calls this "the horror of therapy"—a bizarrely crude process requiring the patient to prove a "coherent gender" to various medical authorities, who then decide whether the request will be granted.

What I'd heard about Matt Farbman was that he'd gotten a sex change; that is, Matt had become a woman. The rumor mill, it turns out, is not calibrated to transcend binary conceptions of gender. As Anne puts it, most people still think in terms of "the big two." And so when a person decides to invent a gender all his or her own, things get more complicated.

"What I like to say, being a very interested party in the discussion, is that because of cultural anxiety about gender and about the stability of gender, you have a phenomenon where people require a hard-and-fast justification for anything that challenges gender further. They need to know that this is a scientifically justified, medically justified kind of thing, and that they are not—by acknowledging it—colluding with some process that calls their own identity into question."

Anne summarizes the conversation she had with the therapist guarding the pills:

"So why should we do this for you?"

"Well, this is where my identity's at."

"Are you going to kill yourself?"

"Gosh, I really hope not."

Then Anne paraphrases the therapist's demands: "'Can you prove that you meet this list of requirements from somebody who has always, in every way, been a girl, and never anything else, never had any unusual experiences for women, or unusual characteristics for women?'"

"Unusual experiences?" I ask.

"Women can't like sports," Anne suggests.

In order to pass the test, she says, she had to "emphasize some stories and not tell others." It was a wrenching dishonesty—and it's partly why she no longer feels comfortable visiting her actual reasons for beginning with the hormones. At one point, she was almost kicked out of the program for not wanting breast implants. It happened that a doctor unaffiliated with the program overheard, and pointed out that breasts do not a woman make.

"It's very difficult to convince doctors to take any kind of non-standard gender identity seriously," Anne continues. "The traditional narrative that is accepted, to a degree, is one of absolute inflexible, stable, and socially normative identity in a socially accepted gender category. It may not correspond with what it says on your birth certificate, but it's one of the big two."

Anne was alone and reeling in Chicago—between two selves, yes, and also between two poles of acceptable identity. She found work as a bike messenger, a job that she says left no time for depression. She also found politics, something Matt had largely ignored—or found overly simplistic—in high school. Anne got involved with Queer Nation, and then the Lesbian Avengers, where, coincidentally, she bumped into Karen Taggart—Karen is the only former Jefferson student with whom she keeps in touch. Anne also fell in with Chicago's homo-core scene, and before long she began publishing what she describes as "a queer punk/gender punk zine." She called it *Unapologetic: The Journal of Irresponsible Gender.*

The summer of 1998 marked the first full year out of college for most of the class of '93. Some of us were still temping or working entry-level positions, others of us had begun early burrows into Internet jobs, others still were in graduate school. It was at this time that Anne "completely dropped out, became a crusty."

A crusty is a punk, but more so: "It's the same thing—you just travel more, don't live in a house, and you steal shit. It's easy to make a cliché out of it: dreadlocks, Carhartts, dirty clothes, really bad tattoos. Riding freight trains and stuff like that."

Anne, once a computer-bound young man, now found herself

about as far from a desk as can be gotten. The peripatetic years that followed were an extra-capitalist tour of a seldom-glimpsed United States. In America, as in high school, the array of cultural options sometimes feels something like one main road, with a handful of smaller roads branching off; in her crusty years, as far as I can tell, Anne went off the main road, and then off the smaller roads, and then full into the woods, and finally through a trapdoor deep inside a cave. But this is not to suggest she belonged to no tradition whatsoever. On the contrary, her adventures are no less than a primer on Americana. She describes such folk standards as her "old traveling partner coming through town," and hopping freight trains, scamming food, and pilfering Dumpsters. Most American of all—which is to say most revolutionary, most singular—she was a tranny doing these things. Imagine Huck Finn on Estradiol.

Here I'm allotted another of Anne's parsimoniously apportioned life stories. It began on a hot May day in Winnachee, Washington, where Anne jumped on a freight train, as was her habit. On her back were most of her possessions: her coverall, wool pants, wool sweater, and her sleeping bag. She was about twenty-three years old. The rain started. Then came more, and more, and more. Around twenty-four hours of it, she says, and the train—and her exposed spot on it—kept moving. During short breaks in the downpour, she'd quickly air everything out, only to have it soaked again. She went to sleep and awoke, still drenched, in Montana. She estimates the wind at forty-five miles per hour. It began snowing.

An easy way to die on a train is hypothermia. "I [was] basically trying to decide if I was going to die or not before the train stopped," she says. Finally, the train came to rest at a grain elevator in North Dakota. The snow continued to fall, and there was a foot of it on the ground. Anne decided to make a run for the front of the train. She would find the engineers and ask them if she could come in—the worst they'd do was call the police, and the jail would be heated. She started running for the front of the train, but the train started moving.

"I'm running alongside this train, and I'm nowhere near the front, and I just jump in the first car I can get in and we take off again," she says. Now she was wet *and* tired. The train ran and ran and ran, in the cold and the snow and the wind, until finally it slowed down again.

Anne ran up once more, almost to the last of the three engines at the front of the train. She threw her pouch of essentials—food, glasses, and other supplies—onto a catwalk. It was just as she pulled herself up onto the moving train that the pouch slipped off the catwalk into the snow. She let it go.

"Ordinarily, when you're on a train, you're in a well," Anne explains. "You're in this little gap between the end of the freight container and the edge of the car, so you're sheltered from the wind, to some degree, and you have something to sit on. Well, I'm actually just holding onto this railing on this catwalk, on the side of a moving unit, soaking wet, forty-five miles an hour, below freezing out."

She pulled herself up to the door of the unit and miraculously found it unlocked and empty. Dragging herself in, she turned the engine's heater up full blast, crawled into the bathroom, and waited to be discovered. "I heard them come through the train—and I know I must have left a big *schlop* mark across the floor—but they didn't knock on the bathroom door," she says. "They must've decided just to leave me alone."

"Why jump on cold, wet trains?" I ask Anne in one of our phone conversations. Often it was activism that got her traveling, she replies—she went to a Food Not Bombs conference in San Francisco, squatted there; "hopped up" to Active Resistance, an anarchist organizing conference, in Toronto—but deep down the commanding principle was a simple and apolitical disaffection.

"It was alienation. I was completely alienated. I didn't believe in or want to have anything to do with anything in society [as long as] I knew where the food was, and I had stuff to keep my mind busy. I really don't feel like it was a protest, or that it was out of a conscious rejection—it was just out of that complete anomie of not knowing what else to do. As far as what it was about society that was particularly irritating, it was purely visceral."

There's certainly a "me vs. them" element to the stories from this period of Anne's life. Sometimes "them" is just a train, victimless; other times a department store employing actual human beings. Crusties call it "scamming," but stealing is often how they came into supplies and food. When I ask how Anne, otherwise an agonizingly ethical person, justified shoplifting, she mutters: "Oh God, *realpolitik.*

"Honestly, everybody justifies post facto, in my experience: 'I want this, how can I come up with a reason why it's good for me to take it?' I didn't have a job. I don't know. It's not something I have a clear answer to, except that I don't live as morally consistent a life as maybe I should."

These days, Anne does more Dumpster-diving than department store scamming. She knows of one Dumpster that gets returned orders from a health food distributor: soy milk, salad dressing, and other nonperishables. She knows where to get produce. Apples thrown out for brown spots get their brown spots cut out. She gets clothing, construction supplies. Of her years on the road she says this:

"I would joke [with my traveling partner] that we were like human rats: We somehow ended up in a human environment with the ability to survive in it but without the regulations or acceptance that humans had. It's a horribly romantic view of alienation, but whatever, you only get to be twenty-two once."

———

AT MINNEAPOLIS'S MINNEHAHA Park, around Minnehaha Creek and the Mississippi River and a freshwater spring called Camp Coldwater, sits one of the most controversial pieces of American earth in recent memory, and surely that with the happiest and saddest of memories for Anne. Depending on whom you asked in the late '90s, the area was either an environmentally significant stand of giant oak trees, sacred property to the Mendota Mdewakanton Dakota tribe, or one more holdout in the pitched battle with rampant capitalism and modern American culture. Or else it was a nice place for a highway, which is how the Minnesota Department of Transportation felt. When in 1998 the state decided to reroute Highway 55 directly through the region, an array of protesters—Indians, Earth First! members, anarchists, assorted sympathizers, and other activists— took over condemned houses, erected tepees, climbed into trees, and generally mounted a permanent opposition that was both blockade and community. As Anne puts it, "A bunch of squatters moved in and took over the houses, and fortified it and barricaded it and turned the neighborhood into something between a protest encampment, a hippie festival, and a war zone." They called themselves the Minnehaha Free State and were said to constitute the largest communal squat in modern U.S. history. It lasted into the year 2000, and from the beginning Anne was at the core.

"That's the high point of my life," she sighs. "Everybody who was actually part of it—there was like a thousand people, total, who came through at one point or another, and a core of thirty to fifty. And of that core, we all keep in touch. A lot of people are a little more normy now, a lot of people have kids, but we all keep in touch. And we joke that we're never going to live up to that again."

It would be awfully difficult to live up to the Free State. For a year and a half, through brutal winters and periodic confrontations with the police, the group maintained an anarchist's utopia. Survival was a full-time job. "There was a lot of Dumpstering, a lot of scamming for essentials. . . . People would shoplift food, or climbing supplies, or building supplies, or whatever the hell we needed. There were always barricades going up. . . . There were treehouses to build, a lot of public relations stuff going on all the time."

And there was the constant stress of impending raids:

"There was one night we knew the police were going to clear out and bulldoze one block. I had known that because me and a friend had hacked into the archives of the city council and so we knew the terms of the contract with the builder [who had the bulldozer]. We wanted to go out there and barricade, and we finally got a crew at the last minute and the [barricade] supplies were late and everybody had gone to a punk show by the time he got there. So of course [the bulldozer] did come in the morning and three of my friends were hospitalized. One person ended up breaking her hip. Another person, who I was dating, had her head smashed against a railroad tie. The third person was thrown to the ground and was bloody all over one side of his face."

Minnesota Public Radio reporter Mary Losure describes the Free State in her book *Our Way or the Highway*. You can see Anne in one of the photos—that's her in the bandanna. (Anne, for her part, isn't crazy about Losure's account. "She takes this condescending tone toward Free State. Like, 'These kids, they were wrong about the Indians, they were wrong about the road, it didn't lead to the end of Minneapolis, the community didn't collapse—but isn't it sweet that they cared so much?' It's her paternalistic relationship to the people involved that I mind.")

What Losure documents, ultimately, is the failure of the Free State to stop the reroute. After a year and a half, the encampment was finally shut down and the highway put through. By this point, Anne was in a "crisis/breakdown kind of thing. . . . A lot of people came out really badly from that. A lot of people came out as drunks, a few people actually got into cocaine and other shit—it had all the same post-traumatic stress disorder effects that any other prolonged, stressful environment would have." When Seattle's antiglobalization protests came along in 1999, the Free State turned out to be a natural incubator, and dispatched many from its ranks to the demonstrations; Anne stayed behind. "I was too completely freaked out from the experience of the Free State," she says. "Living for a year, flinching every time you hear a helicopter, is different [from typical protests]. The helicopter is actually one of the common nightmares many of us still have."

And yet Anne says it wasn't the threat of violence itself that withered so many Free Staters. It was the dismantling of their community.

"I think a lot of it was—and I know this sounds really cheesy—we didn't want to lose. The whole experience of the last summer [at Free State] was just watching everything you've built, everything you've constructed, everything you've organized for and worked for and stayed up all night sleeping in to keep it safe—it's just being torn down methodically. And everybody you see trying to stop it is just thrown in the hospital or jail, one or the other. It's not an easy thing to watch, it's not an easy thing to be present for. It was the stress of watching that happen to everything you've cared about for a long time."

Anne left Minnesota for Tennessee. There she hooked up with the Radical Faeries—a decades-old group she describes as "queer, post-hippie, activist, back-to-the-land"—who operate communes throughout the country. "It's basically just queer people living on land, growing food, doing that thing that crusties all say they want to grow up to do," Anne says. "I just stayed there until I stopped having nightmares."

What came next was yet another protest encampment, considerably less intense. The Michigan Womyn's Music Festival is a decades-old summer tradition beloved among its women-only attendees, but increasingly criticized for a seemingly simplistic interpretation of "women-only." Female-identified trannies, it would seem, do not qualify as women in the eyes of the festival. It was only a matter of time, then, that Anne would find her way to Tranny Camp, the protest crew that has become a fixture outside the festival gates in recent years.

As Anne explains it, the festival "was founded by people from the theoretical lesbian separatists school, who felt that the problems in culture were not based on systems of domination or the cultural interpretations of gender, but that they were actually the physical manifestations of essential, innate biological personality differences between men and women."

Not satisfied just to picket, Anne borrowed a friend's video camera and made a documentary about Tranny Camp. In 2002, she and a friend toured the West Coast, showing the film and giving presentations. She sold all 250 copies of the movie.

ANNE WENT TO Austin in 2000. That she hasn't left, a full three years later, suggests inaccurately a picture of uncharacteristic stillness. In her time there she's started a pirate radio show. She helped found an anarchist-based community newspaper—the *Havalina*. She began teaching a workshop on DIY medicating for would-be trannies. She went on a women's pirate radio tour across the country, speaking at fundraisers. She started writing for the *Texas Observer* and finally began building a career. For three years now, she's been studying to become a medic. There doesn't seem to be a single explanation for the career choice, but Anne suggests it has something to do with bashed heads and broken bones back in Minnesota.

"There were a few events where I was called on, at the Free State, because I had some first-aid experience. It was pretty clear that there wasn't anybody doing that, and that it was something that really needed to happen."

Becoming a medic has meant rejoining the establishment, to an extent—inevitable for someone working thirty-six hours a week and attending school full time. Anne's also had to do a little normalizing, at least on the surface. She describes her looks these days as "pretty boring—I have a uniform, and my hair is its natural color and 'mid-length.' I have no visible facial piercings. I cover my tattoo with my watch.

"When you're in school as a medic, you have to do clinicals where you go on an ambulance for twenty-four hours, fourteen hours, twelve hours, eight hours—whatever that particular rotation is—or you work in the ER practicing skills or assessing people. For that you have to meet the dress code. When I left for the [documentary] tour I gave myself a bi-hawk and dyed it bright red and said, 'This is the last good haircut I'll ever have in my life.' That was how the transition happened."

In the last of our conversations, we end not on tranny life or crusty life or any of those facts Anne finds irrelevant—we end on casts and stitches. She is not theoretical discussing the life of a medic; it seems there's too much to be practical about. A couple years ago, for instance, a pro-Palestinian rally at the University of Texas had devolved into shoving. The attacks of 9/11 happened to follow shortly thereafter, and within hours Anne was on campus with a video camera and a medic kit, should greater violence break out.

The change in Anne these days isn't just a zeroing in on EMT work but a broadening of whom she'll endeavor to help with it—a reimagining, as Anne herself might say, of categories.

"I realized it didn't matter what context I [would be] doing it [medic work]—I would feel okay about it. It's nice to be able to do everything you do for the revolution, or whatever you want to think about it as, but if I spend the rest of my life in Burnett County, Texas, pulling people out of smashed-up cars or reminding granny to take her insulin, am I going to feel bad about that? Is that something I have to chastise myself about for not doing enough to help humanity? No, that's a great thing to do. I have no moral problems about it whatsoever. That itself was enough."

18 "It's All Going to Collapse"

Amanda Rieder had been dating someone casually for two or three weeks around Thanksgiving 2001 when one night he broke down.

"We were in my car and suddenly he just started crying. Sobbing. Couldn't get words out. We went to my house and went inside. Finally he just said, 'My mom was there.' 'Where?' I asked him, dumbly. And he said, 'In New York.' He didn't really say anything else that night. He just cried and cried and finally just went to sleep."

The young man's mother had been on a business trip to New York on September 11, Amanda later found out, and was in one of the towers when they were hit.

"He didn't remember the day. He just remembers calling her cell phone a lot," Amanda says. She broke off the relationship eventually—he had begun drinking a lot. Amanda herself struggled. "I had to stop reading the paper for a while, and I'm not the type to do that. I was getting depressed."

Another classmate, David Lobe, recalls being in Manhattan on September 11. "I was at the corner of 42nd and Fifth with my girlfriend. We heard this loud roar overhead. I turned and said, 'That's really unusual to hear a jet engine so loud,' but I didn't look up. I got to work, in midtown, and found out what was going on. My mom is a flight attendant, and she was in Boston that morning, where one of the planes had left from. I was frantic until I found out she was safe." Here David grows quiet. "Later we found out five people from my company were on the various flights. Several were quite young, and one was with his partner and their baby."

Brenda McEldowney had been inside a church, signing up for an audition, when the planes hit. She didn't understand the magnitude of what had happened, and proceeded on to the Disney callback she'd already scheduled.

"By the time I got to my callback, I think both buildings had fallen. I didn't know what was going on. I was singing in midtown. I got there and everybody was on their cell phones, and they were saying, 'Brenda, we're so glad to see you, but the Pentagon's been hit, and if you don't want to sing you don't have to sing.' And I had gotten a message from [Brian] on my cell phone saying, 'Come home, I don't care if you have auditions.' [But] it just didn't hit me. And they said, 'Well, do you want to sing?' And I said, 'I'm here, I might as well.' So I did my callback, they took all my costume measurements, put me on videotape. I distinctly remember them having a camera and saying, 'Okay, tell us your name and where we are right now.' And I was like, 'I'm Brenda McEldowney, and it's New York City in the middle of the bombing, here's "Summertime."' It didn't really hit me until I was halfway across the Queensborough Bridge and looked to the south end—smoke all over, no towers. And suddenly this exodus, this mass of people walking. I was like, 'Oh my God, New York City's being evacuated.'"

Classmate Justin Romberg was getting out of the shower the morning of September 11 when his wife called. "I watched CNN for six hours straight, then went into school [where] I was teaching a class at the time. It was very tense. We have a lot of students from the Middle East, and no one knew what to say to each other. But then, in the coming weeks, there was tremendous dialogue. It was really good."

Missy Melberger says: "I was in Italy when I heard about the attacks. I spent four days in the Frankfurt airport waiting for the airspace to open again. Nothing in the newspapers ever made it real. Finally, when I was back, I drove past [the Pentagon] and I saw wires and desks hanging out of windows—it looked like a monster had taken a handful out of it. That was the time I got truly scared. There were also planes buzzing overhead all night at the time. At one point my friend Kevin said, 'That's the sound of freedom.' I said, 'No, that's the sound of fighter jets flying over my apartment.'"

"We heard about the plane hitting the Pentagon, and all I wanted to do was get out of there," Becky Earle remembers. "Congressman Wolf sent us all away. He stayed there until the Capitol police officers forced him out. I ended up walking to a friend's house about a mile away, and her dad actually is Gary Bauer, and he came over, and I ended up watching September 11 unfold with a former presidential candidate. It was weird. It wasn't Gary Bauer to us then—it was Elise's dad. He was kind of a comforting presence. Even though we're all grown and on our own, we still look for some sort of authority figure in a situation like that."

It was, quite simply, the biggest thing to happen in our lifetime. Everyone has a story. It's been said a lot that 9/11 gave commonality to an otherwise unfocused generation. Suddenly there was a day we all remembered, a panic we all knew, and eventually, a universe of policy arguments we could all have for a long, long time. But if the terror attacks clarified something about my generation and, by extension, my class, they clouded things, too. *Had* we actually been unfocused previously? The attacks activated notions we'd apparently held about ourselves until that first moment of impact, but they did so retroactively, and it became impossible to remember accurately how things had really been. "The end of irony" was famously announced, as was "the death of postmodernism" and "the loss of our innocence"—but how innocent, ironic, and postmodern were we in the first place? In this and a hundred other ways, 9/11 forced my class to examine who we were as people. In a sense, the aftermath brought us the soul-searching of high school all over again.

OUR HIGH SCHOOL reunion draws nearer as I write this, just a couple months away now. In our ten years since graduation we've seen the world, and our regard for it, somersault into something unrecognizable. Life, for a short while, came to us as a series of diverting nothings—a celebrity trial, a funny new Web site. A decade later, it takes work to find a classmate who doesn't fear the world is truly collapsing in one way or another.

Among the private, guilty reactions to 9/11, one of the more common among people of my generation seems to have been something along the lines of this: *Now we have our big event.* Before the attacks, we'd been known only for what we lacked—a Depression, a major war, an epic civil rights struggle, a push toward revolution. But if terror brought us a shared experience, some kind of unity even, it also ended up fanning old antagonism. Too much changed in America after that initial sadness—inevitably, we took up political positions, perhaps even more fiercely than in high school. For every instance of unity among us—new friendliness, new mellowness, new maturity—9/11 planted ten more of discord just beneath the cordial surface.

"It seemed like our generation was finally going to get the chance to live our entire lives with no major war or social upheaval," classmate Stacy McMahon wrote to me. "We could just work, invest, and build up our estates in peace. Now we can't be so sure anymore, and that's ultimately what pisses me off most about the terrorist attacks. It's terrible that 3,000 people died, but even worse in a utilitarian sense is the decrease in the prospects for the rest of us. Just when you thought you were safe . . ."

For others, the 3,000 people was enough. Recently a documentary about the political implications of September 11 came to town, and I proposed to Charlotte Opal that we go see it. I hadn't gotten the words out of my mouth before she declined. "Nope. They'll show footage," she said, case closed. "I don't watch 9/11 stuff."

For Becky Earle, the attacks brought out a sense of solidarity. "The single most moving impression" she had in her five years on Capitol Hill came when the members of Congress went out to the Capitol steps and sang "God Bless America."

Others felt this solidarity but also unease. "I felt like a New Yorker like I never had before," Brenda McEldowney says. "But it also brought out a backlash of isolationism, which has been horrifying to watch. September 11 was a horrifying thing, but it's become a flag they're waving."

"I work with a lot of firefighters, many of whom resent the symbolic weight that's been handed to them," Anne Farbman says. "On the other hand, it was really disillusioning because of the complete inadequacy of response from people that I really cared about, and people that I thought I had a lot of political commonality with. [There were a] few people who inevitably crop up in any crisis, who become frightened and very identified with the media reporting and indulge themselves in fear—*If Islam is not curtailed, everybody we know and care about will die!* Luckily, those people were very few in my circle of friends. The primary problem was people who were very smug: 'We had this coming. The World Trade Center is in enemy territory anyway, we're just going to watch it come down and laugh, and laugh at everybody who cares.' I was living at an activist house at the time, and there was this guy I had to chase out of the house—I just couldn't deal with it."

Still others saw their anger and apprehension become a permanent fixture:

"I got home that day and threw a tape in the VCR. I've got about twelve hours of footage," Brian McConnell says. "Anytime you start to feel like it didn't really happen, when it starts to take on a dreamlike quality—'Why are we doing this in Afghanistan?' or whatever—you just pop that tape back in and it's like, 'Oh yeah, *that's* why we're doing this.' It's almost like ripping off a Band-Aid—it'll definitely snap you back and make you remember what you felt on those days. It almost makes me shake. I don't go home and watch it every day, but I've watched parts of it since then, because I think a lot of people forget too easily. Then you have something like this sniper crap up in northern Virginia—'Oh how horrible, I don't feel safe!' Well, duh, you shouldn't feel safe anyway, jerkoff. We're at war with a bunch of people who want to see each and every one of us die a violent death."

Ryan Beckwith sees the mainstream media's coverage of terrorism in terms of a vast and ongoing manipulation. "[Americans] come home from work, turn on the TV, crack open a beer, [and] they get strategically released data that's designed to trigger an emotional reaction—an Osama bin Laden videotape, for example. The whole point of the emotional reaction is to cloud the rational faculties. *'They hate our freedom! We're so free that they hate us!'* People turn on the TV and this is what they get. How is the other stuff going to seep in through this shell?"

David Garber takes issue with those who criticized Bush's War on Terror. "I'm not sure what else we'd do, you know? Go bake them a casserole? Say, 'Hi! Let's sit down and talk'? From my impressions of them, they're pretty hardened in their opinions. They're sort of beyond the point where we can talk things out with them."

"The day after September 11," Chris Sununu tells me, "I just knew the Palestinians were going to get it from that point on, from all over the world."

"It took me a while to come to this realization, but it was the best we could've hoped for," classmate Chris Dwan says. "I'd been predicting for several years that it would take something of that magnitude to wake us up to how much the world hates us. I'd always thought it would be a suitcase nuke, and that it would be Washington, and I'd learn about it by my parents' death. It sounds awful, but I was relieved that it was only two buildings in New York. Since then I've not liked being in large crowds. On the way to work, I look at the Minneapolis skyline and I think, *Hmm, nice target.* . . . To have that part of the world tied up with the heart of our economy—petroleum products— well, I don't want to sound like a loony, prophesying the end of the world, but it's all going to collapse. What does a thinking person do, realizing that the empire that raised me is headed toward collapse? It's almost enough to make me go into politics, but I don't see how that would help."

"I wanted to know why [these kind of attacks] would happen," Justin Romberg says. "The troubling thing to me, with the war in Afghanistan and then the war in Iraq, was the shroud of secrecy that the administration tried to hide it in. I really dislike Bush for that reason. I certainly wouldn't call myself a Democrat, but I would never vote for Bush."

September 11 caught us all sleeping, goes the metaphor; the time since, from finally learning about Middle Eastern history to reinvigorating our intelligence community, has been a national awakening. There are implications for my own high school class in this idea. Not only did our decade of comfortable slumber allow us to stroll into dot-com jobs and flop about amid glittery cultural decadence, but it let us relax that adolescent habit of *digging* that's come up so many times in this book. Our arguments over how life ought to be lived, how people ought to *be,* ceased not only because we weren't confined to the same brick building anymore, but also because we were lulled by the relative peace of our early twenties.

Two years afterward, the meaning of September 11 has been jumbled by America's response to it: our wars in Afghanistan and Iraq, the Middle East crisis, the Patriot Act, the Bush Doctrine, newly unsettling tension of varying degrees with North Korea, Iran, Cuba, Saudi Arabia, Pakistan, Syria, and even Western Europe. Whatever unity arrived after 9/11 has all but vanished, replaced by a growing entropy. At the micro level of my high school class, our dusty old ideologies have reemerged after a decade—but with tiny fissures in the foundations. Assumptions of ours have begun to wither and adapt in the post-9/11 world. Or at least that's how it appears; I can think of no other explanation for reconciliations like the one found in the next chapter. It's not world peace, but for two former high school classmates, it's a start.

19   John Doyle

JOHN DOYLE: *"Everybody in high school wanted to be tough. That was the whole persona that you had to build and maintain. But if I had really met somebody that was tough, I'd've had problems!"*

JEAN COOK: "We used to ride the bus together. He was scrawny and sweet the first two years, then he got hard to talk to. Cocky.

"In tenth grade, his father was in the Gulf War. This guy named Bruce started talking about going to the airport and spitting on soldiers. John just freaked out, got really upset. He kept saying, 'My dad's over there.'"

BEN KIM: "He was a bully, I'll admit it! But he's probably changed considerably."

SETH BLEIWEIS: "A lot of people thought he was a bully, a real asshole. And I could see how he'd come across like that, but when you really got to know him, he wasn't always a tough guy. He did have a strong temper, but he didn't take pleasure in fucking with people—not like some people do. A lot of it was unjustified. He was a big homophobe back then. He would make jokes about gays. For better or for worse, he didn't give a shit what people thought."

JUSTIN ROMBERG: "He was very intense, very physical. I remember a basketball game where he had a guy on the floor, punching him. That wasn't the only side of him, though. I had calculus class with him and he was really sharp, too. As far as race goes, I never perceived him as being terribly racist. He would say things, make jokes, but a lot of people did. His big thing was he was homophobic."

WES BLACK: "We were pretty close—we went skiing a couple times. I hesitate to say I knew anybody more conservative, except maybe Chris Sununu. He was anti–gay rights, which at the time was a pretty polarizing issue.

"As far as race was concerned, I can understand where some of his reputation came from. But I don't think he was truly racist in his heart. He would make jokes—and I wasn't entirely innocent of that either—but I know he hung out with other races.

"He was always big into the military, and really into West Point. All his life, he'd lived a lifestyle of discipline. I wouldn't have wanted to cross him. One time we were just goofing around in college, and he ended up squeezing my arm for some reason and it left a big old bruise. He had a strong physical side, and he could get fired up sometimes.

"He was a good guy. He didn't always have a good-guy persona, and he didn't always mind. It's just a theory, but in an intellectual environment, maybe that sets you apart a little from the nerds. Even though he got a 4.0 or something."

■

John was a big old boy in high school, but not so big that you couldn't picture one of those furious pink fists approaching fast. His offensive-tackle physique was intense, his reputation was intense, even his crew cut was intense. Doyle, as his football friends called him, was one of the few TJ students to take occasional swings at people—but I never knew him to be a bully. Virtue and principle were where indiscriminate cruelty might have been, though his virtues and principles struck many as odd. He stood for some combination of patriotism and hard work that seemed, to many, to involve misogyny, homophobia, racism, and the occasional face punch. He loved America and felt others did not. Others wanted to surrender everything to the immigrants, to the fags, to the lazy. Recently I asked our teacher Garfield Lindo what he remembered about John. "Racist? Yes, that was certainly the impression he gave off. I hated that boy!" He laughs. "I don't like to say that about a student, but oh did I hate him. But not for any lack of intelligence on his part. He was extremely, extremely bright."

The football team tended to rally around Doyle, and not just because his father was coach. He was magnetic and brazen; he kept an air of near-danger. Even those close to him knew not to cross him. "We were friends and played football together and everything, and he even took a swing at *me* a couple times," Justin Romberg recalls, laughing. John's reputation preceded him, and sometimes undeserved reputations preceded him, too. "Didn't he once tell Mr. Lindo to go back to Africa?" Adam Rice asked me recently.

John was more than a fabled brute; he was also my nemesis. We were in Mr. Lindo's class together, and there we argued viciously. The class was called Humanities, for no good reason, and on good days it was conducted like a cockfight. Into the ring Mr. Lindo would throw some red meat: Immigration, or Affirmative Action, or Clarence Thomas, or Sexuality, or Environmentalism, and the battle for the soul of America would begin. Doyle and I kicked and clucked our way to the middle every time, angry combs a-flap.

Doyle and I hated each other, and he was bigger. I heard, now and then, that a fight might be in the works between us; in retrospect this must have been wishful thinking. Still, I fantasized alternately about administering a miraculous roundhouse, John Wayne style, or hitting the floor peacefully, as Gandhi might have. Neither ever happened, and the experts will say searching for John ten years later is about closure. Having found him, I would be more interested in hearing the experts on the subject of Doyle himself, who now boggles the mind all over again.

WHEN I FIRST meet him at a noisy bar near our alma mater, I'm prepared with my Wayne and my Gandhi, but mainly I'm just curious. The decade that follows high school is, among other things, a pleasant exercise in *choosing* one's surroundings rather than having them assigned. For me, this wound up meaning ten years without knowing anyone like John. From the safe distance of a liberal arts college, then New York, then San Francisco, the idea of an out-loud bigot almost began to seem legendary, mythical. The notion of getting a beer with one was like getting a beer with a sword swallower or a levitator.

John is smoking a cigarette in front of the bar, one of those big, loud, macho sports bars with a TV screen for just about every patron. He looks the same—short, tough haircut, chest like a barrel—though possibly his face is harder somehow. We shake hands civilly and head inside.

At first there's no mention of our mutual and unresolved antagonism—it would be superfluous, like manure farmers remarking on the smell. Instead we order beers and talk about mutual acquaintances. Things are comfortable, if not exactly playful, by the time we work our way back to high school and to John's recollection of himself. "I know for a fact that there's people in high school who I couldn't stand," he tells me. "I know for a fact that there's a lot of people going out of high school that couldn't stand *me*." When the subject of fights comes up shortly after, I ask if he remembers any.

"One was freshman year. I threw a punch at Joe Poppin because he was fuckin' pissing me off. It was on the basketball court, we were playing basketball. . . . That was stupid. You still see people that act like that, too, even though they're our age. I don't understand that. I look back, and it's embarrassing. What was the point?"

"Did it work?"

"I think, no, it didn't work, actually. I had my close-knit group of friends, guys I played football and soccer with, I had them no matter what. I didn't need to prove anything to them. But what I did by acting the way I did is, I turned off some other people that I probably could've been pretty good friends with. But then, there was also that—what I call the 'cool group.' That whole crowd had some decent people. But I don't think I ever got to know them all that well, because they were put off—understandably so—by the way that I acted.

"But then again, thinking back, I was kind of put off by the way they acted. When they got together in their little group sometimes . . . I just wanted to go over there and smack them all! I thought they were arrogant, selfish, and I thought they were just typical yuppie kids. Running around, thinking that they were a little bit better than everybody else . . . They were the beautiful people, but they really weren't . . . you know? I felt like an outsider to them. I'd never fit in with them. I had really nothing in common with them. It was almost like they would tolerate me, but . . ."

Having already spoken with John on the phone, I knew that the years since high school have made him more candid and approachable. Until now, though, I had little reason to doubt he still had the same basic orientation to the world. I'm relieved of this—this prejudice, I guess—upon asking him to describe the person he was in high school. His answer comes in his uniquely choppy, martial cadence—the kind with which one might demand push-ups from a private—but what he describes is a transformation that few of our classmates believe when I gush about it later.

"Helluva lot different than I am now. Some things I think are the same. Hardworking: Did it then, do it now. Focus. I think the biggest change is that now that I have ten years of world experience under my belt, I see the world in a different light. I like to think of myself as much more accepting than I was back then. Back then, everything was black and white, right and wrong. That doesn't exist, though. You gotta take everybody at face value, respect what others are doing. As long as it's not illegal or infringing upon my rights in some sort of way, who cares? Part of my experience has been outside of [the northern Virginia] area, much more diverse, different cultures, different people. When you get to know them, you get to understand what they went through, they get to understand what I went through, there's a little bit of empathy built in there, and then the respect level is generated from that."

"Different cultures"? There was a time those would have been gag-ging, if not fighting, words for John. When I press him to explain, he suggests that the right-wing posture we saw in him was largely a response to political correctness and other inventions of the looming left.

"I have this problem where I like to disagree with the accepted norm," he offers. The accepted norm at Jefferson, he felt, was liberal-ism, and so liberalism he challenged. But that would soon change. It's the middle of the day, and we order more beer.

HIGH SCHOOL, FOR John, was more like pre–West Point—John's was a military family, and he'd planned early for an army career. "I had a lot of respect and admiration for my dad and what I'd seen him do," he says. "I saw what he did and I was like, 'I wanna do that. I wanna be a leader of men. I wanna serve my country'—it's a cliché—whether that be as a cop or a fireman, or the army. I went to West Point because it was free and it was a good education, and it did help prepare me to get where I was headed."

I don't think anyone was surprised to see John head to the Academy after TJ. Perhaps even deeper than his family reasons, or his desire to serve, John's basic temperament destined him for a place like West Point. As he puts it, he's a hard charger. Grant and Lee became hard chargers at the Academy, as did Eisenhower, Patton, and MacArthur. John should have been in paradise, but when the prevailing winds at West Point proved conservative, "that's when I started to see stuff on the other side. I went from one extreme—where we went to high school—to a completely other extreme.

"I think it really hit me the first year. We were talking in a history class about the use of atomic weapons during World War II, and I was

WHAT REALLY HAPPENED TO THE CLASS OF '93

the only one in the class who didn't agree with it. And I still don't agree with the use of [atomic weapons]. Everybody was like, 'Hell, yeah,' but to me, killing innocent women and kids, no matter what your rationale, is never justified.

"Then I was in a philosophy class talking about the death penalty. Everybody at West Point agrees with the death penalty. I'm fundamentally opposed to the death penalty. I hate it. It's murder. It's vindictive. It's incredibly vindictive, actually. If somebody commits a wrong, they go to prison, they sit there, and they think about it."

But John's adjustment period at West Point wasn't confined to policy disagreements. Before long he discovered the ground had moved—surreptitiously at first—beneath his feet.

"My dad left my mom the day that I went to West Point. It was pretty ugly, their divorce. They were in court for like three years. It was brutal. They don't talk to each other to this day. He ended up getting remarried in about '95 or '96, so it was about a year or so after the divorce was finalized.

"The last year and a half has gotten a little bit better, [but] I didn't speak to my dad for like three or four years. It wasn't until December of 2000—that was the first time I've seen him in a long time. I finally realized that I'm not gonna change who he is now. In the long term, it's good to have relations with your own dad.

"I should've, looking back, seen the signs. It never dawned on me, but my senior year in high school, my dad was gone a lot. Away from the house, a lot of business trips. Legitimate business trips, but I could tell that there was more fighting than was normal. They did a pretty good job of disguising it. But looking back, I should've seen it. He didn't seem very happy. The first year after you're retired"—John's father retired from the army while John was in high school, then began working for the Defense Intelligence Agency—"you're leaving the army, and living and working in this area is something he really didn't enjoy as much—the commute and all that.

"My freshman year there was just a struggle to get through that. You're treated like a piece of crap [at West Point], so it's day-in, day-out trouble. I never had any problems academically [but] I was out of control in college, up until about junior year. And then I finally saw the light and settled down. But I totally got wrapped up into drinking way too much, causing problems. I fought a lot. I broke both my hands in a fight. . . . Random guys coming out of some stupid fraternity at UVA started fucking with us. They were local people from Charlottesville. They weren't allowed into the fraternity for the party, so they're out there drinking and complaining. When we were walking out, they kind of directed it towards us. And I wasn't gonna put up with any of that shit, so one thing led to another and it was a fight.

"Somebody threw the first punch, and the next thing you know it was all over. People flying everywhere . . . It was bad. We got the best of that fight, but had things gone the other way . . . bad. We were trying to hurt them some, and they were trying to hurt us. It started out badly for us; I was flat on my back. Two or three of us were already down. It started with five of them. Two of them got to running because they saw that they were gonna lose, so then we turned the tables on the other three. I'd [gotten] tackled and . . . I held the shirt over the guy's head, and just started elbowing and punching him, and the guy finally got woozy and kind of went limp, and I rolled him over, and that's when I broke my hands, 'cause I punched him like about forty times. It was bad. I realized later that I could have been seriously hurt, or my friends could have. That was a life-altering experience for me. And I haven't been in a fight since then. That was November '95."

———

JOHN GRADUATED FROM West Point and was assigned to a base in Germany, just north of Frankfurt. His duties there were on the scale of running a small town. As time logistics officer, for instance— S-4, for short—he handled all the supply, movement, and maintenance for his entire battalion, consisting of about 500 soldiers. "I was responsible for the supply of anything from fuel to pencils," he says.

In May 2000, John was deployed to Kosovo, and he stayed there seven months before returning to Germany. As scout platoon leader, he led about thirty soldiers as "the eyes and ears" of the larger unit. The job was to "probe deep and try to pinpoint enemy locations, and assist with identifying where they're at, what the strength of the enemy is, how best to engage them, et cetera.

"My particular platoon was given a chunk of land that consisted of about ten towns, with roughly 4,000 to 5,000 residents. Our basic mission was to patrol that on a very regular and consistent basis, and ensure that there were no acts of violence between the different ethnic groups that are down there—primarily the Albanians, who are Muslim, and the Serbs, who are Orthodox Christian.

"When I was at West Point, that's when Bosnia kicked off, and [it was] drilled into our head, 'Hey, at a certain point, one or two of you may end up deployed in a peacekeeping mission.' At the time I said, 'Okay, that's a possibility,' but I didn't really realize it until I was assigned to a unit in Germany. If you're in the United States military these days, you're guaranteed to go on a peacekeeping mission. Bottom line, whether it be Bosnia, Kosovo, or our ongoing presence in Kuwait, or now Afghanistan, you're guaranteed to sometime be deployed.

"When we prepared to go to Kosovo, we did a rotation, a simulated field problem, that lasted twelve to fourteen days. During that whole time, they hired Germans and some Hungarians to come in to act, and we saw it all. We practiced for 100-person riots, 500-person riots, drive-by shootings, bombings that could occur in a town, ethnic-related, for what they call the 'Mad Mortarman' —the guy that runs around and just has a mortar from the war and decides to shoot rounds into the town.

"We were going to step into an area that was still very charged, and anything could happen at any time. It didn't while I was there, but the unit that I replaced down there, five months before we arrived—you probably read about it or saw it in the paper—they were smack dab in the center of one of those riots that occurred in Kosovo. They essentially had to fly in the general to calm everybody down, because a U.S. unit was down making an arrest in a Serbian town and all the Serbs in the town converged on that unit, which only consisted of about nine guys, and pinned them down, and pelted them with rocks and would not allow them to leave the town."

Seth Bleiweis, another classmate who went to Kosovo with the army, describes the typical challenge in Kosovo this way: "It was a lot of he-stole-my-goat kind of problems." Tensions were simmering, John says, and could heat up for any number of reasons.

"When we arrived there, it marked the one-year anniversary of the cessation of hostilities, [and of] the U.S. presence in Kosovo. We had a full alert, we pretty much had patrols running nonstop—the Albanians were celebrating, the Serbs obviously were not, and we thought that would perhaps lead to some violence: Albanians move into a Serb town to try to stir something up, or Serbs getting kind of mad that they're having Albanian celebrations, and on the flipside they go looking for trouble.

"We got an unconfirmed report that there were a large number of Serbs that were gathering in this one town, [and it] seemed like there was a disproportionate number of vehicles that left than those that returned—they were like, 'Wow, there's a lot of people in this town.' They sent myself and another one of my sections forward as scouts to observe.

"So we were out here on a hilltop, the sun's starting to come down, they gave me some helicopter support that I could pretty much control going over the town, making sweeps to give a visual aid of what was going on. And I'm thinking, 'Here I am with reports of 500 to 600 Serbs in this town, and it's me and, like, seven of my guys up on a hilltop.' I won't say I was scared, but I was a little uneasy at first, in that I'm not familiar with the area—I have a map, of course, but I'm not familiar with the specifics of the land, so that was a little bit of a weird situation. Ultimately, it was just something that was blown out of proportion, so nothing happened.

"We also did a lot of responding to domestic disturbances, and one time we had a report of a shooting in one of my towns. One of my sections was already out there and they were the first one on the scene, and they came on the radio and told me that I needed to come out there. It turned out that the owner of the house had illegal firearms, in this case a handgun, and had left it loaded and cocked, not on safe, and his kid had got hold of it and killed himself. We evacuated the kid to the local medical facility, where they tried to save his life but unfortunately couldn't. But the way the parents reacted when we got there was sorta like, 'Hey, are we gonna get in trouble?' It wasn't like, 'How's my son doing?' I don't know, it was kind of weird, the irresponsibility of how the people acted sometimes kind of put me off.

"There's a sense of hopelessness in Kosovo. . . . It's an incredibly poor place, the unemployment rate is in the 90s. What you need to do is get some sort of viable economic solution that puts people to work earning money, get a sense they're doing something with their lives.

And maybe you get these business ventures where the Serbs and Albanians are working a little bit together, and they can see that there's mutual dependence and everybody's gonna prosper, that perhaps that's the way to go.

"The first thing I talk about is just the education. I'd hear from seven- or eight-year-old kids that they hated Serbs. I mean, when you're just seven or eight years old you don't have the *capacity* to hate, you're learning that from your parents, you're learning that from your community, and the only way to get around stuff like that is through education. I said it till I was blue in the face. I would lecture eighty-year-old Albanian men or eight-year-old Albanian kids. I would say, 'You can't say something like that.' In many cases it kind of backfired on me, because the Serbs *did* do something to them. I'd say, 'That Serb that you hate now, wasn't he your friend before the war?' [And they'd say], 'Yeah, but then in the war he did *bad stuff.*'

"It's gonna be a long, long process. I would say 85 percent of the people, when I would talk to them about issues like that, wouldn't even want to discuss it with me. They were like, 'No, I hate 'em. The Serbs killed my wife, I will never like them, no matter what.' How are you going to change somebody like that?"

THANK GOD FOR tape recorders. John Doyle? Talking about poverty and hopelessness? Teaching Albanian children that racism is wrong? Later I play the conversation back to myself in case I've misheard. There was a time, after all, when poverty, hopelessness, and racism would have struck him as little more than squishy liberal contrivances. Eventually, he explains to me how his outlook on life itself could have changed so drastically.

"We don't have time for it [in the army]," he says about bigotry in particular. "We're too busy doing what we need to do to worry about stuff like that. . . . People in the army aren't working for their country. They're not working for that higher cause everybody thinks they are. They're working for the guy to the left of them or the guy to the right of them. . . . And most of the guys, even the white people coming to the military, as soldiers, you know what they all share? They're all trying to make themselves better."

"Back [in high school] I thought I had all the answers. I used to always say, 'Hard work no matter what'—if you just work hard, you're gonna do well, you're gonna be successful. Everything else is an excuse. But that's not true. Hard work is still the fundamental element of any success, but some people, based on their situation, their circumstances, can work as hard as they want, but unless somebody steps in and gives them that boost—whether it be in the form of encouragement, opportunity, money, I don't know—they're not gonna get to that level. And to say that they can I think is foolish, and we're deluding ourselves, in a way.

"Take somebody from a school in Prince George's County. Could be a ball of fire, smart as a whip, [but] maybe they came from a broken home, so they don't have that family support. [They] go to a P.G. County school, don't get a good-quality education, therefore when it comes time for, say, college, this person's ability to apply to go to different universities is not the same as somebody in northern Virginia who had a great family life, went to a good school, drove a nice car, always had good clothes on their back, [and] was in a culture where everybody goes to college. You think that those two people are on a level playing field? Wrong."

John and I talk for another while, mainly ideas about what needs fixing in the world, and find that we've each migrated from our high school positions to a place much closer to one another. It's a strangely emotional experience for me—there must be a German word for the experience of drinking beer with one's former nemesis while he says profoundly equitable and righteous things. John still isn't the emotive sort, so I can't tell if he, too, is affected by our new harmony. Finally, I can't resist asking what he remembers of our relationship back in high school. He lights a cigarette.

"You know, our only interactions, Chris, that really stick out in my mind were in class. I always thought that you were the other side of the pendulum from me, sorta reactionary. I always felt that we were never gonna change how we felt on our views, but that we had some relatively healthy . . . that I knew you would listen, and pointedly disagree with me, just like you knew I would push and pointedly disagree with you. That was kind of my view. I viewed you as as-far-to-the-left liberal as you could find at Jefferson. And I'm sure you probably viewed me all the way on the other side. And back then, you represented everything that I disagreed with. Personally speaking, I didn't really ever know you, you didn't really ever know me. . . . I would say, 'Oh, I don't like him,' but mainly I was saying, 'I don't like what you represent.'"

THE LIFE OF a West Point graduate is determined: graduation, a career of promotions, and finally retirement after twenty years. I assumed John would be out on the battlefield until he was a toothless old general, but he had a different plan. Five years after leaving West Point, he quit the army altogether.

Since July 2002, he's been living in his mother's house and working as production supervisor at a uniform supply company in Maryland. At first, John's slow to explain his departure from the army. A congenitally loyal guy, he first describes it in terms of personal dissatisfaction.

"There are a couple things I didn't care for, and ultimately those outweighed what I did like about it. I guess it's just the constant feeling that you're going to be deployed everywhere—it's something that I didn't really look forward to. To be honest with you, I don't ever want to go to the Balkans again. If my country asked me to I'd do it, but I really don't want to go down there again. I joined the army to be a tanker, man, to shoot stuff and run over stuff, not to maintain the peace."

Gradually, though, something larger comes out—an incisive, thoughtful critique of the military itself. "The army is capable of doing a hundred things okay, but I'd like to see it where you do ten things really well," John says. "Ultimately, it was creating a difficult situation."

The country is nearing its attack on Iraq as we speak, and John continues on into U.S. foreign policy:

"One of the problems I have, America needs to be engaged in the world. Not necessarily militarily, but politically, socially, and economically. One thing that doesn't sit well with me is that we're indiscriminate as far as how we get involved. We got involved in Kosovo because we were already involved in Bosnia, and the reason we got involved in Bosnia is because—well, the Europeans can't handle their own business, and white people were getting killed. Why didn't we get involved in Rwanda, where, what, 1.5 million people lost their lives? There was nothing at stake there. I think there's a little bit of racial undertones. Why are we getting involved in Iraq? Because you and I want to get $1.25 per gallon, not $1.50.

"I don't see the evidence that indicates Saddam Hussein's doing anything different than he's been doing for twelve years. What makes it different today? I think it's that we need an opponent and we need to do something about it, and this is the easiest way for us to do something about it. But I mean, the Middle East is a can of worms. Yeah, we could roll up Iraq, but then who's gonna fill the void of that government? Look at Afghanistan now."

THE WAR IN Iraq has been declared over for two months the next time John and I exchange words—this time via e-mail—though much fighting continues. He was right, of course. So far no one's filled the void we made, and Baghdad is in chaos. But we don't talk about military operations this time. John is done with uniforms—his own and the ones he was laundering—and he's living in Germany. There he works for the government contractor Computer Science Corporation, formerly DynCorp, on a simulation system called the Close Combat Tactical Trainer. The CCTT trains army tank units and can be brought anywhere in Germany that soldiers need it. The first units John trained are now in Iraq, he tells me. "I like to think that we helped them in some small way prepare for what they are going through."

But work isn't the only reason John's back in Germany. While stationed there initially, before Kosovo, he rented an apartment in a small town from a German woman named Kathleen. The two didn't talk much—she was gone often, and anyhow she was married with children. Three years later, that began to change.

"She got a divorce and she moved back into the area, and that's when I really started getting to know her more, and found that we had a lot in common," John says. Soon they were an item. They lived together after John returned from Kosovo, and now he's gone back to live with her permanently.

"A couple years ago, I knew I was gonna get out of the army. I was like, 'Yeah, I'll go into corporate America, start climbing the ladder, I think I'm pretty smart, I think I'm a hard worker, and I have what it takes to get to that successful level.' But the last year, year and a half have really changed my outlook on it. It's not important to me. It's more important to me to be with Kathleen, and her kids also—they're great. So that's more important to me right now, believe it or not."

Back to me now. I've learned this: Spending a year looking for high school classmates—as opposed to, say, leading a platoon in Kosovo, or inventing an algorithm, or bouncing around in freight trains—is the kind of activity that indulges the occasional emotional extravagance. Built in, after all, are not only regular, destabilizing visits to the moldering realm of adolescent relationships, but a direct view of *other* people's adolescences and all that's happened since. It leads a soul to say dopey things. In my final e-mail to John, I let loose a wave of senti-ment—not only that our talks moved me, but that they *encouraged* me, somehow, in a more cosmic sense. His reply is restrained but kind:

"I appreciate what you said in your note. I actually enjoyed our interview as well. I find it ironic that we were 'arch enemies' in high school, because after we spoke I felt we had more in common than not. Oh well, call it the foolishness of youth."

20 Sean Bryant

WAYNE STEWARD: "I first met Sean in chemistry class sopho-more year. He seemed to do well at whatever he was doing. He was very put-together. *Really* into politics, very persuasive, very smart—he just had that personality that would've worked in a political situation. He had principles, and he also understood the realities of getting things accomplished. He captured what you'd expect from a great high school student, but without all the crap that goes with it. He got all the good qualities but dumped all the bad ones."

KAREN TAGGART: "He loved everybody and everybody loved him. I remember him not being in any cliques, and everyone accepted him. He was a genuinely nice person, and totally himself. I remember him showing up places in overalls—God, were they *short* overalls?—and a straw hat and a big smile. The jocks liked him, the computer geeks liked him. And I'll never forget the stuff he did with the school board, it was just so gutsy."

VANYA (SEAMAN) WRIGHT: "I remember we went to New York on a journalism field trip, and we were sitting in a café and I'd ordered a wheat grass drink. It was disgusting. Everybody was talking about how gross it was, and then Sean just grabbed it and drank it. And felt terrible. He was impulsive. And quiet, too. And he always seemed to have a smile on his face, I remember."

ANNE BARNHILL: "He was relentless. Relentlessly engaged. He was really over the top in every way. Strong feelings, impassioned. Rage, too. I think he was very loving, but also very rageful. He just had really strong feelings. When I say rage, I don't really mean anger. He had raging passions of all sorts. . . . He did have this public persona, which was to be very easy to get along with. I think he came across as positively engaged. I think he probably didn't come across as sensitive as he was. He was easily wounded. But he also had so much initiative—he wasn't the kind of easily wounded person who cowered. He had resilience."

S ix weeks now until the big reunion. I've mailed my check and registration form, I've *strongly urged* various classmates to do the same (and pondered my embarrassing new role as class booster)—all that's left to do now is write this chapter about Sean. I think I should come out and say that I don't know how.

The Sean Bryant we knew in high school was so kinetic, so multifaceted, so *broad* of interest and spirit that describing him is a little like trying to sketch running water. Because he struck us as great, or else enigmatic, or else simply *beyond* us, those attempting to explain him eventually throw up their hands and resort to an unsorted heap of adjectives. Sean was a glowing, smiling, insouciant, passionate, adventurous, decent, handsome, outdoorsy, tousle-haired tree-climber of a fellow who impressed everyone who knew him, and many who simply watched from across the room. In a building full of teens grappling rather uncomfortably over what life was meant to look like, here was a young man with a way of being that pleased people in just about every corner.

Bliksem Tobey was Sean's best friend at TJ—in fact, he'd been his best friend since the age of two. "He was a very accepting guy and a fun-loving guy," Bliksem told me when I asked why Sean was so well liked. "He brought people from different groups together. He'd go hang out with a bunch of hard-core engineers, then he'd go hang out with the [student government] circle." Sean's mother, Sallie, told me that he once argued with a teacher about his grade being higher than another student's. "He noted that the other student lacked the confidence to speak up in class and that giving him a lower participation grade than Sean's was unfair when in fact the other student had prepared better than Sean had," she recalled.

This isn't to say Sean was some even-keeled, George Washington kind of person—one look at him and it was clear he lived far out on a kooky and singular limb. Sean broke a cardinal science academy rule: Love, but *don't flaunt,* your inner geek. Karen Taggart summed up Sean's outward presentation well—*short overalls.* His accoutrements asked for trouble, and his grin was nothing if not big and dopey. And then his laugh was nothing if not big and dopey. "HELLO!" he'd say if he passed you in the biology hall. "HELLO AGAIN!" he'd say again if he passed you five minutes later in the math wing—meanwhile, you were busy perfecting your high school scowl. His was the rare teen intelligence that failed to appreciate standards of expression. Bliksem confirms Sean's geekiness. "He and I were kind of the fun, dorky, weird guys. We were into off-the-wall things."

It's not that Sean had a stunted sense of style; his style was a deliberate insistence—and this will sound clichéd until you remember how rare it is in high school—on making his own rules. This iconoclasm might explain his much-recalled inclination toward adventure. It was said, and the look in the eye confirmed, that he would climb, swim, run, and possibly tunnel under, over, and through anything that caught his attention. He did so fearlessly, it's also said. "When we were little kids," Bliksem remembers, "there was a creek behind my house and we'd go creeking, which basically meant walking the creek. One weekend we walked and walked and ended up following it all the way to the Potomac, in Great Falls. We had to call our folks to come get us."

To use a term that feels outdated—outdated and then reborn in Sean's case—he struck people as an all-American kid, overalls and all. In him we witnessed a rare balancing act. He championed causes but didn't mark himself a fringy activist; he excelled at sports without surrendering to all that macho posturing; he followed creeks until they hit rivers; and he also put his head down and did his homework. In the Sean of high school I see flecks of what the rest of us took a decade to become. In his dedication to reform I see Lesley Cook's fighting spirit, but in his gimlet-eyed appreciation for *getting things done*, I see Charlotte Opal backing her fair-trade work with statistics and economic theory. In his untiring ambition I see Ben Kim with his anti-noise algorithm. In his resistance to partisanship and sacred cows, I see former Army officer John Doyle taking on the logic of his own country's recent military adventures. In his soft touch I see

David Garber's unguarded candor, and in his bursts of wildness I see Anne Farbman chasing a locomotive through North Dakota.

Sean had little pieces of everyone in him before, possibly, we even had them in ourselves. In retrospect, this strange trick of Sean's must have had something to do with his assorted successes, not the least of which was his position as student representative to the Fairfax County School Board—one of the largest counties in the country. What's remarkable isn't that he held this post, but the creativity and moral certainty he brought to it. At his very first school board meeting—no sitting on his hands, no waiting to get the lay of the land—he moved that the county's student handbook be modified to include sexual orientation in its laundry list of verbal harassment prohibitions. It was as if a bomb went off. The subject drew incredible attention, and before his motion succeeded there were accounts of the controversy in the *Washington Post* and the *New York Times*. Wayne Steward, Tim Yerington, and other classmates did the work of coming out, but it was Sean who focused a wider spotlight on the issue.

But perhaps more significant than his activism—the harassment clause was just one of his causes—was the grace he brought to it. If the accumulated friction at TJ threatened to rip my class apart, Sean appeared to us as someone who might save us from ourselves. His was the power of reconciliation, the ability to spread calm. With regard to the culture wars that engulfed our class, Sean was neither oblivious to the issues nor convulsed by them. He cared deeply about things but brought a lightness to his caring, too.

The writer Jennifer Mendelsohn wrote a wonderful essay about him in *Washingtonian* magazine a few years ago that captured his quirky compassion, that strange gentleness that accompanied his raging passion and improvident creeking. In the piece she described a trip he took to London with a few classmates and a teacher: One night he rescued a hedgehog that had been roaming Hyde Park and brought it back to the hotel, intending, without hesitation, to adopt it. I happened to be in the hotel room at the time, and what I remember is his hands cupped around the thing like a fragile little, well, hedgehog. That moment with the rest of us crowded around him, come to think of it, might be the most telling picture of Sean I can come up with.

Sean's classmates weren't the only ones to observe his uniqueness. Senior year the University of Virginia offered him its prestigious Echols scholarship *and* its Jefferson scholarship, and the next fall he went off to Charlottesville to begin his next round of achievements. According to the school's newsletter, *Inside UVA*, Sean made the dean's list over the next few years, became student representative to the board of visitors, served as vice president of the student council, was a government honors student, and was even president of the school's cycling club. He also completed emergency medical training in preparation for work with a local rescue squad. (His adventurous side didn't suffer amid all this achievement, Bliksem assures me. He says Sean would, on a whim, make the trip home from school—two hours by car—on his bicycle.) The most prestigious accolade came toward the end of his time at UVA: nomination by the school's Rhodes committee, the first step in becoming a Rhodes scholar. It's a trope among those who nurture super-high achievers, and possibly even a damaging one, but it would be an incomplete description of Sean not to mention it at this point: Widely held among those who knew him was the belief that the future president of the United States was in their midst. Sean was on the right track, he commanded the respect of peers and adults alike, but more than that you could just look at him and *see* it.

In her *Washingtonian* article, Mendelsohn traced the day of December 10, 1996, as thoroughly as possible, though no amount of detail will explain enough. It was halfway through Sean's senior year, and from the outside the day appears to have been unremarkable. He mailed a birthday present to his father, sent a casual e-mail to his uncle, took a study break with a friend, and went to his room for the night. Sean's girlfriend came by twice, they argued briefly, and later she left a message on his answering machine. Neighbors reported loud music through the night, and no answer when they knocked on the door. By 9 A.M. the music hadn't stopped, and, figuring he'd simply left the room with the stereo still playing, Sean's neighbor had the door opened by the head resident. The two stepped in and then stepped back out. Sean was hanging over his bed, from a belt looped to his bicycle hook. He was twenty-one years old.

WE KNOW, BY now, what happens in the wake of a successful young man's suicide. First, his potential swells retroactively—now he'd been *so full of promise*—and though it may well be warranted, the faint suggestion is that we might not grieve sufficiently otherwise. Then there are the hints we failed to parse; every word he uttered, every hedgehog he cradled suddenly overflows with just-missed meaning. Finally, inevitably, we grope helplessly for a theory of *why*.

Few people had been closer to Sean than Anne Barnhill, who dated him for the last two years of high school and then remained his friend into college. "He was definitely overworked and freaked out about the future," Anne told me. "I guess he was upset about his family"—his parents had shocked him months earlier by announcing they were divorcing—"but that's not persuasive to me, because stuff with his family had been going on for a while. It just doesn't make a lot of sense to me. I don't have peace of mind about it. I don't have an understanding that I have any confidence in."

Undoubtedly Sean *was* overworked, and not all his labors were paying off as reliably as he might have come to expect. To the surprise of many—particularly Sean—the state's Rhodes committee saw things differently than UVA's had, and didn't advance him to the next round of interviews. On top of this, as Anne alluded to, there was the divorce of Sean's parents, to whom he'd been exceptionally close. Still, the deliberate death of a young man so *alive* drove some of my class-mates to speculate further. Because the statistics were there to back it up, or because the subject had engulfed my class so long, the question of sexuality arose.

"Everything I ever heard about Sean's own sexuality came from rumors, and I have absolutely no idea if they're true," Wayne Steward told me. "If it is the case that his sexual orientation had something to do with his suicide—if he wanted to be governor from Virginia and knew that a gay man would never be elected—that's just more evidence of the tragedy of homophobia."

"I don't think Sean was gay—I wished he was at the time, God I wished he was," Tim Yerington said to me. "But looking back, I don't think so. I think he would've come out if he was. Oh, maybe he was going to stay in the closet to run for governor, but I don't see it that way."

"Not all young males who commit suicide do it because they're gay, but there's also a very high incidence in young gay males," Karen Taggart said. "Could it have been the pressure of being as perfect as he was? Yeah, absolutely. Could it have been he was gay? Sure. Could it have been a random thought that he had, that he took all the way—like he took everything? Yeah. I don't know."

Though I don't pretend to understand this last theory—how does the significance of the act not register in someone so thoughtful?—it's the one to which many of his friends subscribe: Where a less impulsive person might have taken an argument, family stress, or the Rhodes set-back in stride, perhaps Sean responded with the same intensity that would impel him to bike all the way home from school. Anne, when pressed, concedes that this seems the most likely explanation.

"If I had to say, I think I would say I think he didn't really plan it. That it was rash, and he didn't mean it. There was this way in which he was just less hinged than most people. He was extreme. He had his own experience of reality. He was not modulated by other people in the way most people are. He didn't respect limits. He had reckless behavior—reckless driving, that kind of stuff, stuff that imperiled his physical safety. He climbed this water tower once. I remember him once picking up a stray dog—I came to his house and there it was in the basement.

"I feel like he didn't intend to die, because it just wasn't that consis-tent with his character not to explain it, to not help his family try to understand. He was really attached to them. He was genuinely attached to them. Also, he loved attention—if he was going to do it, it seems out of line for him not to make more of it!"

Among those in the emotional vicinity, Sean's suicide sometimes seems to reverberate as more than just the passing of a sweet and wonderful guy—though that would be plenty. It's tempting to look back and see in him a Kennedy, and in his death a Kennedy-like loss. He was, after all, the closest thing we had to a beloved leader, the only classmate poised for public office, the nearest we had to a vessel for our, I suppose, canny Gen-X hopes. Even those from other genera-tions appear to have had some kind of civic investment in him. Gar-field Lindo, the Humanities teacher who led the London trip and a close friend of Sean's, recalls the day a school assembly was convened following the "Kill all niggers and Jews" graffiti found on the adjacent elementary school. Amid the confusion of the whole thing, Sean rose to his feet and spoke. He was "steadfast" in his message, Garfield says: "Everyone . . . must stand up and say, *No, we will not abide this.*"

"He was directing himself to a life where he represented everyone, a life in the public eye," Bliksem tells me. "I think everyone who knew him felt he'd be president, or at least joked about it. Sean himself would mainly joke about it because it was too far away, but at the same time it seemed like it was in the back of his head, like that's where he was heading. You know, if you look at his steps and Bill Clinton's, with the Rhodes and everything, they were on the same path."

"Part of him really wanted to have this political life, and to be a successful politician," Anne says. "But I'm not sure it was a love of politics so much as ambition. He was incredibly ambitious. He wanted to be everything. A lot of people want to be very good at something, but he wanted to be good at everything. In retrospect, I think maybe there was a little desperation in that too. Never being satisfied. Wanting to be everything."

TEN YEARS OUT of high school, it turns out our class has lost not just Sean, but a young man named Mark Glaeser, who also committed suicide in college. I didn't know Mark—as his friend Stacy suggested to me, he kept a low profile at TJ compared to Sean. When, at our upcoming reunion, we mill around comparing accounts of the last decade, we will do so with only the faintest resemblance to the kids we were in high school. Our words are kinder, our perspective richer, our paunches heftier. As obvious as it sounds, the idea that Sean and Mark have been excluded from this still feels stunning. They've now been frozen for us at the young age of their deaths; with every successive reunion, the gulf between us and them will only grow.

This, of course, is the heart of it. In Sean's case—and I feel more comfortable speaking about Sean, having never met Mark—the ultimate sadness isn't that we lost a potentially great leader, someone who might do something amazing for a world many of us agree needs his brand of compassion and strength now. The sadness is that his family and friends don't get to witness the turns of a special person's life.

I don't intend to overstate the repercussions Sean's suicide has had on our class. I was always surprised when I stumbled upon a classmate who hadn't heard. Marcus Groenig, the ex-boyfriend of Brenda McEldowney, mumbled a "That's too bad" and went on to express his surprise that only one of us had died in ten years. But for others of us there's no question as to Sean's impact.

"You see his picture and it's like, 'How are you dead?'" Karen Taggart says. "I kind of put him in my River Phoenix file—*You're not dead, I'm just not going to see you anymore.*"

"For quite a few years I was thinking about him every day. I don't anymore," Bliksem tells me quietly. "I still have his photo, and my parents still keep a picture of him with all the other photos of our family. I remember his birthday every year. Now it's more that he comes to me at random moments. It affects me the way losing a brother would, I think."

Anne Barnhill has the same quietness to her when she talks about moving on without Sean: "I go through times when I think about it often. It's pretty well integrated into my worldview. It's conceivable now, to me, that people I love will kill themselves. It's a possibility."

Sallie Bryant, Sean's mother, wrote this in a letter to me:

I admired Sean tremendously. He constantly amazed me by what he would attempt and what he could achieve. He was also a nutcase—silly, impetuous, and fearless. One moment we'd be talking about how to apply management techniques (my thing) to student council meetings (his thing). The next, he'd drag me out in the dark to lie on an open hill in the cold and find the constellations. He would stop on his way to school in the morning with Bliksem to play on a rope swing hung from a highway bridge beam over a stream; then he'd put on his suit and visit a special needs center to help him assess school board priorities. While at summer camp, he refused a phone call from the *New York Times* because he was busy canoeing—said he'd call them later. He habitually wore hats, suspenders, and bow ties but also showed up for a seminar one day in sweaty, muddy biking clothes because he didn't have time to change. He grieved over the divorce that marked the end of the family life he had relished, yet initiated my new husband-to-be by decking out his 200-pound, 60-year-old body in biker nylon and putting him on a racing bike for a trip to DC. He was a finalist for the Rhodes scholarship; he threw a bottle of rubber cement against the wall of his room when he didn't get it—then called me and laughed about the mess he'd created. He mingled among the UVA board of governors in their sky box and then left early to take Mike and me canoeing on a rain-engorged river; we returned to "the lawn" two hours later soaked, having not quite made it through the final rapid. He drove like a maniac but held my hand when I got too close to the side of a cliff. He cried at plays and danced in cafés. I was really proud of him, and I loved being with him.

21 The Reunion

On a rainy November night, 170 members of the Thomas Jefferson High School for Science and Technology's Class of '93—240 including dates—convened nervously, or in some cases struttingly, or in other cases drunkenly, at the Army-Navy Country Club in Arlington, Virginia. The reunion took place the evening after Thanksgiving. We'd spent the previous twenty-four hours reacquainting ourselves with the habits of adolescence—sleeping in the skinny old bed, sighing over parental advice, sliding into the back seat with the sibs, et cetera. With semi-teenage hearts, then, we made our way to the festivities. I'd come with my girlfriend, Amy, my fiancée by now actually, and from the clogged nametag station we set forth into a sea of intimate strangers.

Stepping into a vast ballroom jam-packed with one's former high school classmates, one can feel—what was Adam Rice's word for Lorraine and me?—*unresolved*. Those initial sensations made for an odd mix, classmates told me later: a nervous exuberance, a thrilling nausea. Meanwhile everyone wore roughly the same expression, one of those electrified but perplexed half smiles reserved for occasions of uncertain appeal. In every direction mingled eyewitnesses to the follies of our youth, the people who saw us at our squeaky, muddled worst. As classmate Jen Rice put it, "They know a part of your experience that only people in your high school graduating class can know."

Immediately we were all hugging. Then shaking hands. Then stealing glances at each other's nametag just to be sure. Flanked by a cheesy DJ and a nostalgic slide show, we arranged ourselves into as many conversational configurations as four hours would permit. Content-wise, these micro-exchanges barely even qualified as chitchat—*Hello, where're you living now and what do you do?*—and yet we couldn't get enough. We studied each other's faces, reviewed archival footage in our heads, and performed hasty reconsiderations of one sort or another. Meanwhile, at round tables here and there, bored partners and spouses pouted into their cheese cubes; periodically they received consolation from their apologetic but not-quite-ready-to-leave other halves. As we used to say back in high school, the evening was *so random*. One moment we were reminiscing with old locker mates—how tall they'd gotten!—and the next we were exchanging e-mail addresses with men and women once too scary or perfect to approach. The event saw no official ceremony or structure—certainly nothing resembling what one classmate told me she truly wished for: a huge circle of us, each explaining conveniently who we've become in ten years. Nor was there spoken acknowledgment of Sean and Mark, the two members of our class who didn't live to see this reunion. Their portraits sat on a table near the front of the big hall.

Of the sixteen people profiled in this book, half didn't show. Becky

Earle Middleton was on a long-planned trip with her new husband, and others lived too far away to make the trip. Only Anne Farbman volunteered anything resembling a *position* on attending: "High school reunions are one of the only socially sanctioned, ritual forms of humiliation we have." Brian McConnell and his wife braved the humiliation, and he reunited with Pete, his one-time partner in pellet gun crime. ("Pete's wife wouldn't let me talk him into doing anything stupid," Brian reported later with displeasure.) Adam and Lorraine Rice—Lorraine very pregnant with a second child now—found a sitter for Ian. Brenda McEldowney brought boyfriend Brian, and Karen Taggart brought girlfriend Salua. Ben Kim came from Pennsylvania, Charlotte Opal from California, and Lesley Cook, in bright magenta hair, showed up with a much fawned-over Jacob in tow.

If there's an essence to high school reunions, it's this: Alan, whose hair stands on end in our yearbook, is now an economist at the EPA. Suzanne, always witty and kind, works as a speech pathologist. Mike, who used to keep a crew cut and a dark, self-deprecating wryness, now wears long, Fabio-like locks and repeated several times to Amy and me that he was "evil, evil, evil" (eventually he conceded that his work had to do with nuclear weapons). Joe, who wrote a song about almost everyone in our class years ago, now makes a living as the singer and guitarist for a band called The Hint. Jen, our ebullient class treasurer, is an ebullient architect in Manhattan. Seth, who'd protested the war in Iraq months earlier, was leaving in three weeks for a three-month stint in Baghdad as an economic analyst, getting schools and roads built for the Coalition Provisional Authority.

For every mention of Iraq trips and rock bands, the reunion offered a dozen more familiar life stories. Consultants abounded. Doctors abounded. Government IT contractors abounded. Ph.D. candidates abounded. At one point, I wandered into the men's room to find someone barking actual business commands into his cell phone—a stern nod in my direction. One classmate told me of another who'd complained, in their brief exchange, about the difficulty of earning $500K to $600K now that his company had gone public. There were nonconsultants and nondoctors, too. Jessica Mitchell, who used to read for the entire duration of our school bus ride, now teaches AP history in a Virginia public school. "Now I'm a cheerleader instead of a drama/choir nerd," she told me. She meant it literally. "Every spring, we have a students vs. faculty basketball game and I'm part of the cheerleading squad. My cartwheels have become famous among the student body." Jean Cook, an immensely talented violinist who I'd seen perform in New York earlier in the year, manages to run a nonprofit, manage an opera company, and coordinate various musical undertakings, all while keeping a full-time job at Lehman Brothers. "What I value: being smart, efficient, and productive," she'd told me so efficiently she didn't even need a complete sentence. I met a good number of mothers and fathers, and a good number of single people who bragged that they didn't even have houseplants. Some classmates didn't make it to the reunion, but their stories circulated nonetheless: Paul Bishop had nailed the lead in a production of *Dracula* his freshman year of college, and scarcely objected in rehearsals when the director demanded that a real five-inch knife replace the less-realistic retractable stage blade. On the second night of the show, before a full house, Paul stood in his coffin and felt nothing as the knife missed the stab pad under his shirt and collapsed a lung instead. "He won't make it to the hospital," he heard an EMT say backstage later. But a decade— and a temporary chest tube—later, Paul is as good as new. When we spoke after the reunion, he mentioned his recent starring role in a local production of *Seven Brides for Seven Brothers*.

Is this what brings us to high school reunions—collapsed lungs and $500K salaries? If conventional wisdom has it right, we come to find out how we stack up, or else to show others how *we* stack up. Almost a year before the reunion, my classmate Rebecca (Lamey) Gray told me what was behind her decision to attend.

"I want to see how everyone turned out, and I want people to see how I turned out. I think I became something different from what people expected—I'm finishing my degree, I'm a mother, and I actually *like* being a mother! [People] probably thought I'd be homeless. I was voted most likely to not go to college. . . . I think I'm going to surprise people, and I think people are going to surprise me."

A week after the reunion, though, Rebecca says the most surprising aspect of it was the *lack* of surprise.

"No matter how implausible some things might have seemed back in high school, it just felt like nothing was much of a shock at the reunion," she wrote me in an e-mail. "I stay home with the child that I never expected to have; someone else who did expect to have children is completing her doctorate and is single; multiple people brought their same-sex partners; the jerks have mellowed; the preps have chilled, and we all seemed to just shrug off what would have shocked us about each other ten, or even five, years ago. If anything, I guess that was the most surprising, and most enjoyable, part of the night. Just the fact that everyone seemed to have fun catching up, have released their grudges, and weren't shocked by the path that anyone else has taken."

Which isn't to say there weren't tiny moments of revelation amid the general ease. One classmate found the woman for whom he'd held a bit of a candle all these years. The long-awaited conversation, he told me later, was a bust. "The rest of the room didn't exactly fall away, and the one time she might've mentioned whether or not she's currently dating anyone, I couldn't hear her over the DJ." My own revelation involved asking Geoff Campbell, a former football player and now a dapper lawyer, why we'd so gotten on each other's nerves in high school—Geoff's the one who hated my Free Pee-Wee T-shirt. He rubbed his chin and finally said, "We came from different worlds. Now, though, there's really only one world." We shook hands and smiled for the first time ever. Then there was classmate Pete Shannon, a tall, genial fellow who reflected on perhaps the greatest adolescent profundity of all: waking one day to find he'd begun to transcend acne. "I started getting handsome!" he exclaimed with the pure joy of an unearthed memory. "Every day I was better looking!"

As far as I could tell, and purely by accident, the individual classmates I'd profiled—Brian, Lesley, Brenda, et cetera—managed to avoid one another the entire night. Only briefly did I consider corralling them for some kind of corny group closure. It wasn't dignity that stopped me so much as fear of awkward silence: As emotionally loaded as it may be beneath the small talk, a reunion doesn't lend itself to closure or other explicit forms of substantive communication. Among even the most candid and thoughtful classmates I'd interviewed over the previous year and a half, a general superficiality pervaded the evening's interactions. Even where there'd been significant tension before—I'm talking about Lorraine and Adam here—we found only casual banter now, and perhaps the subtlest glance acknowledging our earlier awkwardness. The high school reunion, one learns only at a high school reunion, is an often-dreaded and often-thrilling but ultimately hollow affair. Part of this, surely, owes to the impossibility of explaining all that has happened since graduation. All those long talks at college, the parties in our early twenties, the middle-of-the-night phone calls from family, the breakups, the looks from across a room, the hairstyle variations—all these get flattened into *Good thanks, I'm doing consultant work.*

In the days after, Ben Kim e-mailed a more involved report than the reunion itself had allowed. Ben, who expects to be receiving an offer from the Johns Hopkins Applied Physics Laboratory shortly—it'll bring him closer to D.C. and to his family—wrote, "It was truly great to see that nerds really do win in the end. Typical male nerds from high school ending up with great jobs and extremely attractive and well-spoken wives/fiancées/girlfriends wrapped around their arms. It was very reassuring. . . . Makes me wonder how things will turn out for me to that end—it may be the litmus test that reveals if I myself was a nerd then. . . ."

Others wrote, too:

Lesley Cook: "I enjoyed it way more than I thought I would—I *did* have some great conversations and with people I wouldn't have expected."

Brian McConnell: "The people I talked to at the reunion were for the most part people I'd been friendly with at school, but it takes a lot more than that to be a true lasting friend. A lot of them fall back on the standard questions like, 'So, where do you live now?' or 'What do you do?' Not to sound blunt, but I don't think many people that asked those questions will remember what I told them in a week."

Brenda McEldowney: "I was reminded how few people in our class I really knew at all. I had a very short list of people I really felt I knew well and was looking forward to seeing, and at least five of those people weren't even there. . . . I really hoped to get more of a chance to chat with [my ex-boyfriend] Marcus, but that didn't work out. I'm not sure if I was looking for some kind of closure or what, but I was definitely disappointed that we didn't get to connect."

Lorraine Rice: "It was good to see everyone. Not scary or intimidating like I thought. I thought it was interesting how all the guys who were so full of themselves in high school looked really beaten down by life. . . . I guess it was interesting that the people I enjoyed talking to the most, or felt the most at ease with, were people I barely knew in high school, but now they are parents or are pregnant just like me, and that connection alone was enough to get us talking and laughing together. . . . I would have loved to have brought Ian. You know everyone was talking about what they are doing, and the most amazing thing I've ever done was sitting at home, and I couldn't even share him with everyone."

If one truism extended to everybody in that ballroom, and no doubt to many who avoided the reunion, too, it was that we still find our deepest selves wrapped in the folds of high school. Adulthood notwithstanding, dark corners of our souls can still be found checking for zits periodically in some private locker room mirror after gym class. It's not for nothing that America's coming-of-age stories take place at high school, and that its midlife crises return there, if only for a moment of nostalgia. It's why every inch of the place has been mapped and mythologized by American culture, from the locker room, to the principal's office, to math class, to the back seat in the parking lot. We have *The Catcher in the Rye, A Separate Peace, Rebel Without a Cause, Fast Times at Ridgemont High, The Breakfast Club, Heathers, Dazed and Confused, Freaks and Geeks,* and so forth. It's the last official shared experience we all have together, and a part of ourselves gets lodged there for good.

As I made my circuits around the room, hello after hello, I had the same thought we all must have had: What a strange ten years it's been. How mightily we'd once concerned ourselves with issues and ideas and other stand-ins for life itself. What would we have said, at the height of adolescent *turmoil,* had we glimpsed ourselves embracing at a country club ten years later? What was it that happened in that time, a decade that saw a homecoming queen make herself into an instrument for a greater good, but also saw a young man, dedicated to change and compassion, end his life in a single, awful moment? From pellet guns to heads butted over sexuality and race, we had always known messiness all along; at the start of the '90s, though, we were also a serious and enterprising bunch. Debate was our province at TJ, and we were perfect teenagers about it, for we saw no reason our words wouldn't change the world. So many classmates I've interviewed echoed that mantra: *I wanted to be everything.* We expected good things, because we were kids or because the signs generally pointed to yes. We graduated and lived our indulgent college years under a young and idealistic president, amid domestic squabbling but also unprecedented peace. We fretted in coffee shops just briefly, and then the Internet economy snatched us up and insisted we, and the world, would indeed see great new things.

The window was tiny, of course. The economy imploded, and the country was rocked back on its heels by terrorism. But at a more abstract level, that invisible certainty of ours—of so many people's—slipped away a bit. Even when our personal traumas didn't coincide with the nation's, our individual lives still tended to rise and fall along roughly similar lines. We're more anxious and cautious now, even those of us not directly touched by 9/11. We're less assured, despite the number of Ph.D's. It's conceivable, my classmates have said to me with sighs, we're getting older.

Eventually the country club closed its doors. A few hugs and some shouting happened out on the sidewalk, and then what remained of our high school reunion had no choice but to wrap up. We took off in our different directions, a mini graduation's dispersal all over again. Amy and I drove to an after-party at a nearby bar—more of the same, but louder—and then on to my parents' house. We talked, as people fresh from a high school reunion will do, about many things at once. We talked about the decorations and the bad DJ, about the former activists and the former geeks and the former basketball players, about Sean and Mark.

As we drove, and then as we parked and just sat in the car—like high school kids, I suppose—we tried to figure out what high school *is.* Such a line of thinking proves fruitless, not just because high school *is* just about everything, but also because it's always at the point of change. *We are transitioning,* every valedictorian intones at every graduation across the country. And they're right. In high school, we're at brinks. The brink of graduation, the brink of adulthood, the brink of independence. The brink of kegs, and of sex, and of paying rent, and of finally getting out of town to get away from all the brink clichés. If high school perches us on the edge of something, the decade afterward sees us leap. We leap from the tidy grid of high school and just sort of *flutter* until we land on whatever solid ground we find: family, a home, career, faith of some sort, a better set of ideas—or maybe just the next reunion.

Acknowledgments

Thank you to Becky Cole at Broadway, who's wise and knows about getting rid of dumb parts and adding good parts. Thank you to Gary Kamiya and Lisa Chase for terrific editing help, to Elizabeth Kairys and John Allspaw for artistic and technical help, and to Betsy Stroman for mother-in-law help. Thank you to Daniel Greenberg at the Levine Greenberg Literary Agency, and to Pat Groves at Thomas Jefferson, and to Carol Lloyd from way back. Different kind of thank you to Mom, Dad, and Nick, and to the Oakland, Brooklyn, Petaluma, Piedmont, and Suriname friends.

Thanks to Amy Standen for bringing home scratch paper from the office and things like that.

Finally, my deepest gratitude to the Thomas Jefferson class of 1993. With nothing to gain, so many of my classmates agreed to let an almost-stranger into their lives. There'd be no book without their trusting and patient and generous cooperation.